Aquarius-Genesis

*«Whenever to my mind somebody's comparisons and
analogies are going too far, I got to ask myself:
«... – or is my own view too narrow, perhaps?»
And if I deem those insufficiently founded, I got to ask myself:
«Did I myself reflect sufficiently to judge them ... ?»*

(Muhammad Khorchide, Islamic Theologist and Sociologist)

«The Lord, God, created everything through symbols»
(Apocryphal Gospel of Johannès)

Hat-Hor – Ancient Egyptian Venus-Ourania feeding to Pharaoh the Milk of Wisdom (see. Appendix 5-B: Legends to Pictures, note 1).

COMPENDIUM CREATIONIS:

THE UNIVERSAL SYMBOLISM OF

AQUARIUS GENESIS

12 THESES ABOUT THE ORIGIN, FALL AND RENEWAL OF HUMANITY

EXPLAINED BY P. MARTIN

WITH THREE FABLES:

WHY EVE WAS CREATED
CAIN AND ABEL TODAY
EVE AND LILITH: THE SECOND WOMAN

AND A PHILOSOPHICAL TREATISE:
ABOUT THE ESSENCE OF BEING

EDITION ORIFLAMME 2018

IMPRESSUM

The Universal Symbolism of Aquarius Genesis
12 Theses and Scholia about origin, fall and renewal of humanity.
With three fables:
Why Eve was created
Cain and Abel Today
Eve and Lilith: The Second Woman
and a philosophical tractate:
About the Essence of Being

Original: © 2016: Edition Oriflamme, CH-4002 Basel, ISBN 9783952078709.
Compendium Creationis – Die universelle Symbolik der Wassermann-Genesis:
12 Thesen und Scholien zu Entstehung, Fall und Wiederaufstieg der Menschheit,
mit vier Zusatztexten: Warum Eve erschaffen wurde; Kain und Abel im Heute;
Eva und Lilith: Die Zweite Frau; Vom Wesen des Seins.

With a table of symbols and 50 illustrations, partly full-page
plus notes to the pictures and notes to the text

*It is impossible for a book author to translate this book into another language
without making some minor changes and additions !*

Vignette on title leaf : A pre-columbian symbol for Man and the Universe

SEARCH TERMS:

Genesis – Gnosis – Aquarius
Quantum philosophy – universal Symbolism – Theory of Ideas

ISBN 978-3-907103-02-9
© EDITION ORIFLAMME, CH-4002 BASEL (SWITZERLAND), 2018

Printed in Germany

Production, get-up and cover :
Adhoc-Organisation, CH-4002 Basel (Switzerland)

CONTENTS

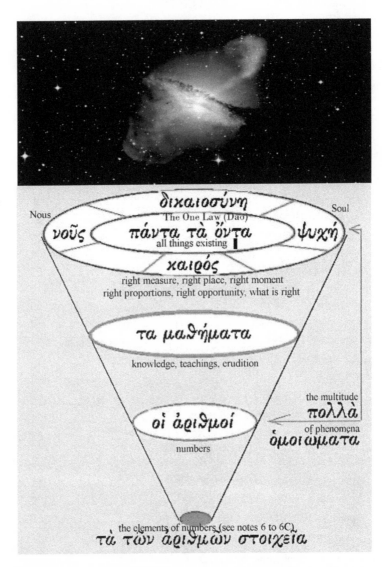

Pythagorean views about the roots of Creation correspond precisely with the first thesis of the Aquarius Genesis: Number, good measure, good proportions and rhythm contained in Nous (Spiritus Mundi, Mind) and Soul (inner perception) – all these ruled and harmonized by the One Universal Law: ‹KARMA›. (Image source: Internet).

Introduction by the Editor

The present book brings the *«Aquarius Genesis»*– an inspired text with in-depth commentaries combining ‹scientific› tenets, primary symbols, spiritual perceptions and old myths so as to give a true *«Compendium Creationis»* in a holistic synopsis. – How can such a multidimensional view be made acceptable to our poor intellect?

More and more scientific discoveries during the past three centuries led ordinary people to adopt an ‹illuminated› contempt for all mystic teachings: Myths – once the cultural, moral and ethical pillars of human societies – were smudged, smirked at and disposed of as being *«merely symbolic»*. – But: is not everything in this world ‹merely symbolic› – namely: *a symbol of the Godhead?*

The new millennium brought with it – right from the beginning and even shortly before – wide spiritual openings demonstrating that *a New Era* has begun: Many a process in this world will soon produce results quite different than expected! Already the language of numbers explains the new impacts on a human plane:

The Number 1 of the *past millennium* lead humanity from its prime *collective soul* to an *individual* EGO, beginning with personal individualization since the 11th through the mystic 13th centuries (3 = NEPTUNE: mystical endeavours and Alchemy), and the inventive *century* of the number 14 (4 = URANUS), with its discovery of forgotten continents. The male EGO reached its apex at the end of the century with the leading number 19 torturing the World with constant wars (9 = MARS, 10 = PLUTO; – see Appendix 1).

The Number 2 of the *new millennium* calls up *and* the soul *and* the *female* EGO which, *if lived adequately*, fosters development of the YOU – i.e. synergy and understanding – and deep spiritual development of the soul. Such astrosophical aspects could be enhanced considerably, but at this point they are just meant to waken the understanding for the development of human consciousness.

The same new psychic aspects promptly showed up even in academic Science – especially in theoretical Physics named *Quantum Physics*: Purely physical (materialistic) understanding of the Universe was *transcended* in favor of a more spiritual view — promptly birthing *Quantum-Philosophy* as well.

Many physical experiments challenge classical theoretical Physics in a most appalling manner. They prove our almost complete ignorance concerning matter and its behaviour, dramatically relativizing conventional ‹knowledge›: Highly developed measuring methods led to objective perception of *Spirit* ‹inside› so-called ‹dead matter›: Particles of matter and energy show a *learning capacity* (hence a memory), a certain *freedom of choice* (i.e. some sort of ‹will›) – and thus a kind of *consciousness*! – It is now only a question of time until also the *soul~life* of ‹dead things› will be detected. – However: *What truly is* a ‹SOUL›? – And ‹LIFE›?

This means that our thinking and learning behaviour *must* be greatly widened! It means that finally the moment has arrived where mankind – after thousands of generations, after centuries of *fake-knowledge* and *research lies* — begins to truly *cognize* our Universe, so as to fulfill the original task given to Man according to classical accounts of Creation of several cultures, namely: Not just to «multiply», and dominate and exploit the Universe, but also to realize, and *physically* fulfill *in Love,* the high *spiritual and mental responsibility* towards Creator, Creation and creatures!

This higher perception and consciousness also asks for a new world picture – in other words: new ways of contemplation, experimentation and formulation regarding this world so greatly misunderstood by most humans. The present book may spark such a new understanding. Outside of personal, family related, romantic and atavistic concepts, it develops an *almost intellectual* view. But if lectors will follow its outwardly strict and sober Symbolism not only with their intellect but also with an inner, blood-related understanding: with the *Reason of the Heart* – they will revive a reality soulfully spiritual and therefore intensely alive. Earlier views are not all wrong, really, but in many ways inadequate. And some are not just «*merely symbolical*», but even *complete nonsense*! – The new – the *Aquarius View* arises from *well-founded insight, inner perception* and a *well-reasoned choice in freedom of will on the basis of a new, truly human consciousness!*

Thus, the *Aquarius Genesis* is not meant to wipe out earlier concepts and myths about Creation: Authors of *relatively young biblical Genesis* didn't do that either, when combining the essence of oldest precursor-myths. The *Aquarius Genesis* may serve as an enlargement of insight into the Mysteries of the Universe, quoting old myths and their *purely spiritual* essence on the level of Symbolism – and so we come back to antique Initiation to the Mysteries as revealed and understood *merely on a symbolical level.* – The *twelve Theses* of *Aquarius Genesis* were conveyed to the author by way of a dream as he says, and so it is through sort of a *dream-consciousness* that really *modern,* i.e. open minded and well-prepared lectors may and will understand this new garment.

The *Book of Genesis* best known throughout today's ‹civilized› world (as publicized by Jews, Moslem and Christians alike) stems from a Babylonian Tradition of at least 4500 years ago. Its text was laid down only from ca. 350 b.C. onwards, and ‹definitively fixed› around 150 a.C. It was no new invention or inspiration but developed from much older Traditions with in parts exactly the same wording: in Old India of the Rishis, the Veda and Upanishads, and besides Sumer and China also in Old Egypt, in the Mayan Popol-Vuj, among the Hopi's, in Polynesia, and so forth ... – Some of them are quoted in the present book.

However, each of said traditions got its own character in harmony with its time and culture, with the ideals and religious teachings their priests wanted to promote – and of course according to their relative language and Symbolism: the colorful image-language of the ‹Indio's› of Central America: the ‹charla›, amiable chat among gods; – the awesome Mesopotamian tale of wonders; – the most juicy imagination after Nature in Egypt ... – The judeo-christian Bible instead makes a parallel and inevitably inconsequent attempt to insinuate an *anthropomorphic Monotheism since the Beginning* – an effort clearly doomed from the start: Scripture shows that this was achieved during the 4th century b.C. at the earliest. The dream since Antiquity of a national identity of Judea (based on a clan's blunt hegemonic claim openly declared in the Talmud), is forcibly implemented by brutal transformation of the *region of Canaan* with its coast-line abundant in resources and fertile land: Old *Philistina*, today named *Palestine*. – During the 20th century this led to a world-wide dominion by this same single Clan. The final goal would then have been: *One ‹Elite›* – a *selected blood-line governing the world!*

Looked at it cosmologically and astrosophically, the biblical clan story evolves during the Eras of *Taurus, Aries* and *Pisces.* Its origin however is much earlier – probably in the last period of *Capricorn*, well 20'000 years ago.[1] The era of *Aquarius* will soon show what decision *the True Lords of Destiny* will take – on the grounds of consciousness developed by *the new humanity*.

At the end of the era of Pisces, families, clans and nations were zealously built up – and decomposed again in order to replace them by an *elitary ideal of oligarchic globalization*: This is the old dream of a ‹*Reign of Thousand Years*› to be established during the era of Aquarius, according to some prophesies – but conceived in its basest form. Concurrently, the same forces ignite nationalism, racism and religious fanaticism. But in parallel, and thanks to humans awakening to true consciousness and sane mental capacities, activities developed in a decisive way to unmask this Great Power-play: On one hand, archeology, space research and academic

science have almost completely ‹de-mythologized› the Universe. –
On the other, esoterical movements and modern Quantum Philosophy define a completely new spiritual consciousness: During the
20th century, acknowledged Sciences cried: *«Who will still believe
the fabulous stories of old!?»* – while at the same time presenting
new ‹historical facts› and ‹scientific models› openly offending
natural common sense: Idle modern myths!

Since the beginning of the 21st century instead, quantum-phys-
ical observation has ‹reanimated› archaic legends related to appearance, essence and main goal of the Universe as seen from a different point of view. – Immediately after this, above mentioned *objective recognition* of the presence of ‹Spirit› in ‹Matter› set in. – But if
we look closer, suggestions in the sense of Quantum Philosophy
occur already in the *Corpus Hermeticum* (1st century b.C. until
1st century a.C. approximately), and in the Veda's!

Such developments re-animated the old questions of humanity:
«Where from …? – Whereto…? – What for…?» . – Today, the
answers to these questions are no exclusive task for people on an
esoterically spiritual quest any more, and even less for the
‹elites› originally formed to the purpose: Theologists, Socio-
logists, Anthropologists etc. – Today these answers are the *duty
and responsibility* of *philosophico-scientific institutions* yet to be
formed. – Part of them are going to be religious groupings and
serious independent esoterical researchers: All those who are on
a sincere quest for Light, for The Spirit, for Truth and for Life:
Those who ‹hermetically open› (Ritman) strive for the highest
spiritual, moral and scientific goal, growing in *true spiritual
Knowledge – Gnosis – through experienced spiritual facts!*

The *Aquarius Genesis* we present here offers a basis for such
new, valid and plausible answers. Like all earlier creation myths,
it is connected to elder versions, the roots of which in turn stretch
back as far as *Atlantis* , viz. to even older *Lemurian eras*. –
These names designate not just some geographical regions but
two so-called ‹prehistoric› world periods[2-A]. Therefore, the present
book includes the old classic Symbolism with its *silent significations*. And even the Mesopotamian family tale about Adam and
Eve, Cain and Abel, Isaac and Ismael find here their relative significance – but now as symbolic images along modern psychological
conceptions and thought-strings showing that whatever exists is
WAVES: Material and immaterial things – thoughts, words and
deeds – if in time or in Eternity – if in human disgrace or divine
glory: All can be perceived as a specific vibrational quality, and
on this basis all may be understood in a deeper, more adequate

way. Thus above mentioned *primary human questions* may be answered in a more definite factual manner.

Now, the title *Compendium Creationis* – i.e. *a summary and ‹Musæum›* of different myths and models relating the appearance of Creation – has a profound double meaning:

Firstly, the *twelve Theses* of the *Aquarius Genesis* do not present themselves as a pleasant story, but as an extremely condensed kaleidoscope, rotating in different speeds at a time. And each of these theses needs deep individual meditation.

The *twelve ‹Schollia›* interpreting the Theses are a most needed help to understand the latter. At the same time they contain the complete ‹Universal Doctrine› of world-wide *Spiritual Science.* The present book thus develops – irrespective of *preconceived visions and traditions* – an *independent,* i.e. *autonomous* conception put down in the highest possible density of information: It attempts to develop sort of a *hologram* of the spiritual structure of the Universe – scarcely lifting the symbolical robe by present-day explanations, tailored as it were from a tissue of interwoven blunt facts and holy Mysteries ... – in one word: a *Compendium.*

Secondly, the center of gravity and focal point of this ‹Compendium› is Man: Once, Man as the *Compendium* of the whole Creation, and *«in likeness of God»* as once we were, and are meant to become again. – Then also Man as *degenerated creatures* amidst today's world – both completely non-paradisiac due to human demeanour: a mere shadow of themselves; – and lastly: Man as a Mediator between Creation and Creator; *pioneer and servant* to universal Creation on *its way back*: A *pioneer,* for Man precedes all other creatures in the development of *individual consciousness* as well as of *global consciousness* of the whole Universe and – as a last consequence – in *new likeness to God*! – And as *servants* in so far as Man will no longer antagonize the divine Plan of the Universe and its creatures as pompous and arrogant ‹Mister Adam›, but now further the *One Path of all creatures* in loving brotherly devotion, achieving renewed godliness.

Such is the actual *Path of Redemption* which today is in reach of anybody, anywhere in the world – thanks to world-wide communication and to the universal impact of The Christos – *whatever His local denomination*; and this has almost nothing to do with official Christianism! This Path is real for *every creature.* It is – expressed in occidental wording – the *Imitation of Christ,* as heralded since eons: *in pre-christian and non-christian ‹gospels›,* proverbs, ‹acts› and myths. Many such texts were excluded from acknowledged Sacred Scriptures: some at the time of the latter's first canonization, some in later and even very recent times – as e.g. the four *Books of Maccabees* and the *Book Jesus Ben Sirah.*

The commentaries to the Aquarius Genesis – i.e. explanations relative to its *twelve Theses* – show the ‹first› surging of the Universe along with its ‹fall› and ‹redemption› as *scientific realities.* They shed a new light on the fact that Creation – especially that of *True Man* – is no myth parched by time, but an *everlasting Presence.* – Yes, there is, as already alluded to, a responsibility that today *must and can be understood «by all humans of good will»:* Divine GRACE and LOVE give us the opportunity of a new start. The *macrocosmic vibration of the* UNIVERSAL CHRIST donates us with the capacity and force to persevere. *–Individual efforts of every human* will finally lead *each creature* to its dignity; and Spirit will produce the final result: *Unity of All-in-All!*

Now, what indeed is the precise meaning of all this?

High academic Science today finds itself back at the threshold that centuries ago it crossed in an opposed direction – namely: the doorstep where once again in a *philosophically scientific* way will be given the proof, that the only real driving force in the Universe – since ‹*The Beginning*› and until the ‹*End of Days*› – is THE unconditional, all-embracing, all-nourishing, all-protecting and all-renewing LOVE! – The present book will at several occasions emphasize this fact, and more in detail.

Deep insight into inter-relations of all creatures – from a neutrino over a bee ‹up› to a human – this *insight,* and the faint notion of an *absolute reality flowing from it* will produce a ‹new› understanding of God and the World, culminating in a *consciousness* finally worthy to be called *human.* Only few pioneers will dive into this new *Kratèr* of Wisdom, says the *Corpus Hermeticum.* But they will encourage more and more others to follow – just as the universal plan of God intends it for Man and Nature.

This dynamic may seem to be set for a very far future but really is just a recurrence on a gigantic, for human conception ‹infinite› spire. – Nothing really new is it; but ‹only› a renewal issuing from the plenitude of todays' conditions, possibilities, and processes.

Acknowledging this cyclic pattern the text of the *Compendium* in a speech freed of stiff conventional conceptions speaks even of ‹future things› as of a ‹past›. Seemingly without motive, it changes from one temporal form to another, crossfading from mythical metaphors to real images a.s.f. – This should neither confuse nor irritate readers: In fact, each moment here is past already ere we can perceive it; and thus, what to one person appears as an obvious presence, others will see as already past – or else as a far-off and dubious future. All these impressions are true as much as they are false. For in the perspective of an unrestrained view, *everything is Presence – everything happens* NOW!

Thus we like to share this book with renewed open minds and courageous hearts of all those readers who already have found the answers to said primal questions of Humanity. And we like to hand it over also to those who only have the questions, but no conclusive, satisfying answer as yet: Not that ‹the final answer› could be given here: Silly and arrogant would be an author daring to state that he himself possesses it: Every ‹last answer› can be valid only individually and for short moments. And as a logical consequence, it can disclose itself only as an individual *revelation*. –

Innumerous changing ‹realities› and ‹truths› swarm through the microcosmic universe of every single creature! – But the *One Last Truth* so much hoped for by every typical seeker – it will never be found in human hands. Blessed are those who from time to time are hit by a divine spark of which they *must know* – because «*it cannot be otherwise*» – that this or that reality *has to be* an impregnable truth. But this, then, is no intellectual understanding anymore, nor either some ‹esoteric knowledge›: It is a ‹blood-certainty› that cannot be shared but among those who are *tinged* by the same *blood*: By the true blood of the intercosmic CHRISTOS irradiating this World. – This *eternal blood* flows to all *bona-fide seekers* of all cultures who *receive Him*:

To all who received HIM ... HE gave the power to become ‹Sons of God› again!

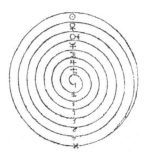

Interlude

Creation of the World as exposed by Hermes Trismegistos
(Corpus Hermeticum – ‹The Sacred Speech of Hermes›) [2]

The glory of All is God. He is the divinity of whatever is divine, the universal Beginning: God, Spirit, Essence, Deed, Destiny, End, and renewal of all.

Namely, there were in the Abyss an immeasurable shadow, and beyond it: Water and a subtle spirit like a thought: These were contained in the Chaos, by divine omnipotence. – But then, there blossomed up a sacred gleam of light: this blended into the sandy masses and amongst the moist force of Nature the Elements. And all gods revered these seminal natural forces – for they were not yet perceptible. But soon all that is subtle sored up to the heights; while all that is heavy instead stayed beneath the moist sands.

When all things were separated from each other, receiving their momentum, they were carried along by a fiery spirit. – Up sprang there Heaven in seven steady orbs: Within the star constellations with their signs, the gods became visible. – Calculated were then the stars in accordance with those who inhabit them. – Stronger on its orbit did Heaven move the gods in lofty circles, in harmony with divine Spirit. Each god out of inner virtue fulfilled the work attributed to them. – And now were born all living beings: Quadrupeds, reptants, aquatic animals as well, and the flying ones. – The sowings also – all the green that multiplies by seeds; – and herbs as well and sprouting flowers. – And all those carried in them the seeds for their rebirth. – Evenly generation of Man: for knowledge about the divine works, and as a testimony for Nature – as sovereigns over whatever is roofed by Heaven; for discernment of the Good; for the thriving of all generation, and for numerous proliferation. – And each and every soul, veiled by the light shadow of the flesh, so that they should have a subtle notion of the orbiting of heavenly gods, and comprehend the works of God, and progression of Nature, the auspices of what is good, as well as the strength and potency of God.

Some are much too confused to be capable of discerning Good and Evil, and to acquire artful skills for manifold good things. – And yet it comes to life within them, so that step by step they become aware of the wisdom of the motions of orbiting gods – and that moreover they themselves are involved with them: – Thereof, abundant memorials will be found, and admonitions by Masters of Arts from throughout the world to their elect in the course of times, through bringing forth herbs, and generating live flesh. – All that is rotten will from the seeds of fruits – and thanks to the Work-master of Nature and Art – rejuvenate itself. –

Finally, born of the need to survive, and during renewal of the gods as well as of the cycles of multiple Nature, reappeared Divinity and, mediating Spirit, conflated, so to speak, the complete assembly of the world, while Nature, once more, flourished again.

And, soon, in its true divinity Nature was again established. [2-B]

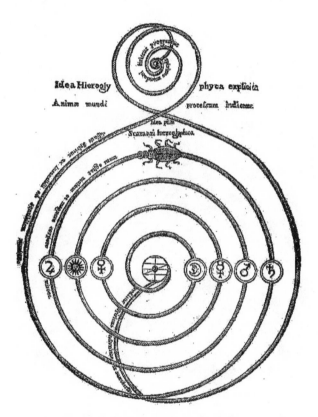

Figure from Kircher's *Œdipus Ægyptiacus* (1652). — The inscriptions say:

Explicit hieroglyphic image elucidating the movement of the World-Soul. // Hieroglyphic image of the sphere of the scarab // spiral of advancement of the Mundane Spirit // Spirit moves the mass, and a physical [?] lodestone mixes // spreading of Spirit by stirring up what is insensible, it to become sensible (i.e. *sensually perceptible*) *// Return of Spirit curved back to [its ? origin?]. –*
Idea hieroglyphica explicita / Anima mundi processum indicans // Idea pilæ Scarabæi hieroglyphica. // Spiritūs mundani helicus progressūs // mens agitat molem et magneta corporea(?) miscet // diffusio Spiritūs ex insensibili ad sensibilem agitando // reditus Spiritūs ad iniciata (?) suæ contortūs (?) —

17

According to the image source on internet, this image represents a stele in memory
of the restoration of the Temple of SIN (Moon-God) by the «last king of Babylon –
Nabonid {Nebo = planet Mercurius ☿}, around 550 b. C.». – In fact we rather
recognize there an old priest-king: terrestrial representative of the Governor of
the World, with his rod of power. His Left holds the same secret object (power tool)
as seen in Egyptian Statues of Horus, Ramses, etc. – In front of him (left to right):
MOON (Sin); second: MARDUK: The ‹unfinished› cross stands as a hieroglyph for the
SOLAR SON – the CHRISTOS, hinted at by a soaring ‹crucified› *Eagle* (a solar God or
Angel) descending from the Heavens. – And, third: The SUN, resp. SIRIUS-SOTHIS (as a
leading star with eight rays, and a Sun Symbol in its heart). These three symbols together – arranged in a different way – add up to the symbol for Mercury again: ☿

18

THE 12 THESES

1. In the Beginning, when there was nothing created yet at all, God created NUMBER.

2. In the second place, God created the UNIVERSE OF PLENITUDE: – this was the pure, absolutely divine, completely spiritual Universe: Space without forms, without thoughts or words, with neither light nor darkness. Its figure is the Circle O, that is All-in-All; for God was One with this World, and this World was in God, and God was this World, and there was no single limitation – neither of Space nor of Time: All was God; All was WISDOM, STRENGTH, LOVE and SPIRIT; – and All was perfectly good.

3. Within the UNIVERSE OF PLENITUDE shone up now the LIGHT-CROSS ✕: This is the Love Force of the CHRISTOS. – And thus was inspired a first PARADISE: ⊗. – There was just Spirit, Plenitude of potentialities, and Light. It was the all-one Sphere of Existence – all Light, Goodness and Harmony. No Evil dwelled therein, for no Evil existed; – and there could not dwell any Evil outside either, for there was no outside yet. – All was One. All was Spirit, Love and Light. God was in All, and All was in God.

4. Thirdly, God made the RHOMBUS ◊. And with the RHOMBUS was created also the CROSS ✚ always contained within the RHOMBUS: ◈. – This is the spiritual potentiality of the FOUR ELEMENTS.
In the RHOMBUS ◊ the Triangle of FIRE △ and the Triangle of WATER ▽ were still united – but lacking consciousness. – AIR and EARTH instead were still dwelling in Secrecy. – This was the Plenitude of potentialities within the wholly spiritual FIRST PARADISE:

5. Fourth, God made the SQUARE – ever-maidenly Mother of all material manifestations: ☐. And inside the SQUARE again flashed up the CROSS always concealed in the Square ⊠ – the LIGHT-CROSS ✕ of the CHRISTOS.

6. Within the harmony of primary paradisiac occurrences, a FIRST SEPARATION happened: The Elohim of the archaic Trinity △ created EVE, and with her they engendered CAIN AND NORIYIA *(another cosmic Triangle, △!).* The ELOHIM OF THE TETRAD ☐ instead formed ADAM. As The One of them ordered ADAM to mate with EVE, sprang up for him ABEL ▽. CAIN was a son of the ELOHIM OF FIRE: *divine.* – ABEL instead was engendered (at the directive of the Seventh – ‹The One›), as a son of ADAM and EVE: an Earthling as it were – still spiritual, but elemental according to the ◈. – This elemental separation became the FIRST FALL

7. From the separation into a spiritual and an elemental Creation, there resulted contrarieties between the Light Creatures among them, and in each of them as well. And thereof arose – as a dominant Spirit – the GREAT DISTRACTOR – alienated of the paradisiac harmony of the divine World of Love, albeit yet dwelling in it. For: from the separation into ADAM and EVE, into CAIN and ABEL, the World experienced

envy – and also gleeful gloating, anger and sufferings, violence and Death. *This was the* SECOND SEPARATION – *the* SECOND FALL. *Thus, the* FIRST PARADISE ⊗, *within the all-one, divine spiritual Light-World was transformed into an etherically elemental* SECOND PARADISE – ⊕.

8. The DISTRACTOR – issued from negative thoughts, emotions and desires of elemental creatures as he was – out of himself now generated negative thoughts, emotions and desires as well. In him arose the lust of power. – And so ‹EVIL› was born. – In order to establish his own kingdom he misled the dwellers in Paradise to follow his will: So, from the ⊕ came forward – in a THIRD SEPARATION – the physical World ⚭ with its properties known so well to all humans. This was the so-called EXPULSION FROM PARADISE – the THIRD FALL. Physical creatures as well as the DISTRACTOR were expelled from Paradise; and thus the DISTRACTOR got his own kingdom ‹outside› the paradisiac divine world. – Thus appeared the dark KINGDOM OF WRATH.

9. The dwellers in the KINGDOM OF WRATH were completely subdued and dominated by the latter's Lord. They were separated from the Sole Good like he, in quarrel and anger like he, in Darkness and Death like he. – In one thing however they differed from him: Abel's sons as well as Cain's sons preserved – hidden in the innermost core of their hearts, but more and more unconsciously – and imperceptible for most of them – a divine core-vibration issued from the Kingdom of Light and Love.
This divine core-vibration the Lord of the Kingdom of Wrath did not have, him being of no divine origin but emerged as a consequence of division – from negative thoughts, emotions and acts by the creatures within his reign as well as by himself.

10. Those others however, albeit being immersed completely in the darkness of ignorance, were touched from time to time by the luminous, fiery love-vibrations issued from the pure divine world ⊗ that irradiates and penetrates the Kingdom of Wrath, any time. Whenever such a beacon of Love-Light hit one of said kernels of remembrance, the latter flared up – for a short instant or longer. – Such flashes of reminiscence of the original Light-World kindled in human hearts an undefined LONGING to return to the original Kingdom of Oneness.

11. This LONGING produced the REPENTANCE of the lost Paradise. That is the ardent pain consciously felt because of the ignorance relative to the ‹Path of Return›. – REPENTANCE became the turning-point: the point of conversion from the dynamics of Death to dynamics of Life. – Whoever faithfully follows this dynamic born from INSIGHT, LONGING and FREE WILL, will finally be allowed to return to the Kingdom of PURITY, WISDOM and LOVE, as a child and brother of God – a god himself.

12. Thus became true the curse uttered by JHVH in Paradise: «Whoever will eat from this tree, will die by Death!» – But evenly, the promise

by the SNAKE : «*You shall be like the gods!*» has – through the grace of the Father himself – become a reality: *While Creation fell into Death, the DISTRACTOR fell into his own traps. For the Light descended until reaching the deepest Darkness. And through POWER, WISDOM and LOVE from above – and through PAIN, LONGING and REPENTANCE from below – the Path was laid free, and the doors opened, for elevation into the Light: for the return of all humans into the glorious Union with the pure, entirely spiritual Kingdom of Love of the Father:* ⊗ – *through GRACE – but BY EACH ONE'S OWN ENDEAVOURS – and into greater Strength and Glory than what they had enjoyed ever before.*

THE COMMENTARIES
TO THE THESES

The origin of Academies, of their faculties and usages may be found at the Courts of Persian High-Kings, of Grand Moguls in India, Chinese Emperors and Tibetan Dalai Lamas with their permanent surroundings of Sages, Savants and Dignitaries: There, on specific occasions, sat in counsel the so-called DARBAN or DURBAN, where the tribe kings or/and Eldest assembled, in order to answer the questions of their Lord, or to deliberate over complex questions regarding the empire. –

The same institution and its usages might also have been the motive for the world-famous alchemistic tract entitled *Turba Philosophorum* (numerous editions in print in *Theatrum Chemicum, Deutsches Theatrum Chemicum, Mangeti Bibliotheca Alchemiæ, Tanckii Promptuarium Alchemiæ*, etc. (all between end of 16th and the early 18th century; one of them even ascribed to Roger Bacon). In this widely quoted text the most famous philosophers and Adepts of the Philosophers' Stone discuss issues regarding God, the Plan of the Universe, and the Great Work of Alchemy.

24

Three things the Bard is bound to preserve:
Symbolism – Language – Tradition
(From the Druidic Triads)

Foreword to the Scholia

Schollia› – σχολια, especially during the 16th to 18th centuries, used to be elucidations and argumentations through scholastically and rhetorically polished comments meant to reinforce theses, antitheses and/or syntheses proposed by academic authors. They were the Humanistic Academy's method to enhance dogmatic conceptions, using innumerable ‹*dissertationes*› – i.e. philosophic and scientific tracts on every academic domain – happily ornating them with Platonic and Aristotelian axioms and dogmata. Preferably religious tracts and ‹letters› – ‹*epistolæ*› – were expounded by such critically didactic ‹*Scholia*› to fasten them within the dominant systems of doctrines – or to be brought into relation with them.

Even the *protocols of papal Counsels* were but a sumptuous editing method to fix more or less important axioms for the use of ecclesiastic power – *Scholia* accompanying or ‹legitimizing› a handful of theses, some of them resulting from irksome disputes, some even culminating in a physical row. – Theses which until today have remained obliging landmarks for Universities and Churches alike. There are good reasons to think that this system of *Scholia* was brought to perfection by the Jesuits of the 17th and 18th centuries – methodically based on *Platonic Dialogs*.

Similarly, the *Scholia* to the *Aquarius Genesis* given on the following pages would like – as a *Compendium Creationis* – serve as elucidations and helpful supports for this new ‹account of Creation›. Its external form is not the classical myth, but the language of the modern world. – However, in order to explain what finally cannot be expressed nor understood in any ordinary speech, the so-called *Language of the Initiates* is required – i.e. of those who through live experience bear in their soul a glimpse of «*what all this is about*», having developed an adapted language and understanding: A language that – until immediately before the so-called ‹Age of Enlightenment› – was present not just in Sacred Scriptures but also in Science and Arts. Today, this language is called *Hermetic*. – By right, for it still uses conceptions, mythological elements, sacred glyphs and timeless old symbols as preserved by Gnostics and Hermetists long before the Christian era – and this in spite of all defamations, debasements and persecutions.

It therefore seems quite appropriate here to dedicate a few words to antique Symbolism: to precisely *that Sacred Speech* hieratic *Universal Doctrine* has endowed to Initiates of all times, and which is still valid today. Architects in Ancient Egypt along with their epigones in Greece and Rome of Antiquity as well as those of Gothics, Renaissance and Baroque, used the same symbols: some consciously, others unawares; but all mostly obeying age-old rules: Classical Freemasons in their temple-workplaces, Alchemists in their *LabOratorium* along with old or new Orders of a spiritual background and with esoteric goals. The same goes for enigmatic texts and images in gothic churches and prophane buildings, everywhere [3] . – Even the ecclesiastic doctrines (dogmatic concepts skillfully built on symbols) use the ‹occult language› of classical Symbolism. – Most of them can be traced back to, or condensed into, relatively few graphic elements, resp. pictorial ciphers – or woven into some vivid myths and fables.

«Since the Beginning», and certainly until *«the End of Days»* as well, phenomena around human life were, and are, and will be, scrutinized in view of a significance *transcending* their sensually perceivable, i.e. *physical* impact – in order to explain and, so to speak, justify their appearance. These literally *meta-physical* and *trans-scendental* interpretations – along with daily experience confirming and thus reinforcing them – have formerly produced, and are renewing in our days, *metaphysical awareness* of more and more Initiates – i.e., of *«Those Who Know»*.

Both vulgarization (i.e. divulgation among people with an ordinary state of consciousness) and debasement out of evil will, successively produced empirical popular beliefs, then ‹peasants maxims› – and thereby again shamanism, Magick, new priest-privileges, and ‹modern Science›. The latter, however, is again but a system of myths and beliefs revered by many, but taught by very few ‹Initiates›: ‹Priest-Magi› of a *scientific creed.*[3-A] – Its value depends on faithful adherence to empirical axioms and ‹laws›, and on *niftily arranged* ‹scientific› doctrines. These doctrines were, and still are, adapted to the aims of the ‹Establishment› in power – and to an imposed ‹consciousness› defined, shaped, judged and rewarded by the same. The guardians of this system as a whole then exploit and administer – as they did in all times – the relative privileges endorsing the whole game ... –

These sad observations are proven by the fact that religion as well as natural sciences, together with social, economic and cultural values (partly defined by the same ‹elite›) depend absolutely on such official viewpoints of ‹elite› Schools, Communities, political and cultual circles, and imposed trends which *from time to time* change – by themselves or by governmental decrees.

Such arbitrary changes very seldom are to the advantage of the Majority. They have pushed aside most of ancient knowledge and wisdom, and therefore arch-old symbols as well. As a result, primary spiritual insights and conceptions could be preserved and forwarded only within small, and often secret (i.e. «occult»), circles of persons with similar inclinations and interests.

Old symbols were often declared as ‹heathen›, or even cursed as ‹devilish›, excluded from official spiritual knowledge (‹religion›), then outlawed as ‹Occultism›, and finally wiped completely off collective human consciousness. – Finally, they were replaced by modern *Symbolism of Electronics*, where all subtleties went extinct, and binary alternatives exclusively accepted: Or «ONE», or «ZERO»; – or «YES», or «NO»; – or «BLACK», or «WHITE»; – or «GOOD» (e.g. *profitable for some*) or «EVIL» (e.g. *autonomous*). –

Worldwide aggressive christianization with its ‹Enlightenment› (i.e. *extinction of Traditions*), «rational»-ization, and indoctrination have systematically perverted, prohibited and erased Symbolism and, in an early way of biological war, even evinced from the blood of the peoples: Knowledge of the soul is anchored in the blood; and that is why invaders everywhere ever encouraged their rudest soldiers to mate with as many women of conquered nations and countries as possible. Even the Balkan War at the end of the 20th century followed this same pattern, while top functionaries worldwide observed all in utter silence and apparent placidity. – Thus, Every ‹superstition› – i.e. every *preferred*, or *superior*, way to explain first causes and inner truths regarding the Creator, Creation and creatures – was crushed: Not only explicitly alternative teachings were overpowered, but also their forms of expression in images, names and idioms: Since then, the potentates leading the world-wide concordance of Science, social politics, world-religions, mass media a.s.f., define what and who may be believed and taught, and in what form. All the rest was eliminated as idolatry, heresy, devil worship a.s.f., and persecuted as being against the law, against nature or good faith, or even as sorcery – and chastised accordingly. Excommunication, dungeon or death menaced new dissidents and the relapsed alike: Torture or exemplary execution through hanging, drowning, beheading, or on the stake … – no beast is as inhumanly cruel as is ‹Man›!

New times have *only changed* this global strategy of despotism, by modernizing expressions and using new techniques; but the result remains the same: Free thought, speech, belief and behaviour are suppressed – not in view of peace, joy and prosperity for everybody, but for idle profit of a scarce minority of ‹Chiefs› – as it was in olden times. Thus disappeared openness of both heart and spirit, and got stunted the experience of the oneness of humans with their Creator and Creation – as well as among themselves. And thus also fell silent those world-wide symbols – once sprung from the original harmony with the All-in-All, serving it without words, understandable as they were for all, and commonly used: Thus died the era also named *The Golden Age.*

Today, the collective soul of Humanity is deeply impoverished: Instead of dwelling in the original paradisiac wealth of *one divinely pure Mind,* Man errs through the slums of general demoralization, social neglect and spiritual waywardness.

Meanwhile it is impossible for any human to live *without symbols,* as it is impossible for any human not to believe in *anything at all*: In every human there lives the hope for some human, super-human or *supra-human* magical power or support, and lies asleep an arch-old reminiscence of those earliest paradisiac ‹days› – in hope for some mainstay to straighten the human soul: faith in God, in gods, in natural spirits; and a memory of magical Symbolism (on whatever basis). – Colors, forms, sounds, smells find their resonance in the human soul. The latter appears to still remember in its profoundest depths the original Harmony, and to react on the original harmonic vibrations of *The Golden Age* – as it was *«in the Beginning»*. – The human drama as described in official Historiography, in old myths and in new Religions alike, is reflected in popular tales, in fables and parables, and especially in the old idioms of common people: *Vox populi vox Dei – People's speech is God's speech*!

Much of this has survived until today. Still more can be found in ancient geographical or personal names: names of lakes, fields, mountains as well as written tradition, and mythic figures as preserved in fairy-tales and in children's plays: Their linguistic roots and origins – and their inner (esoteric) meaning – often surprisingly spring to the attentive eyes of the independent researcher, or, so to speak, «drop into his lap› (see pic. 37).

Much of that also goes back to very old times, often conveying some old ‹heathen› expressions as do popular customs or festivals of all nations. And much of it, again, points back to the first eras and cultures remembered by today's Historians (or even further back): In today's official view, the most differentiated of old cultures was the one of Ancient Egypt (after Babylon/Sumer!).

Now: does this mean that the origin of Symbolism known today in East and West lies in Egypt? – This may well be if we look at cultures since only about 5500 years; but even in that time we are unable to find any *experimental attempts* – any, so to speak, clumsy or rudimentary examples of today's Symbolism; and many a scholar is certain that the roots of symbolic language as still accessible to some, and preserved by them, stretch back as far even as the beginning of the Atlantean culture.

Moreover, we might suppose that this Sacred Language did not originate on our Planet Earth at all but was, during a ‹prehistoric› past, brought to humankind by some intelligent beings from Space (gods, angels, Nephilim «from Heaven», ET's etc.), together with many other insights and things: plants, fruits, animals, technical and metaphysical skills ... – Some people even affirm that specific human races appeared on Earth through the influence of intelligent extraterrestrial (GMO resp. implantation). –

Even academic Scientists begin to yield to the evidence they reluctantly produce themselves: Archeological finds reveal technical knowledge in, and objects of handicraft from, very remote times, at the sight of which today's technicians and artists are forced to humbly bow and admit their incompetence. The true age of the *two Sphinges in Egypt* (as reported by Solon, but only one still known today), looked at from this point of view, suddenly ‹grows› from ca. 3500 years to 15'000 and even 35'000 years – and so forth. Some name here Hermes-Thoth the Atlantean ...

Such theories may be contested or approved at leisure; and the discussion will for sure remain alive for still some time as is usual for all human learning and experience. Nevertheless, and for us today, the origin of Symbolism lies back in such a very old past that it can truly be said: In our days each and every human microcosm incarnated has (during one or several earlier incarnations, maybe even thousands of years ago) been in touch with the complex ensemble of symbols. It therefore is obvious that basically every human living today carries in his or her Aura the immeasurable wealth represented by the Symbolism of the whole World, at least as a primary memory – one might as well say: as a blood-memory – conveying it thus – all unconsciously, too – to the blood of all their descendants.

So, how come that so few humans consciously remember these things? – How can it be that even people of great spiritual openness, education and expertise are unable to correctly handle symbols – or that at the most they accept and use them in a materialistic way, and only where symbols are directly connected to their daily spiritual, material or artistic activities? – Or that even some of the best among those look upon the antique language of symbols as something obsolete – something valid only for past conceptions, and of no use for us today? – We even know some individuals with some spiritual background who are proud to «have outgrown» the Symbolism of cloudy Antiquity and the blooming Middle-Ages – ‹thanks› to intellectual ‹evolution› (degeneration, indeed), and thus to stand high beyond such ‹poppycock›! – Now this is not just a sad way to sum it up, but a tragic and even a dangerous one, as soon will become evident from what follows.[3-B]

If the construction of the ‹Tower of Babel› occurred the way the myth wants it – or not – is no crucial question: Everybody has a right to their personal opinion. But that there was (or *is* for that matter, time being an illusion of the physical world), a *Speech of Oneness*: this is certain. According to Spiritual Science, all humans are One. And this Oneness must, logically, also have possessed one common language – the language of Oneness, so to speak. Now, the word *language* comes from «*tongue*»; but today we currently speak also of *image language, body language, sign language*, and more: *Symbol language* as well is nothing but an *universal means of communication*. And it is obvious and needs no discussion that especially symbol language is sort of a communication bridge linking all cultures, idioms and times.[4] That in our modern technological era this is not only *still true*, but even *more and more true* (although sometimes in a perverted way), may be demonstrated by three examples:

1° All occultist groups use the most ancient symbols. If they strive in good faith (‹*bona fide*›) towards union with the SOLE GOOD, or if in disbelief, resp. in gloomy *ignorance* they vow themselves to black Magic – they all use the oldest symbols and rites, albeit sometimes with different interpretations. Even Churches use Stars, Circles, Triangles and Crosses in their arch-old rites like e.g. baptizing›, and ‹Eucharist›. – Some shady organizations use black-magical Symbolism ranging from pervert baptism (using Crosses and Pentagrams) to pervert sex-rites, ritual child-murder and -cannibalism. – These are no phantasms, but a sad, hard reality in *today's* so-called civilized and cultivated West – especially in England and USA)!

2° On every street, train station, airport etc., symbols direct the behaviour of *each passenger* in one and the same way. Every controll system, too, functions with *fixed information units*. All these use their own *symbol language* (convened signs or numbers) to which some live humans or/and automatic devices are drilled resp. adjusted. The very old basic symbols or derivatives thereof (Circle, Triangle, Square and equilateral Cross) still serve as basic elements. – Street traffic is most typical for that.

3° In the year of 1972, were launched the space capsules Pioneer 10 and 11. Both were equipped with a gilded aluminum plate, engraved with some *intercosmically understandable symbols* – namely information units from Mathematics and Physics, together with the outline of a naked human couple. It is quite significant, by the way, for the *schizophrenia* (one could as well say *hypocrisy*) of our time, that of all nations people in the U.S.A. whence sexism, pornography and commercial sexual exploitation are spread throughout the world, protested against the sober, harmless outline of two nude humans on said aluminum plates. This must appear especially deviant for a *spiritual researcher*, to whom Man even today – notwithstanding his degenerate state of existence – has remained *«at the image of God»*, and to whom, correspondingly, a normal human couple is still equivalent to a *Compendium* of the ‹dialectical›, i.e. double-natured, World with its innumerable pairs of opposites (complementary Duals really) so well-known to our humanity, and certainly likewise to all other reasoning beings throughout the Universe.

Meanwhile, classical symbols increasingly reappear in our society – but are mostly given a material *function* only. The *virtues* of the old, classical symbols instead are not limited to aspects of daily life (to which they perfectly apply as well, however): They extend to every physical and metaphysical, material and immaterial aspect in the whole Universe: Whatever there exists can be expressed by some primary information unit of antique Symbolism. – Or, the other way round: There is not one single *modern* application of the antique symbols, where the latter would *not* have the timeless lawful impact they had in antique times. – Thereby (and this must be emphasized again and again!) it is completely insignificant if symbols are attentively observed and ‹experienced›, or used ‹incidentally› and unconsciously – or while disregarding or even denying them!

On the other hand, a human who re-becomes conscious of his or her primary blood-remembrance of symbols *«since the Beginning»*, and therefore consciously perceives the vibrations of this universal language imprinted into everything in Nature – the Kingdoms of minerals, plants, animals, humans, plus spiritual and divine realms; – that such a one is able to sense, and then become aware of, each and every subject and its live interactions within the Universe. – What remains however, is that his or her knowledge, findings and conclusions can be shared – thus communicated and made understandable – only among persons equally keeping up their own individual link with, and understanding for, that universal symbolic language: Not everybody draws the same information from the same image or experience; not all reach the same conclusion from the same elements.

Or, expressed in a positive way: Humans who deeply meditate the innermost metaphysical interactions, being conscious of antique universal Symbolism and able to become conscious of more such informations by way of hypersensual (‹spiritual›) awareness, may not only *share and exchange* their perceptions with others: While everybody – according to the gifts of each personality – interprets the same signals of information differently, they can *add up* their fractional insights in a way that may not be expressed in any conventional language. So they will produce a new total sum or complete image – a new symbolic synopsis. – Enhancing their own spiritual evolution (and thereby that of the whole Universe!) they progress, step by step and in harmony with Natural Laws, until *inevitably* achieving a *supra-human* – and even *humanly divine* – level of consciousness!

Or, expressed in other words still: Who *does not* nourish, strengthen and use the universal symbolic language – the language of Oneness coming from the dawn of humankind – will *fall out of* communion with the archaic knowledge of the Universe – and thereby loose even the last remnants of Humanity's originally divine omniscience. And as a last consequence, they successively let die down completely the already so terribly parched roots of their own Tree of Life – lightly and unforgivably!

To sum up what has been said until here, and to emphasize it in the context of the *Aquarius Genesis* and its *Commentaries*: If such high spiritual truths and experiences could be expressed in ordinary *conventional* speech instead of using symbols and some neologisms – i.e. by common conventional verbal compromises – it would have been done that way. – But conventional formulations always are insufficient: They cannot but render spiritual relations, processes and interactions in disfigured ways,. Therefore, the primary universal symbols were applied again, albeit tinged here and there by some modern interpretation. – Both classic application and modern presentation or interpretation are easily understood by whoever still (or again) remembers the old symbol language *physically*, i.e. in said blood-consciousness: Pure intellect – by nature of the subject – cannot do the job.

That those who ignore this inner presence of what is «long past» may permit the content of the present pages to reawaken said deep inner understanding in their hearts, is our earnest bidding!

Consequently, the *Aquarius Genesis* along with its commentaries is accompanied by a wish, a hope and an encouragement:

May lectors *in inner freedom* oppose the arrogance of modern ‹Illuminates›, and, in awe and joy remember and revive for themselves the original language of Symbolism. The fact that since the early 18th century this universal human language went lost to a great extent – resp. *was stolen from the Majority* – is not exclusively due to scientific ‹Enlightenment› and academic or ecclesiastic dogmatism as such, but to the instance of world-wide systematic suppression and forceful eradication of old traditions and independent thought (today already during pre-scholar childhood!) by an usurpative ‹authority› in favor of a dominating materialistic strategy for idle ‹almightiness› of an ‹elite›. – These facts long ridiculed as *«conspiracy theory»* need to be acknowledged before it is too late!

Whoever achieves to reestablish union with primary Symbolism as explained; – who approaches it again: today in innocent, childlike openness as long ago they did in a state of dream-like semi-consciousness, and at the same time in modern «soberness of the mind» – those will be given to enter the adytum of the most cryptic secrets. – Those who will learn to *«suck the milk of wisdom»* that flows from the archaic oneness of universal Symbolism, since the beginning of time, and surely until the *«End of all Days»* (see frontispiece to the present book), those will be able to preserve inner freedom of thought and imagination despite all (spiritually ever poor) systems of power and manipulation of this world – even if those were construed in the most subtly treacherous way: He or she will then find again the primary, unpronounceable *Language of Oneness* — this *common speech of Initiates*[5] – and thus reunite with the innermost core of the Universe, in an intimate communion born of *comprehension and Love* – i.e. in silent dialogue and mutual understanding between all creatures, and with the Creator Himself! (see Appendix 3-A).

Furthermore, let us dedicate two thoughts to the phenomenon, or dimension, of TIME: The *Aquarius Genesis* as well as its *Scholia* use forms of speech in present, future and past tense alternatingly and *almost* arbitrarily as it may seem. – We bid lectors of these pages not to be *scandalized* by this fact: Time is a conception valid only within the tridimensional physical world, and applicable only there as part of the illusions of this world: ‹MAYA› or ‹SAMSARA›. – Esoteric Science always confirmed this fact; but during the last century it was ‹proven scientifically›, a.o. by Einstein and his magic of formulæ – albeit in a contestable way:

‹Relativity› expresses itself differently on different levels of the Universe: in supra-cosmic, macrocosmic, cosmic and the microcosmic consciousness of every individual. What one person sees as a far-away and even improbable future, another one sees as present or even past. – To others, then, past, present and future seem quite equivalent: They see them as being so intricately interwoven that they appear to them like an unlimited *sea of time*, or one NOW, named ETERNITY – something like a plasmatic space-time-fluid. Their *time-illusion* is, so to speak, *suspended forever*. Creation to them appears no more as a historical fact reported by pseudohistorical or mythic records, or by traditions using a ‹logical› *sequence* of time: They see an *actual, multifaceted reality* floating through the unlimited sea of Time, without beginning or end[5-A]. – This view of time relations however may be expressed and explained uniquely by timeless symbols – hence in a way where conceptions, numbers and ‹things› – times, space and worlds, can neither be unrolled nor interpreted separately anymore, but only as superposed sheets, or planes, or as spheres complementing and interpenetrating each other, until appearing like fused into eternal Oneness: unlimited in time, space or numbers.

For: NUMBERS, too, are used here not just according to conventions of school-arithmetic, but as playfully combined symbols, destined to express otherwise what cannot be said in words – as numeric symbols, or ciphers really, *«as it was in the Beginning»*. At the same time one should remember that numbers and arithmetic belong to the highest level of the highest plane of *Devachan* (see picture on page 8; where this hierarchy is visualized).

This is how the *Twelve Theses* of the *Aquarius Genesis* and its *Scholia* are to be understood, the kernel of them having been conveyed to us more than ten years ago. They describe both formation and reality of existence of all Worlds as well as their ‹Fall› – but also the idea and reality of the ‹Path back to the Father›, as heralded by all traditions regarding redemption from physical life. This *good tidings – euangelion* — is valid for every single conscious creature as well as for the universe of Creation as a whole!

One last remark, concerning the PICTURES IN THIS BOOK:

They were not planned, actually: The *Aquarius Genesis* is about *invisible things*. But pictures and pictograms arrived spontaneously while editing the *Scholia*, and it would have been a pity not to ‹listen› to them and forward them. They demonstrate that whatever in the wording of the *Scholia* may seem strange or out of place was already hinted at in earlier times – verbally, or «visibly hidden» by images. On the other hand, these old traces translated here into words for a very first time asked for new expressions in an English as close as possible to their symbolical and physical impact for our *New Era* which has only just begun.

One should also remember that every new *macrocosmic* era in its beginning repeats in a ‹short ‹summary›, so to speak, the previous cosmic eras – as explained by Max Heindel and Dr. Rudolf Steiner, between 1906 and 1924. – It therefore is self-understood that in the course of the *Aryan epoch* this recapitulation of earlier periods is unforgettably documented in ‹primitive› art and symbols. Especially the *Double Helix* ⊚, and light symbols derived from it unto the *helicoidal Triskell,* are to be understood as memories of an early consciousness until the submersion of *Atlantis.* The *helicoidal Swastika* ⊕ is a *post-Atlantean premonition* of the Rosy-Cross ⚘, while light symbols built from straight lines (the Cross, the straight-lined Swastika and Stars) are early Aryan symbols for *then* contemporary *consciousness of* THE LIGHT. –

Due to both the complex system of symbols and their polyvalence along the text, APPENDIX 1, as a help to readers, offers a separate INDEX OF SYMBOLS followed by a minimal INDEX OF SOURCES. And in order to purge the main text of special excursions, APPENDIX 5-B unveils some special aspects in pictures of APPENDIX 5-A. Actual footnotes to the text – philosophical, linguistic and bibliographical – are collected and outlined in APPENDIX 6.

The Scholia as such quote both ancient Sacred Scriptures and 20th century spiritual literature since Papus, H.P. Blavatsky, M. Heindel, R. Steiner, C. de Petri, J. v. Rijckenborgh, and others – along with most recent publications. Their parallels, correspondences or contradictions are mostly left for the lector to assess.

To close these preliminary remarks, we admonish all lectors to be *earnestly aware* of the fact that LANGUAGE – i.e. *each conscious or unconscious* THOUGHT *or spoken* WORD in any form – is MAGIC in its highest precision and power – and linked to unavoidable ETERNAL RESPONSIBILITY of whoever speaks: It is HERE that begin higher consciousness and responsibility of every human — for:

IN THE BEGINNING THERE WAS THE WORD!

The tattoo of this Australian Shaman clearly shows the features of the *Double-Helix* evoked so often throughout this book: ⑨ as well as the course of its two counter-bending branches in the ‹*solar S*› as well as in the curve named *Clothilde* (pic. 15-B). The origin of the feather pinned into his hair – here as well as in today's Turkish Altai region, and in the case of North American Indians or certain tribes of African Negro's – is a secret; – it might also be a reminiscence from the long disappeared lands of KASSKARA (MU) resp. LEMURIA, or even an allusion to communion with bird-like gods.

The Scholia

1.) «In the Beginning, when nothing was created yet, God created NUMBER.»

What Number? – Boundless indeed are Numbers! – Meanwhile: at the absolute *Beginning of a new Day of Creation of Brahma* – of a new ‹Eternity› that absolutely needs an *exclusively spiritual* first act – NUMBER is no ‹creature›, but as yet an all-embracing *quality of some indefinable density* – expressed mathematically as a «total aggregate»: ∩ or Ω (a philosophico-symbolical ‹Matrix›, or *womb*), whereof, like on *stroke* ONE, all numbers, proportions, rhythms, vibrations and harmonies are born. – This silent total sum of all numbers – THE NUMBER – therefore forms an all-comprehending, sublimely high *divine ordaining abstract principle* (see pic. p. 8).[6]

Elaine Pagels in her excellent book *Reading Judas: The Gospel and the Shaping of Christianity* comments: *«For Astronomers of Antiquity, the possibility of a mathematical description of the Universe proved that divine intelligence (not some chance or necessity) directs the Universe».* – The late Platonic tract: ‹*Epinomis*› even names numbers *«the first cause of all things».*[6-A]

The term ‹*to count*› – i.e. ‹*to number*› –means *to delimit, define and name something by its number* (*numerus*). – For: everything is ordained by NUMBER, in its appearance, existence and disappearance: ‹Kosmos› is sacred *Order* – hence *numbered and defined* (*numen = divine will*). – In short: Whatever occurs in the Universe can, looked at with ‹the eyes of Spirit›, be seen as a mathematical operation. The fight among ‹Determinists› and ‹Creationists› around this statement results from a misunderstanding: Mathematical or otherwise ‹scientific› description never affects divine nature, neither of the whole Universe nor of its smallest particle. – On the contrary: It manifests the divine will to be known by all truly thinking humans, as He knows *them* (comp. *Corpus Hermeticum: Hermes' Key for Tatios*; loc. cit. fol. 25-v.). This clarifying remark was necessary as an opening to this chapter. – And from it follows:

THE NUMBER God created in the Beginning was the ONE – His own number. For He is ONE, and whatever is in Him, is ONE with Him, hence ONE itself. – ONE alone remains undivided and un-multiplied, and is – as taught the Pythagoreans – *even and odd at the same time*.[6-B] — ONE is the root of all divisions and all multiplications – «by the will of God» – i.e. *‹by its own will›* : I. – All other numbers were born from division or multiplication of the ONE – fractions included. – IT, the source of all numbers, the ‹DOT› – is also the *«infinite straight line curving back to its own origin»* and finally ... forming that *«Sphere, the circumference of which is nowhere, while its center is everywhere».*[6-C]

Opposed to the ONE – and akin to it – there is the ZERO: not created, but arisen; – not NUMBER, but NUMBERLESS; – indivisible and not to be multiplied. – As the ONE is *perfect undivided Presence* in essence and consciousness, so the ZERO is *perfect Non-presence* – but quite different from *non-existence* or *Nothingness!* – Just as ONE is *dynamic immobility* in perfect presence, so is ZERO – that is also a CIRCLE – as the *static plenitude of the Forethought* (‹PRO-NOIA› of PLEROMA) *in its constant motion*; and in the meantime it is perfectly ‹invisible›: shapeless, spaceless, immeasurable.

Thus, ZERO is no opponent of the divine ONE: It is rather its inversely polarized *counter-part* – and therefore its true complement, just as the ‹Female› is the inversely polarized *counter-part* of the ‹Male›. – This interplay of opposed ‹Duals› sparks the dynamics of the whole Universe: Only the most sublime ‹Highest Father› is, and remains, ONE and unopposed.

From interaction between ONE and ZERO are built up today's data processing techniques, which are almost immaterial – mainly etheric – and increasingly ‹magically spiritual› in substance and dynamics. – From the union – resp. the ‹infinitely rapid› interaction between ONE and ZERO thus arises no conflict but – correctly understood– appeasement of all contraries: Sacred Marriage of the first numbers – *out of* themselves, and *by* themselves.

In fact, from the union of ONE and ZERO immediately arose the TEN: 1+O =10 – that is the supra-cosmic Father-Mother, which generates all: The ONE here stands for creative will and creative potency (Wisdom and Power): NOUS. – The ZERO is the latter's *revelation*, but as yet, as the PRONOIA, hidden in the PLEROMA containing the *«germs of all created (or yet uncreated, or never to be created) things»*, as says the Æonology of Valentinian Gnostics (see pic. on p. 152). – On the other hand, the 10 is expressed also by the top Sephira in the *Tree of the Sephiroth*: KETHER – the ‹Crown› or ‹Dot› or ‹Aiyn› – is equally undivided yet, but indeed intrinsically bipolar in its perfection.

Earlier (so-called Arabian numbers are a young but very magical invention!), the FATHER was symbolically *drawn* as I, the MOTHER as —, the SON as ✕ ,– that is the universal Light-Cross which also forms the Roman number TEN. Adding to these also the *macrocosmic divine* SON OF MAN: IX (the macrocosmic NINE: 9), this

Symbolism surprisingly produces the well-known Word of Jesus in Jo. 10:30: *«He is in Me and I in Him»* – resp: *«I and the Father are* ONE*»*: I + X = IX ; but also: I + IX = X = 10 = I. Adding to these ⟨*Holy Spirit*⟩ *as a fourth component,* the cipher of which is a H (like the front of many gothic cathedrals, hence the *aspiration* H), the group of archaic numbers is almost complete: ONE for the *One-and-All;* – TWO (by the 10) for the *Father-Mother* as a prime foundation for the dichotomy of the physical Universe; – THREE for the eternally universal Trinity of the ⟨Holy Family⟩: FATHER, MOTHER and SON. – FOUR mirrors the Pythagorean TETRAKTYS as FATHER, MOTHER, SON and HOLY SPIRIT. – The NINE (9) stands for perfectly divine (earth-born) Man: ADAMAS PROTOGENOS in the Beginning of Creation. And NINE shall be also the result of perfect earthly Man (9) *overcoming matter* after his purification, renewal and transformation, in the process of rebirth from Water, Spirit and Fire, – i.e. after his actual *Transfiguration* (see THESIS 12).

IO thus is also the first manifestation of the NUMBER TWO – not for ordinary thought in the *Separation,* but resulting from *fertile Union* of I and O. As the ⟨fruit⟩ from Sacred Marriage of I + O must give X, there appears, with the SON (X or +), the NUMBER THREE – *Synthesis from Thesis* I *and Antithesis* −. The inner meaning of the THREE is the △.[6-D] So the SON becomes the Mediator between I and O: between God and World, hence also △ between O and □, giving ⊜. The following chapter will show the impact of this statement, and why it is universally applicable. Even the Druidic Triads are to be read with this as a background. Guyonvarc'h and Le-Roux in their book *Les Druides* express it like this: *«The Triad is ... a manifestation in Plurality as a subordinate conception of Unity»*.[6-E]

In these highest interrelations thus, numbers are not used according to scholarly arithmetical conventions, but, in a consequent enlargement of views, *arithmosophically* in a free *play of numbers,* similar to what Hermann Hesse named *the Glass Bead Game.*[6-F]

In order to prepare readers for the *multi-layer system of Creation* of the Universe, the following fundamental ⟨planes⟩ should be well understood: 1° *Kosmos* as the sevenfold living being of the World as we ⟨know⟩ it. – 2° *Microcosmos,* the complete system of every human being, representing a miniature *Image and Compendium* of God and of the World (thus, in the following chapter the term *Microcosmos* always means *a complete human entity*). – 3° *Macrocosmos* as the totality of all Universes with all the *kosmoi* or worlds they contain, with the latter's Reigns and inhabitants; – hence, the total sum of all *presently, in the past, or not yet,* manifested Worlds. – And 4° the *supra-cosmic plane,* or ⟨*Sphere*⟩: the unlimited, all-one *inner-most and outer-most Cause of all Causes and all manifestations* including their dynamics and effects: the *all-one, Alone-Good God* – the (supracosmic) ‹Father›. (see 1ˢᵗ book of *Corpus Hermeticum: Pymander*).

Because the trains of thought of the *Scholia to the Aquarius Genesis* describe relations never mentioned before, occasionally new terms had to be «invented», moreover borrowing some from the *Kabbalah*. But unlike kabbalistic tradition, meanings of the AIYN are not mixed up here: According to mentioned cosmic, macro-cosmic and supra-cosmic ‹planes›, they are differentiated as cosmic AIYN, macrocosmic AIYN-SOPH and supra-cosmic AIYN-SOPH-AUR. The teachers of Kabbalah appear to use the same differentiation and planes, but keep silent about them. They often express themselves very cautiously and in polyvalent ways, so that readers may easily be confounded.[7] – It makes good sense to adopt these four planes, their effects and new causes into the *Aquarius Genesis*, and to describe them, beginning with the AIYN-SOPH-AUR:

On this most sublime ‹plane› stand – from this prime causal space emanate – the first three Theses of the *Aquarius Genesis*: This is the unlimited Space of THE ONE, unreachable for any human understanding, and which one may at best get a faint hunch of: This inner-most ‹*Nothingness*› that ancient authors also named the *All-in-All*, may be symbolized in the closest way as ◉ – a *glyph* occurring in some rare cases on ancient Egyptian monuments. This *glyph* in Arabian Tradition is named AIYN – ع, that means at the same time: EYE, SOURCE, AND NAVEL. – Within the frame of Genesis this gives the cabbalistic ‹DOT›, in German: ‹ORT› (lat. *ortus – origin, begin, [sun-]rise*, and also *garden*). From it, God Himself ‹conceived› or ‹exhaled› Himself as the macrocosmic ‹FATHER›. – That ◉, the *Compendium* sees it as the absolutely (for humans) inconceivable All-One Father Principle: Prime cause and ground-foundation – spaceless space, invisible light, dwelling within Darkness – named by the Kabbalah «*Aiyn Soph Aur*» i.e. «*fiery source of wisdom*»; – unmanifested presence of all attributes that as yet are no attributes, because there is nothing that could mirror – let alone ‹see› – any ‹facets› of God as do, for example, the Sephiroth (recall the phrase in old myths of Creation: «... *even before the gods were created ...*», and similar). – As the One supra-cosmic Father, HE is also named «Spirit», the «Sole Good», and «Light of Lights» (*Aur* and *Or* = Hebr. *Fire* and *Light*, Lat. rad. ur-).

This immeasurably sublime vibration of God may be perceived by humans only when, as the *macrocosmic Father*, it descends from its highest heights – at first perceptible as *an inner light* only. And that is how, in the *Aquarius Genesis* as well, promptly appears the Light as soon as there exists anything like ‹space›, wherein what so ever can ‹exist›. For – says the *Sohar* – «*the Eldest of Elders descends, worlds leaping from him and dying again, like the fiery sparks from under the hammer of the blacksmith*». The *Aquarius Genesis* sees this *macrocosmic Father-God* – the *Aiyn-Suph* of the Kabbalah – as the ‹*All-seeing Eye*› within the Fiery Triangle: △. – Western Theosophists also name that one – in a *macrocosmic* sense – the LIGHT OF LIGHTS which reveals itself to the Candidate as a *light-spot* (*Pingala* in Hindu Initiation).

The *Fiery Triangle* △ – also named *macrocosmic Trigonum Igneum* – thus contains the *macrocosmic Trinity*: All-Father, All-Mother and SON (LOGOS, the macrocosmic CHRISTOS), and fourth, as its *central Dot*: HOLY SPIRIT.

To help understand this, we need to emphasize that the ‹MACROCOSMIC CHRISTOS› must not be seen in the frame of any specific Religion, but as an energy, a dynamic, a macrocosmic *effectiveness* of the *supra-cosmic*, all-embracing, all-penetrating, all-preserving *power*, which continually presses onwards everything contained within the Universe: The *macrocosmic* CHRISTOS is, then, the *Love-Radiation of the Father* as the LOGOS. – That is why He is also named the *macrocosmic Christ-Force*, or – as says Rudolf Steiner – the *universal Christ-Intention*.

On the first, the supra-cosmic plane, but penetrating all planes, thus ‹stands› the FATHER as the spiritual originator and preserver of ‹His› Universe, which in cycles He ‹exhales› and, at a ‹given moment›, ‹inhales› again, retiring Himself into His innermost *Source*. On the second plane, there is the AIYN-SOPH: Kabbalah and Valentinian Gnosis also name it in short: the DOT, the ‹*master builder*› and *the Old of Days*. This is the *macrocosmic Fiery Triangle*: △.

At his side, there stands the ●: This is the symbol of the *macrocosmic Mother* aspect within the △, figuratively expressed as the *Prime Source within the Universe*: CHAOS, the absolute *Zero-Point of Energy* (before that, no Zero-point and no manifested energy exist) – the Prime Foundation, or *Non-Foundation* (Jacob Bœhme), whence every Kosmos «*comes forth by Day*», – and whither everything will return at the periodical re-union of all Worlds inside the «*New Jerusalem*» – «*at the End of Days*» – at the end of a ‹*Day of Brahma*›. – The ● gives birth to everything, *revealing* whatever the *macrocosmic Father* as the *Aiyn-Soph* ‹thinks out›, visions or ‹imagines›. She is the womb wherein everything ripens; – She is the Great Mother: *macrocosmic Plenitude* (Pleroma): As the daoistic ‹De›, She contains the ‹germs› of all created – and of all never to be created – ‹*ten-thousand things*› of Daoism: material

41

creatures, spirits and animated spheres: First living as formless ideas, then etherically shaped by the Master-Builder, and finally appearing as physical manifestations (comp. Thesis 5, and also Appendix 4 hereafter). – And She – DE – is the One Universal Law. *Pymander* names Her : *The first Child of the Father.* – On the cosmic plane then, She is also denominated as NATURE. –

«Descending to the cosmic plane», now, in the Tree of the Sephiroth we find the *cosmic Trinity,* named Chokmah, Binah and Dath. This triplet illuminates – as the *«Head»* – the *«Body»* of the so-called *Tree of Life* – the *Tree of the Sephiroth*. The symbol for this cosmic Trinity is the ♀ – a symbol primarily known from Ancient Egyptian Monotheism, with three aspects as well: OSIRIS, ISIS, HORUS. – A different way to express the cosmic Tri-Unity *«at the Beginning»*, is the symbol of the Sun: ☉, understood as: ⌒ (comp. ‹Osiris›, the eye of the Father) with ◡ (‹Isis›, Moon) as the maternal womb, and with ✕ (*cosmic Christos* as the Light *for the World*, and also as the WORD *in the World*). – ✕ is identical with the Dot in ☉, the cosmic Christos *as the turning point in the cosmic Destiny*, in and by whom the macrocosmic Fire-Ether shines up through the resplendent *solar* dynamics of the Father: *Jèsoūs, the Fiery One,* according to His Word: *«I am the Light!»*

Above mentioned *Tetrad* shows in the four Top Sephiroth of the TREE OF LIFE: 1° KETHER, or Holy Spirit, dominating as the ‹CROWN› – ‹pure divine Idea›, or ‹abstract Thought›, with 2° CHOKMAH, i.e. ‹Wisdom› SOPHIA – as the ‹Father›; – BINAH – *‹concrete thought›* or ‹Science› as the ‹Mother›, and, finally, DATH in its meaning of *virtue, potency and effectiveness* – i.e. the SON as the LOGOS.

Before leaving the Tree of the Sephiroth as an image for the main facets of manifestation of God in His Creation, it is worthwhile to mention that the somewhat ‹arbitrary› representation of the *Threefold Crown (‹Tiara›)* consisting of Aiyn, Aiyn-Soph and Aiyn-Soph-Aur on top of the Tree of the Sephiroth, finds its *microcosmic* correspondence in Man's so-called ‹higher Thought-members›, which only by very few exceptionally blessed Initiates undergoing a complex spiritual process of Transformation have been brought to live maturity: MANAS, BUDDHI and ATMAN.

One more addendum is indicated here: To the aforementioned *Abyss* or *Non-Foundation of the Aiyn-Soph-Aur* ◉ corresponds the Babylonian Apsu, the Egyptian Atum.

Phonetic Cabale may have changed APSU into *Ab-Shu* – *father of* SHU; for the latter's Egyptian ‹descendants› – his Creation – are really SHU and TEFNUT. This pair of siblings then corresponds to the *macrocosmic* Father-Mother. TEFNUT in fact means *Itef-Nut* –

father of NUT – hence *father of Heaven.* The well-known ‹Feather of SHU› shows that SHU as the ‹Pillar of Heaven› equals a *macrocosmic Law*, inscribed (so to say) *with a gilded feather* in the ‹belly›, or ‹book›, of ATUM. – This is the Great Law – MAAT or KARMA.

Macrocosmic ATUM hence becomes *cosmic* TEN: *At-Um* (from *Ata, Father*, and *Umma, Mother*), is the *Father-Mother so oft mentioned by Jesus:* bipolar Unity. – Logos, or the Christos as the Son from the union of I and O – their ‹cross-over› ✕ as Light, Truth and Life – is, thus, really ‹One› with his Father-Mother: X = 10 = 1. Here symbolic ‹values› appear to flow together in polyvalence.

At this point, there is no more question of the *supra-cosmic* plane in which no individual thing is discernible yet at all – but of the *macro-cosmic* plane. *Aquarius Genesis* in Theses 4 and 5 names this purely spiritual *potentiality*; – but only in Theses 6 through 8 consider it as manifest *realty:* ‹Paradise ⊗› of Thesis 3 is not vulgarly discernible at all. Theses 9 through 11, then, speak of Macrocosmos, cosmos and microcosmos in *overlapping parallels.* – And once more let this be emphasized: Said ‹Glass Bead Game› is *no speculation,* but precise spiritual reality !

But let us return once more to the *supra-cosmic plane* where, by the NUMBERS TWO through FOUR, all manifestations, from the most sublime to the grossest one, are yet just prepared as *spiritual potentialities*, as divine powers, as *Virtues:* This is to emphasize said *Tri-Unity* which will be emanated by the macrocosmic Aiyn-Soph – and ‹later› by the Aiyn of the *cosmic* ‹Fiery› Triangle △: Western Tradition has several names for the three divine Virtues within the Flaming Triangle – e.g. Will – Wisdom – Impact (or Effectiveness – comp. *Pymander*, loc. cit.). These give again the mentioned triplet of Sephiroth: Chokmah, Binah and Dath .[7-A]

Macrocosmically, the THREE represent the universal creative power in its perfection: *cosmically* speaking the triple perfection of the world of manifestations. The Candidates of the Gnostic Mysteries in turn ‹see› the SON rise from the central point of their *microcosmic* Fiery Triangle (see above) – as *the effectual living* WORD *of Redemption.*

In *Thesis 1* of the Aquarius *Genesis,* this really inconceivable process with its entire dynamic is still veiled within the TEN: in the IO as well as in the WORD – ✕; – and the THREE is veiled likewise within the One. The TEN as the purely spiritual ✕ stands (as the DOT and the axis of elevation) in the Prime Source of the AYN-SOPH-AUR (thus in the «*Innermost of the Innermost*»), *and* in the Innermost of the AYN-SOPH, *and also* in the center of the AIYN): This in turn is the ‹NOTHINGNESS› of the Kabbalah, from which will arise the WORD as the *cosmic and microcosmic* SON: The AIYN-SOPH, thus, is «*the innermost of the 24 Mysteries*», whence according to the famous text of ‹*Pistis Sophia*› arose the Christ, and whither He re-entered after taking back His Light-garment[8]. –All this serves as preliminary explanations to - Theses 2 through 12. —

From the *supra-cosmic* plane, macrocosmic dynamics of the SON ✕ had yet to come forth as the timeless *dynamically static* revelation of the *macrocosmic Light-Cross* ✕ contained in the ○. – As for now in Thesis 1 however, this manifestation cannot be spoken of – neither in its rest, nor in its motion; for there still goes on the process of perfection of THE NUMBER which, as first creation, appears on the plane of supra-cosmic divine consciousness. This is the *vibrational level* of the Primary Source of *sound, warmth, movement and light* – the phenomena really effecting LIFE. –

‹Higher› even than all conceivable and unconceivable Kosmoi vibrates this supra-cosmic Source – this Primary Source of AIYN-SOPH-AUR – this «Eye of God» ☜, inhaling and exhaling all *potentialities* of the Macrocosmos and of IT-self, while IT ‹*thinks out*› *as a vision* all realities adapted to the actual inhabitants of every world – created by the latter's consciousness – IT donning such realities like one robe after the other, such as IT – through actual Creation – projects from its innermost Mystery.

Nevertheless: supra-cosmically – and long before any physical creation takes place – the Dual of the ‹FATHER-MOTHER› and the Triplet or Trinity of the ‹divine Family: ‹FATHER›, ‹MOTHER› and ‹SON›, are present in their creative *potentiality*; and they become manifest realties out of the will and the mercy of HIM: the AIYN-SOPH-AUR in His descent as the AIYN SOPH, ‹clad› in the AIYN of the ‹TREE OF THE SEPHIROTH›, and with as IT's robe's trail the ever actual *Path of Return from cosmic and microcosmic Exile*, available to all creatures – especially to *all humans of good will* …

The ‹*Hymn of Repentance*› of creatures then conjures descent of the SON as the CHRISTOS who clears the Path of Return for the bizarre host of *physical worlds of manifestation*: the Path back to Oneness of the souls – the highest manifestation in our sevenfold Universe, named as well ‹*Union of the Pure*›; –and from there, in absolute Perfection, back into ‹*the Fathers House*›.

2) *«In the second place, God created the* UNIVERSE OF PLENITUDE: *this was the pure, absolutely divine, completely spiritual Universe: World without forms, without thoughts or words, with neither light nor darkness. Its figure is the Circle* O, *that is All-in-All; for God was One with this World, and this World was in God, and God was this World, and there was no single limitation – neither of Space nor of Time: All was God; All was* WISDOM, STRENGTH, LOVE *and* SPIRIT; *– and All was perfectly good.»*

The very first Creation – the (as such, for humans) entirely inconceivable NUMBER – became ‹seizable› only when there appeared ONE, TWO (Dual), THREE (Trinity). Thence immediately followed the infinite host of all other numbers. And thus the boundless *plenitude of potentialities* within the Universe – PLEROMA –already is a reality – but as yet just as entirely formless, unseizable ‹divine thoughts› (see *Appendix 4*). The total potentiality of PLEROMA instead (see pic. on p. 152), already contained MEASURE and PROPORTION, including all Spirits, Demons and gods. – When these descended from the supracosmic field of *potentialities* (as macrocosmic and cosmic realities according to the commentary to *Thesis 1* here-before), the ONE LAW OF NUMBER, MEASURE and PROPORTIONS immediately became a macrocosmic and a cosmic reality (Life!) as well: That is how the seven *fundamental Hermetic laws* were born – like, e.g., *«as above ... so below ... »* etc.

Regarding the origin of the physical world as described in the biblical book of *Genesis* (definitively edited only around the beginning of our Era), there may be distinguished three ‹planes› or ‹octaves› of the UNITY *of God* : God as the *supra-cosmic* FATHER, the ‹All-One-Good› (AYN-SOPH-AUR) – ◉, *macrocosmically* as the AIYN-SOPH △, and *cosmically* as AIYN – ᛉ, i.e. the Sephirah KETHER. – Secondly: TRI-UNITY of the macrocosmic Fiery Triangle; – and, third, PLURALITY of the ‹Elohim› as the ‹Seven Lords›, or the ‹Seven Spirits before the Throne of God›.

If now the *macrocosmic Trinity* of ONE, ZERO and ✕, viz. the *Tetrad* I, O, ✕ and H as developed in *Thesis 1*, also called into being the *cosmic* ‹TRINITAS› ♃, i.e. the classic Triad of FATHER, MOTHER and SON, then this second Trinitas, nevertheless, is ‹of a much lower ranking› than the former which, in turn, becomes ‹seizable› only if seen as part of the whole Plan of the *macrocosmic Creation* with its numberless cosmic manifestations, like the ones «we know».

Now, re-defining the symbols used earlier for the *highest plane*, the same *Triad plus Tetrad* may also be understood (relatively!) as the cosmic Unity (Union) of the *Seven* Spirits before Gods Throne, who, being also *Seven Virtues*, *immediately* direct the appearance of the *cosmic plane*: *Three* of them are contained in the *Triad* of the macrocosmic Fiery Triangle – but *Four* in the divine name of the ‹*Tetragramma*› יהוה. – *These Seven* form – as long as united – the seven-pointed ‹*Star*› △, as realized by a true *Christ-Man* who – in full consciousness of both his four lower, physical bodies and his three higher, spiritual ‹bodies›: MANAS, BUDDHI and ATMAN – would stand in this World as a true Human: Having completely outgrown all typical cosmic phenomena, he or she – after deposing their physical body – continue their cooperation in the Divine Plan – now out of the spiritual world of the Universal Brotherhood of the Redeemed: Perfects within the Heptad △, one with the One, welcomed joyfully inside the ZERO: O. They have made manifest, *microcosmically*, the *cosmic* CHRISTOS, and thus have realized the *New-Divine Human* ☺ – the SON OF MAN. – Now they operate *into* the World, and *for* the World, as ‹Angels›: not as human personalities anymore, but as pure *force-entities*. – However, they also may re-incarnate in a new human form if ‹the Divine Plan› demands for it. – This is what recurrently happens with the Entity called *Christian Rosencreutz*.[8-A]

There is also a description by Leadbeater[8-B] directing our attention onto these four main ‹*planes*›, or *levels*, or ‹*octaves*› of spiritual vibrations showing the presence of God in the Universe:

1° The *supra-cosmic* ‹womb› enfolding the *macrocosmic* ‹plane› and the cosmic worlds it nurses just as it does for all other thinkable or unthinkable, actual or potential, past and future systems: On this plane of a *Space-Time-Continuum* stand *Theses 1 to 3* of the *Aquarius Genesis*. — Here, where no shaped idea occurs yet, there now appears unlimited, unshaped LIGHT and its symbol: ✕. Within the UNIVERSE OF PLENITUDE O indescribable as such, there appears ‹for the first time›, illuminated by the Christ-Light, the universally divine, entirely spiritual LIGHT-PARADISE ⊗, where ✕ also stands for the SON emanated by THE NUMBER, and here also for the WORD as the LOGOS.

2° The *macrocosmic plane*, which along with ‹our› world also contains all other worlds comprised in the totality of galaxies (the Universe): They all are vivified and animated by the macrocosmic ‹black› Central Sun – out of the maternal *macrocosmic Zero-Point of Energy*, ● as mentioned earlier.

All these relations are indicated by *Theses 3 and 4* of the *Aquarius Genesis*. – To this *macrocosmic*, still ENTIRELY DIVINE SPIRITUAL LIGHT-PARADISE corresponds the Glyph ⊗ again. –

Today's Gnostics in this respect also speak of a (macrocosmic) ‹*Sixth Cosmic Sphere*› (a vibrational level) and of an *extremely bright, divine Light* (All spheres interpenetrate each other).

3° On the *cosmic plane* will thus ensue: FATHER, MOTHER, SON and *originally divine Man*, all still united in an *elemental, only pre-determined, and as yet* ETHERIC, PARADISIAC WORLD ⊕. This corresponds to the *biblical Paradise*. – The *Corpus Hermeticum* in its *Key for Tatios* uses the following wording:

«*These then are three: God-Father, the [Sole] Good – and the World – and Man. The World is maintained by God, and the World maintains Man. The World is the child of God; Man is a creature of the World. – And God knows Man very well and takes care of him; – and evenly He wishes to be known by him*».

In *Chinese Gnosis* as given by Lao-Dse in his *Dao-De-Ging*, DE corresponds to the MOTHER; – Hermes names it *the World*.[9] – At this point however, all forms are present only as mental and astral *idea-shapes* (see Appendix 4, and Leadbeater, loc. cit.).

This cosmic plane also holds the [in a limited way] sensually perceivable, ‹natural› solar system with its perspectives towards further Kosmoi. This is the plane where stand *Theses 7 through 11* of the *Aquarius Genesis*. – Within etheric, *but still paradisiac*, Creation ⊕, divine idea-shapes reach their first manifestation. – It is only now that the Elements begin to condense physically: FATHER-MOTHER, SON and Creatures split up: This is the so-called ‹THIRD FALL› – amidst spouting sparks of Spirit (see later).

Voluntary descent of Spirit to meet lower and lower frequencies of physically ‹gelled› *Prima Materia* continues today, due to odious degeneration of humanity. Only original Man in his first Paradise – ‹*Adam Kadmon*›, or *Adam Protogenos* – despite being etherically condensed already, was celestial – and *androgynous*.

4° *The microcosmic plane*: Here, thanks to enhancement of an *inner-own awareness*, human individuals begin to consciously *perceive* the *inseparable communion* with the three higher planes, then even learn to *reactivate* this communion *with their Self*, embarking on the process of Transfiguration – until finally achieving to *live this communion* in the ‹ETERNAL NOW›. This is *New Life* – «*new Heaven and new Earth*» of the *biblical Revelation*. But as this process needs *a living physical body endowed with consciousness*, Man *had to* become a physical being, shaped by the Moon-Angels of JHVH-Yaldabaoth.[9-A]

Based on these differentiations, Spiritual Science ‹discerns› several degrees of consciousness which typically are encountered again in «practical Esoterism» (the spiritual process) as *four levels of consciousness of the Christ-Light* [10] – namely:

a. *Worldly Christendom* on our Earth, also denominated as *Pastoral Christendom.*[10-A] – The latter is mainly based on the Gospel of *Luke* (*Lux* = *Light!*): The symbol for this Gospel is the bull (*Taurus*) – an animal going well with stables and pastors, embodying in the Zodiac the *Element Earth* and ‹governed› by the *Goddess* (i.e. *Virtue*) named Venus.

b. *Cosmic Christendom* named *«of the Three Sages»* with their Babylonian *«Star-Wisdom»*. The latter is described in the *Gospel of Mathew*: This is – so to speak – a *scientific Gospel,* (Greek *μάϑημα, máthèma – knowledge, tuition, teaching*). Its allegory is *Man* figured as the ‹*Pregnant Blind Seer*› we encounter in *Revelation,* and in myths where he appears e.g. as ‹*blind Homeros*› (literal meaning: a *Guarantor*), or as the ‹*Seer Theiresias*›. The element of this Gospel would be *Air* (the *god* or *Virtue* named *Hermès-Mercurius*).

c. *«Messianic»,* or *«Michael's Christendom»* according to the *Gospel of Mark* conveying especially the wonder-deeds attributed to Jesus – hence *concrete facts,* meant to fulfill the *Old Testament's «prophesies of old»* and to legitimize Jesus as the expected Messiah. – It is quite logical that this Gospel's insignia are the *Lion* as a symbol of royal power, and also the *Fiery Sword* of unconditional, supra-personal *Love in action* (*Uranus* as higher octave of *Venus*): The ‹*Lion of Judah*› moreover is a synonym for the (in Jewish Tradition) expected messianic offshoot from the mythical «House of David» – i.e., *microcosmically* and in Terms of *Transfigurism: triumphant achievement thanks to human effort and divine grace.* — The Element of this *spiritual Christendom* is: the Solar Fire.

d. The so-called *Johannis-Christendom* is the state of consciousness that welcomes the universal macrocosmic Christos *in the heart* – thanks to obtainment of a *new understanding and new Thought* – the so-called ‹*Jupiter-consciousness*› which ‹connects›, or even permanently unites, a human with Spirit, elevating him or her beyond terrestrial bonds, until reaching to pure divine spheres. – This Gospel is rightly symbolized by the *Eagle* appearing *«in the clouds of the sky»,* as in the famous ‹dream› of Emperor Constantine II, the ‹Great›: *«In hoc signo vincas* – in Him you will overcome». – The Element of *John's Baptism* is Water – the Element of so-called *Johannis-Christendom* instead is FIRE-ETHER: ♁.

Regarding the cosmic *(solar) Christendom* with its ancient *Star-Wisdom*, there remains to be added what Werner Greub in his book[11] writes about this old Tradition, largely quoting *Wolfram von Eschenbach* : The ancient Star-Wisdom was based on a consciousness far from today's exaggerated intellectuality of over-excited individuals, but close to the imaginative consciousness of individuals endowed with an inner view, having direct access to the *collective Wisdom-Memory* of the Universe (‹*Akasha*›).

In earlier times, the carriers of Star-Wisdom were the *Sabeans* (*sab-* = *light*, same root as *Savant*). Their main centers were in Mesopotamia (Haran) on one hand, and in Ethiopia on the other (comp. the *black Queen of Sabah*: *Sulamit* is the female form of *Sulaiman*, i.e. *Salomon*).[12] – It also is worth-while mentioning that here is a hint to the so-called *Era of Taurus*, – hence to the time from ca. 4'500 b.C. to 2'200 b.C.: This is the begin of the highly developed civilization of Old-Egypt, where the *Apis Bull* – or *Sun Bull* – played his important role: In order to be eligible as a *Holy Apis*, a bull had to fulfill certain conditions, among others: to wear a divine signature on his forehead – the sign of a god (Hat-Hor) or a Planet (*e.g. Sothis*), or the Moon – or even that of the *Sun*.

The Judeo-Syrian Christendom of the *Manicheans* (with its *Chaldeo-Persian* influences) taught the old Star-Wisdom as well, until the Manichean Apostate and ‹Saint› *Augustinus* with his consequent persecution of Gnostic Christendom achieved almost complete extinction of Star-Wisdom throughout Europe.

The biblical account myth around the Accadian *Abram* who from *Haran* went westward in order to «*serve the new Sole God*» as says the myth, means the young Chaldeo-Sumerian nomad tribe averting from *solar Star-Wisdom*, favoring the new monotheistic cult for *lunar Jahweh* – a conversion fully achieved only ca. 500 b.C., i.e. some 2000 years after the time in which biblical ‹History› places the relative myth (the geocentric world picture replacing the heliocentric one until ca. 1600 a.C.).

So-called ‹Jewish› *Kabbalah* and Jewish Gnosticism as they exist today are other relics of the old *macrocosmic Wisdom of the Gods* as learnt during the Babylonian Exile: It was transferred from the *Cushites* to the *Chaldeans*, from those to *Assyria*, *Accad* and *Babylonia* – and further on to Egypt: Still consequently taught in pre-islamic Arabia, in medieval *Islamic Persia* and its Universities

(*Ibn Ruchd, Ibn Sîna, Dar al Hikmèt in Baghdad*), this sort of magic was almost completely pushed to the underground during the ‹christian› Middle-Ages. In the Occident, the most important *underground* (i.e. *occult*) continuation of this old lore, mentioned also in the *Corpus Hermeticum*, is the *Grail Tradition* preserved still in today's esoteric Orders in the ‹West›.

NUMBER, PROPORTION and GOOD MEASURE are, as shown earlier, the highest *hierarchy of the Heavens, supra-cosmically* culminating in the ‹*Love-Will*› of the all-embracing, all-effectual, all-vivifying One Eternal ‹Arch-Father›-God: AIYN-SOPH-AUR – the *Fiery Source, Navel and Eye*. – In the *supra-cosmic Trias*: ONE–ZERO – TEN, the symbol of NOTHINGNESS (i.e. Plenitude of the ● ‹in› the primary AIYN-SOPH-AUR), arose (through inversion of the ◉, and after a second step), third, the definitely evolutive dynamic Triskell ✿. Thence wells then up the *macrocosmic Trias*: FATHER-MOTHER-SON, united in the macrocosmic *Aiyn-Soph*: △.[12-A]

The *universal aspect* of △ makes of every ‹thing› a spiritual realty. – From its ‹all-*motherly*› aspect ● every ‹thing› «*comes forth by Day*». – Through involution of the self-contracting Double-Spire ◉, a cosmic night falls, and everything – *even the idea* of FATHER-MOTHER-SON – returns into all-absorbing Non-Being. –

The *macrocosmic* FATHER who from the △ issues as Its ONE, is, e.g., Babylonian ANU. – Him too, the *Aquarius Genesis* simply names «*God made* ...», whereas the *Corpus Hermeticum* relates God to have *visioned* the World embedded in the *macrocosmic* ZERO of all *Non-Beings*: – The latter ZERO is the GREAT MOTHER-GODDESS (MOTHER OF GODS) who to everything donates *existence* – but *no shape yet!* – As PRONOIA she keeps, within PLEROMA, Her Plenitude of germs which will eventually *become manifest*.

The *macrocosmic* SON as well springs ‹directly› from this ‹Black Madonna›, the ●: If ONE and ZERO represent a DUAL of THESIS and ANTITHESIS – and also, as the *supra-cosmic* TEN (IO), the (as such dual) dynamic unity named by Jesus of the New Testament: «my FATHER-MOTHER in Heaven» – then the *macrocosmic* 10 is the creational SYNTHESIS to reach *Union in Perfection* of all contraries (Duals) of which, therefore, none can «exist there».

Biologic Science speaks of *cross-overs* e.g. of different sequences of chromosomes. In the sense of the Spiritual Path, *crossing* consists in that the contraries of all existences are dissolved by a process in which the Candidate pacifies and unites them, *crossing*, or *crucifying*, his personal *differentiation/discrimination /‹separation› /di-vision*, as explained above: All these terms actually have the same effect. – This process cannot be achieved through stout *personal will,* but only when the momentarily or permanently illuminated Candidate of the Mysteries, in an ALL-EMBRACING VIEW, experiences the deep-inner Oneness in all aspects of all things as a permanent reality enfolding all in sublime LOVE.

By this ‹crossing› (sacred marriage), or ‹crucifixion› of opposites, the Candidate *becomes a Synthesis himself* – hence, a *higher unit* (Roman TEN: ✗) as a ‹Son of God›, a so-called CHRISTOS – anointed by his own Love Force). The LIGHT-CROSS ✗ – Greek *Chi* X –, is, and ever was, the simplest hieratic glyph for *a star* – and thus for THE LIGHT whose most important visible representative within our Kosmos is the Sun (comp. pic 17).

This train of thought leads back to the WORD as the *supracosmic* LOGOS: Unmanifested Himself but, as the synthetic dynamics of the 10, resolving (‹redeeming›) all manifestations out of the ● (microcosmically: out of ☉). On the *cosmic plane,* this turns into the manifested WORD. – And with IT as *mediator* (METATRON of Jewish Tradition), resuscitates NEW DIVINE MAN, in his perfection as the NINE (9), resp. as SON OF GOD *and* SON OF MAN: **IX.** – Seen as a ‹closed system›, this looks as follows:

Macrocosmic spiritual relations in the Universe, and especially in so far as planetary and interplanetary worlds and humanities are concerned – are described in unique comprehensiveness by Emanuel Swedenborgh.[12-B] – It would lead too far to quote an adequate abstract of this already very succinct booklet: We recommend in-depth study of its pages as a self-rewarding task.

From the *macrocosmic Trias* proceeds the well-known *cosmic Trinity* ♀ : GOD-FATHER (e.g. shown as ZEUS) – MOTHER-GODDESS (*Mari-Isis-Ceres-Dana-Venus* etc.) – and the *cosmic* SON ✗, in-carnate in *Horus, Krishna, Mithras* ... and, finally, in *Jesus Christ.*

The supra-cosmic or ‹primary plane› is not described by the *Aquarius Genesis.* It cannot be described but only grossly pictured – ‹imagined› – through analogies and symbols. On it, there dwells a fully ‹abstract›, i.e. mystical, threefold Unity as the triple *Power and Wisdom of God* (comp. *Pymander*): invisible, inconceivable, unthinkable. This Triad becomes noticeable only in and across the manifestations which It produces on the macrocosmic plane – and thus IT *must do,* too!

Why ‹*must*›? – Firstly: because the (for humans) still unnotice-able Plenitude, this abundance of the ‹germs in PLEROMA› *is pressing* towards manifestation. – Secondly: because the power of the *supracosmic Trias* of I, O and ✕ in Its never-ending dynamics *pushes those germs* to become dynamically active (see *Corpus Hermeticum*, in «*The Mind* (NOUS) *speaking to Hermes*»: «*Will you stop talking so much, oh thrice greatest Hermes ... *»).

When mentioning the *four Elements* before, there was also question of *three Principles* (no «*either – or*» as in vulgar base Nature, but a «*both ... and ...* » of macrocosmic divine Nature). For: the MOTHER is at the same time the *One Divine Law*, also named DE, or KARMA, or ASHA (Hebrew: HALAKHA) – and of a three-fold nature as well.[12-C] This Law cannot be explicitly explained here, but only be hinted at. Its visible, symbolic ‹form› instead can be seen in the *cosmic Sun* ☉ – like this:

The verbal summary for above said Trias is the *One-and-All, the* «*Center and Circumference*» forming the ☉. – The latter's *intrinsic Trinity* however is this: ⌒ (an eye) as the ‹FATHERLY› aspect, ☽ (Moon) as the ‹MOTHER› Aspect, and ☉ resp. ⊗ as the aspect of the ‹solar SON›, resp. the ‹WORD›. – And it must be emphasized that the principle needed to complete the Tetrad – HOLY SPIRIT – on all four planes (including the plane of the *microcosm*), whenever it appears at all, *is always the same*. – For: Spirit remains one and indivisible, into how many aspects and individuals it might be apportioned – from a god to the tiniest grain of sand!

Too long an excursion would be required to faithfully elucidate the above shown concept of the *macrocosmic Trinity*. It is corroborated however not only by the sum of all sensually noticeable manifestations, in the center of which always stands a *cosmic Sun* – but also by new insights of Physical Science along with numerous impressions and inner experiences that cannot be clearly verbalized but since eons are linked to the symbol of the Sun: ☉. Therefore, to *quasi-split* the Sun-Symbol into a macrocosmic *Triplet* after naming it a divinely indivisible *One-and-All* just a moment before, is acceptable only in symbolic language of very old initiatic Tradition: The Theogony of the *Quiché-Maya* has the ‹three persons› of the *Heart of the Heaven*. – European kabbalistic Theogony has the ‹all-seeing Eye› inside the *Triangle* : AIYN SOPH: △, which as a ‹*cosmic* AIYN› (KETHER) ‹contains› the same three aspects: CHOKMAH (FATHER, wisdom), BINAH (MOTHER, intellective will) and DATH (SON, LOGOS, effectual Act) – with KETHER (Aiyn, Holy Spirit) ‹completing› a new *cosmic Tetrad*. – Gœthe in his *Doctor Faustus* ‹translates› the term LOGOS as «*Tat*» – *action*; – remembering his Saxon dialect, this is: DATH. – And we now understand why ...

The FATHER – as Sacred Scriptures emphasize – can be known only through the SON. But who knows the SON also knows the FATHER –

and who knows the FATHER and the SON, will know the MOTHER as well (see pic. 13: the DOT amidst the O ‹completes› the ☉.

The *macrocosmic God-Son (Sun-God)* is therefore always a *Sun-Spirit* or *Sun-Hero* – cosmic personification of the macrocosmic *Love-Force* of the CHRISTOS as *Sun behind the Sun*: As the ‹WORD› that – like a fifth Dimension – breaks through *so-called Time*, He is really *sent out* from the *focal point of the Light-Cross* ✗, as the *turning point* for all higher states of consciousness of the Light, and as the vertical axis for spiritual ascent (growth). –

Ancient Alchemists named Him their CHRIST-SALT (*Hals Christou* or *christal*; comp. Mt. 5:13). – The SON who results from the ‹Sacred Marriage› of ⌢ and ⌣ can therefore, on the cosmic plane too, be adequately represented [only] by the Sun-symbol ☉, of which He really is the *pivotal center* and inner-most ‹Virtue›.

Even in the Symbolism of ⌢, *Father and Son are One* – as all Gospels repeatedly maintain. Another representation of the same state of being, the same effusion of force, the same live reality, is the Egyptian Hieroglyph ⚹, read by Egyptologists as ʿAabd. — Its meaning in terms of time is «*month*», but it is also linked to «*teaching*», and to the term ✶ – *sab* – Light, Star and *Illumination*.

The repeatedly occurring formula in Egyptian hieratic texts: «*pʿrjt-m-hrw*», is read by Egyptologists as «*coming forth by day*» – a phrase rather void of any meaning at all: We prefer the literal «*come forth from the Light*» – or «*entered into the [kingdom of] Light*», resp. – a formula in tune with the earlier mentioned «*Mysteries of Pistis Sophia*, where the Christ declares that He has «*entered, and come forth from again, the innermost Mystery*».

The hieroglyph ⚹ however can not only be interpreted as *Light* or *Enlightenment* but also as SOTHIS: She who as the *Morning Star*, announced *the flooding* of the Nile – hence *Renewal and new Life*. On the level of the ‹New Soul›, this is indicated by the *five-pointed Star* – the ‹Star of Bethlehem› or *Pentagram*. Moreover, the symbol ⚹ is even linked to the so-called *Gate of Light*: This appears to be analogous to the Sephirah *Jesod* («door› or ‹access› – a threshold or actual *door-step*) – according to the word of Jesus: «*I am the door ...*» – and: «*I am the One Light, the Truth* {true reality, true teaching, the true WORD} *and the [One] Life*». – Thus is proven once more the *one-heartedness (Con-cordia)* of language and Symbolism throughout all worlds and eons!

The triple descent of the *supra-cosmic* Trinity as deep as the material plane (positive antithesis to the ‹Fall›), for all cults throughout the World culminates in the appearance or ‹wondrous birth› of a ‹divine child› (Horus, Buddha, Krishna, Zarathustra, Jesus ...) – *macrocosmically* The SON – or LOGOS. Sacred Scriptures address the latter's *Advent on the cosmic plane* as the WORD again, or as *Spirit of the Sun* (comp. old anglo-germanic roots: both *Sunna* for *Sun* ☉ and *Sun* for *Son*). This explains His denomination as a *Sun Spirit* (or *Sun Hero*) who is – and remains – ONE with the FATHER, and returns *into Him*, the FATHER who *is indeed the One-and-All*. – Literature of ancient Theosophists, Rosicrucians and Alchemists named HIM the *All-in-All*.

On the *cosmic plane*, the FATHER as well was represented as ☉. Ancient Mysteries of *Dionysos and Kybélè* show the SON as the *«descended {descendant!} Son of the Sun»* – and also as the *Morning Star*. – Hellenic *Evos* or *Dionysos*, from Celtic (*«Bacco» – the Little One*) became Roman *Bacchus* and *Liber* (the *sonny!*).

Microcosmically, the *cosmic Christos* descends into well prepared humans ready to receive Him. That is why participants in the Christ-Mystery – from Antiquity to the Rosicrucians and Alchemists of the 17th and 18th centuries – named themselves *Sons of the Sun* as well. – In other periods, too, Initiates presented themselves as *Sons of God, Sons of the Father, Sons of The Light* – or simply: *Sons of the Sun* (comp. Aztecs, Incas, Chinese Emperors, Sun Kings of France (= Khazarish Kagans), Pharaons, Jesus etc).[12-D]

The three Triads of FATHER, MOTHER and SON on the three planes form a *divine Ennead,* which must not be understood horizontally but, like the *Tree of the Sephiroth,* ‹stereoscopically› over *thrice three Dimensions,* all interpenetrating each other. These nine dimensions meet, or touch one another in a *tenth, divine Dimension,* as shown in *Appendix 4*. – This, then, is again HE who in *Theses 1-3* of *Aquarius Genesis* is simply named «*God made ...*» – i.e. that same «*Father who dwells in Darkness*», in the DOT or in the ‹*void center*› of the Double Spire ◉ – i.e. in the ●.[13]

In Ancient Egypt said *divine Ennead* was expressed as *The Nine Gods of Heliopolis*. – This shows once more that polytheistic religions (lightly sniggered at by modern Theologists) all over the World really represent the full view of the multiple aspects of the Godhead on all ‹planes›: supra-cosmic, macrocosmic, and cosmic. – In spite of this, since such a multidimensional view is too strange a picture for them, ‹modern› humans with their ‹exact Sciences› continue to indifferently talk about *Polytheism,* mostly being themselves captives of some idolatrous concept where – like in anthropomorphic pantheons of Ancient Greece and Rome – Gods, Spirits, and personifications of divinized forces of Nature are mixed up and disfigured past recognition.

So the Divine Ennead of Ancient Egypt holding a mystic Trinity on each of the three planes went lost: *then* more or less *willingly blurred* by degenerated castes of priests, but *today* by sterile ‹members of the Academy› attempting to *naïvely interpret* it on an erroneous basis – or proudly in complete ignorance.

For the *supra-cosmic plane*, elucidations to this subject – verbal or in imagery – are hardly found. On the *macrocosmic* and *cosmic planes* the same goes for material or immaterial physical manifestations of any *shape* in so far as one might name ‹shapes› even such ‹macrocosmic forms› as are the cloudy or spark-like atmanic ‹divine thoughts› – and entirely vague mists of monadic Prime Matter (pure divine Love Substance) alike. –

Ancient Egyptian Tradition renders the Trinity of FATHER, MOTHER and SON by more symbols than **I**, — and **X**: M. Hirmer in his book *Ägypten* (in German) gives this comment (transl. ad-hoc):

«*The Ennead [of Egyptian gods] represents a theological system ... This system includes divine powers from the pre-existent Creator-God to the living King. On its top we see* ATUM, *The Arch-God* {comp. our ☜} ... *As a pre-existent being he is androgynous and generates ‹out of himself› the first divine couple,* SHU *and* TEFNUT: *airy Space and Humidity which are separated by* SHU – *he «who lifts up – or shores up – the Sky»* {comp. the *Rune* TJU ↑ and the hieroglyph TJW ⟋, an eagle or ‹eagle-buzzard›}.[13-A] – SHU *and* TEFNUT *can also be seen in a pair of lions near Heliopolis* {the two Sphinges? – the ‹Memnon Colosses›?}. *Their next generation are* NUT, *i.e. Heaven, and* GEB, *i.e. Earth ...*». – Unquote.

Note: In Antique-Egypt, unlike well-known Cosmologies, conventionally masculine Heaven becomes female NUT, while in GEB (same root as female Greek *Gè*, lat. Gaia), Earth – conventionally defined as a Mother – here becomes male.

Leaving to our lectors to answer the question why here *The Sky* unfolds only *after the Supporter of the Sky appeared*, a remark is due here: It is possible that ancient priests purposely inverted ‹male› and ‹female› in order to hide better the real Mystery – just as in hieratic Scriptures they inverted *right* (male) and *left* (female). It could also be that the change from Matriarchate to Patriarchate had caused this ‹inversion›. – In a similar way, since the end of the 19th century, Theosophical cosmogony inverted *Mercurius* and *Venus* at the transition from the ‹Earth Epoch› to the next: This fact will be shortly discussed towards the end of the *Scholia* to our *Aquarius Genesis*. – At any rate, the ‹male› and ‹female› poles would have been inverted, silently but willingly. – In analogy to this inversion, the glyph ♈ (female SOTHIS, male SIRIUS) again becomes the eye of macrocosmic FATHER – hence, the focal point of macrocosmic △. – Heed that this is no playing around with symbols, but a deep look into the *Mystery of genders*!

Some pages earlier, the *pair of Sphinges* in Heliopolis were mentioned. These originally two Sphinges may be looked upon also as the *Two Natures* – one divinely static, the other non-divine and ever changing – and evenly as the archetypical *poles of ‹opposed› Duals*, in China seen as *complementary Yin and Yang* – with all the meanings and impacts linked to these terms.

With NUT and GEB thus being created, there was already reached the *cosmic plane* – but still in the state of a purely divine, paradisiac (etheric) form, like ⊕.

Maybe this is the reason why, in Egyptian Theogony, a mythological personification of the SON has not appeared yet: Until here, uniquely the dynamics of a neutral play between natural powers, viz. negatively and positively polarized states of energy according to the ‹Good Law› (DE, KARMA, ASHA, see above) seem to direct all processes:. This corresponds to a *«Lemurian state of consciousness regarding The LIGHT»* – as characterized by the *Solar S* (see there).

NUT and TEFNUT instead will not generate *two* children, but *four* – namely *two pairs*: Opposed to the pair of OSIRIS and ISIS, stand SETH and NEPHTHYS: SETH could be characterized in one word as ‹The Evil One› – in short: EVIL. His element is Darkness!).

NEPHTHYS as a protective divinity would then be ‹The Good One›. Thus discrimination and judgment (the ‹Tree› of ‹Good› and ‹Evil›) come into play, and into the World as a pair of Gods. The original Harmony of ⊕, with the sisterly couple OSIRIS and ISIS as the cosmic *Father-Mother* will be disturbed permanently by SETH (this corresponds to the ‹GREAT DISTRACTOR› in Paradise, resp. to *Expulsion from Paradise* following the judeo-christiano-islamic *convention*) – thus realizing the physical Universe: ♂.

This *Disturbance* the *Redemptor Omnium*, SON HORUS, will dissolve or neutralize: that is what *cyclic History* relates of the past, and promises for the future. HORUS thereby becomes the Christ Figure. In fact, the linguistic root of *hr-* for *Horus*, and *khr-* for *Krishna* and *Christos* are equivalent. This can be shown even more clearly in the following example:

Hieroglyphic imagery represents spiritual re-birth by a crocodile (Msj, pic. 41), over which a phial with anointment oil is poured out. One of Pharao's eponyms was: Re-born HORUS –HR-MSI – thus quite clearly *the One anointed as a divine king (or as a priest-king), named* HORUS – or HORUS-MESSIAS!

The root MSJ in Middle Egyptian stands for *«give birth»* and for *«to be born»*. Græcisized, the term HR-MSI (*reborn Horus*) appears as the Greek HERMES who in his astrological symbol ☿ unites ☽+☉+✝ , thus soul, spirit and body, Mother, Father and Son in a perfect synthesis. The Romanized name *Mercurius* can be derived from *Hermes* by phonetic transmutation: $Ms \leftrightarrow Mr$, $- Hr \leftrightarrow \chi\rho \leftrightarrow cur$, viz. $\chi\rho\mu \leftrightarrow mrc$, the way Romans and Hebrews use(d) to permutate ‹outlandish› expressions in order to obtain ‹Roman› ones.

In Persia, to HR-MSJ corresponds HORMUZD. The latter may be derived from AHURA MAZDĀO (a *Father-Mother*). The term *Ahura* is used *and* for the Creator-God, Lord of The Light, *and* for divine AHURA'S created by Him (see ASURAS of INDIA) who are most akin to the biblical ELOHIM. – The Counter-Gods created by the Prince of Darkness – ANGRA MAINYU (or AHURA MAINYU whose name later became AHRIMAN) – are not named AHURA'S, but DEVA'S, FRAVASHI'S and KHRAFSTRA'S.

Integrating the Egyptian Ennead into Philosophy and Theogony of *Aquarius Genesis*, we may say: ATUM reflects the supra-cosmic ●. This is Babylonian APSU, Greek and Roman *Abyss* {Ab Is, Father of the Moon?}: the unknowable, non-representable *Non-Foundation*. Following the above-shown system the latter gives birth in Egypt to the sisterly couple SHU and TEFNUT, i.e. the macrocosmic FATHER-MOTHER, with SHU as ‿ and TEFNUT as ⌒.

ATUM in Ancient Egypt was imagined as elemental, or as a humanoïd. – Him who stands higher than all Gods we may take as a proof that original divine Man – an image of the highest Creator as the *Crown of Creation* – represents the latter's *Compendium*. In-depth study of the human microcosm confirms this. Thus the two go hand in hand: the *fabulous system* of the 21st century b.C. and the *analytical system* of the 21st century a.C.!

The fact that Egyptology – and maybe also the Priest Language of Egypt – may have attributed somewhat arbitrarily the ‹male› and ‹female› aspects of this Pantheon, should shock nobody: Contradictions (so-called ‹mistakes›) in mythological and symbolical messages (images too are to be read as texts!) *always* have a deeper import, and be it only to animate lectors' curiosity for deeper reflection, and thus enrich them with new perceptions according to his or her spiritual capacities.

About the *cosmic plane* in *Thesis 2* of the *Aquarius Genesis*, one more remark is required: NUMBER, PROPORTION and GOOD MEASURE are contained in the *musical sounds of celestial spheres*, culminating in their union: *conscious Harmony*. – NUMBER, PROPORTION and GOOD MEASURE therefore were reproduced *consciously and in wisdom* in the Temples of Egyptian Pyramids and in obelisks, in gothic cathedrals with their harmonious cosmic proportions; – but also in all shapes and proportions of every single creature in the Universe: each limb of them as well as their whole organism. And all this culminates in an all-embracing Union – everything communicating and interacting in joyful obedience to the GOOD LAW – in the NUMBER TEN – cosmic NUMBER OF PERFECTION. And their impact penetrates and rules all planes : *macrocosmic, cosmic* and *microcosmic;* – created, eventually to be created (or not at all) – or long past!

If the present analysis of Egyptian Theogony displays such a detailed systematic consciousness, this is no arbitrary interpretation, as clearly shown by the example of the *Tower of Babel*:

Its numbers, proportions and ground measure not only reflect the celestial hierarchies and the sacred numbers *Phi* (Φ) and *Pi* (π), but also names and conceptions of God {*[i]S(e)m – the Name*} along with the whole system of Cosmos and Macrocosmos.[14] – The latter resulted when, like in the so-called *Chrisma* ⊗, the *sacred* SIX *of equilateral trigons* for the six solar Elohim (three Duals) *in Pleroma,* was joined by a seventh, lunar one, (see comments to *Theses 2, 4,* and *7;* viz. the legends to pictures 27 and 37).

Original Man was *earthly divine Man* – «*Deus et Homo*» – the concluding synthesis and «*crown of achieved perfect Creation*»; – and this is what Man will finally become again when overcoming the once inevitable, foreseeable «*Third Fall*», and after accomplishing the sacred «*Path back to the Father*».

Remains to note that the phenomenon of TIME, too, is a result of the ‹Fall›: a consequence of division and splitting (multiplication) of ONE, ZERO and NINE; – and that is why «*in the Beginning*» there was no ‹before› and no ‹after›, neither ‹now› nor ‹then› (except *potentially*) – and that «*at the End of Days*» those will not exist anymore, either (except as past *experience in perfection*).

When the first ‹prehistoric› sacral monuments – megalithic constructions of the *Golden Age* – appeared, consciousness of the original divine Union was generally present. Those «*Monuments*», i.e. sacred *Memorials* (root *Men-*, see p. 16, para. 4) were conceived, built and consecrated as *reminders* of Divinity (→ the end of book *Pymander*). But Man lost that union with, and in, the paradisiac NUMBER ONE. He *forgot* it when he *left Paradise* (following the SOHAR Man himself *evinced God from it!*). Since then, he considers himself as *forcibly separated from It,* as clearly show the following linguistic facts:

Due to today's ‹orthography› – i.e. manipulative *orthodoxy of writing* – most humans live in *complete unconsciousness* amidst divine Nature, considering Nature as something completely different and estranged from them, and even as an absolute *contra-riness*. So, as an example, a neutral counterpart (God) of a thing (Man) is no more seen as its complement, but as its antagonist, thus insinuating a sheer opposition of humans and Godhead – of an *entity* (lat. *ens*) and its *identity* (specific *essence*). –

Consequently, i.e. as an inevitable consequence of the Cartesian *«dubito ergo sum»* – and of critically ‹enlightened› aversion from the Sole Good, whatever today's humans invent and build cannot but express this sadly destructive – or angrily resigned – human separation from Angels, gods and GOD!

The *supra-cosmic* (supra-divine) and *macrocosmic* (supra-human) ‹celestial› *Harmony of the «Beginning»* immediately after ‹perfection› of Creation, has – alas! – become an *ungodly cosmic* and – as compared to the *Beginning* – perfectly in-human INFERNO: This is the HELL *of the physical World*, a place of *disorder* and *distress*. Literature, arts and music since mid-20th century more than clearly illustrate this complete loss of sense, sensibility and intelligent harmony.

Thus – if we compare the whole with the elliptic orbit of a cel-estial body around its Sun – the World and humanity have now reached the *apogee*: the point most distant from God – and in the meantime the Nadir of stupidly brutish human unconscious-ness: the point where Humanity is the farthest away from said divine harmony of ‹the Beginning›, having inanely bereaved themselves of the one perfect focal point and divine origin ●, and of its sublime harmony. – But exactly there: precisely in the apo-gee or *ap-hel* of an orbit, the accelerating *force of return* towards the opposed *peri-hel* is at its relative maximum! With regard to present reflections this is what effects the *momentum of reversal* – the begin of the *sway back to the Father*.

The *«Beginning, when there nothing was created yet»* is described by many ancient traditions. In today's common language it is best ‹known› under the name of CHAOS (TOHU-WA-BOHU). This is – in a cosmic view – the Arch-Mother: She who is praised in that old Sumerian hymn the Church of Rome has annexed as her own, disguised as the *Litany for Mary «for the untroubled seizure of Spirit»* (as alluded to earlier – and opposed to what says the Gospel: Jo. 1:5,11): *«Litania in immaculatam conceptionem bea-tæ Virginis Mariæ»*:

«The Lord possessed me in the Beginning of His ways. I was ere He made the first creature. I was there since all Eternity, even before the Earth had been made. Still there was no abyss, yet I was engendered. No source sprang out of the Earth yet; – nor was there piled up the great mass of the mountains. – I was born even before the hills. – Neither soil nor rivers had He created, nor had He fastened the World on its poles. When He spread out the Heavens, I already was there; – when He surrounded the abysses with their limits, and laid down an inviolable Law for all Worlds; – when beyond Earth he fastened the Air; – when to the Waters of the sources He gave their balance; – when He confined the Sea within her shores, and when to the Waters He prescribed a Law, lest they abandon their shores ... – when the foundations of Earth He put down, I was already there with Him, and ordered everything.»

The Mayan *Popol Vuj* describes conditions before the Beginning in similar words as above litany:

«... Still was invisible the surface of Earth. Only the quiet Sea was there, and Heaven in all its immensity ... Nothing was joined, nothing was there that would have made a noise, nothing that would have moved, nothing that would have made the faintest sound in Heaven. – Only immobility and silence were there in deep darkness – in the night. – Only the Creator and the Shape-giver, TEPEU *and* GUCUMATZ: *They who generate; they who give Life – these dwelled above the Waters, enveloped in clarity. They were concealed under green and blue feathers – that is why they are named* GUCUMATZ, *the being among the greatest Wise Ones. In such a condition were Heaven and also* HEART OF HEAVEN; *for this is the name of God – thus is He named. – Then the* WORD *appeared ...»*

A Polynesian hymn about Creation also chants this state of matters – like so:

«In the Beginning there was only Emptiness. Neither darkness nor light were there, nor the Sea, nor the Sun, nor Heaven. – Then Emptiness started to stir ...».

In the Nag-Hamadi scroll: *The Secret Book of John,* there is asked the question: *«Why – and how – did Arch-Mother stir?»* – And Jesus answers (captured into a few words): *«Because she – Sophia – was tormented by self-reproaches about her actual state».* [14-A]

The Babylonian way to describe CHAOS before Creation (i.e. the model after which was written down biblical Genesis), says:

«When Creation was not yet named from above; – when solidly founded Earth hat no name yet; – when solely the Arch Father, APSU, her awakener, as well as the Arch Mother TIAMAT who gave birth to All, mingled their humors; – when no swamp was formed; – when no island could be found; – when not a single god had appeared nor been named by his name – then the gods were created therein ... »

At the side of *All-Father* APSU there stands his *all-motherly* aspect: TIAMAT (*Mat* for *Mother*, *Ti* for *Life*) – as the *Mother of Life*, or also as a *mother-wave*, or *fundamental law* for the preservation of Life and cosmic Order: DE, or MAAT. – Thus, *Ti-a-mat* is at the same time *Life born of the Good Law.* — Egyptian MAAT, i.e. *Law, Order* and *Justice* has the same signature – the same big Maat-Feather ᛁ as SHU, the *«Pillar of Heaven»*: Without *Order* (Kosmos), *no Life* – and *no World*! The counterpart of MAAT however is SETH: 𓎡, the DISTRACTOR, lawless *Father of disorder* (see Thesis 6).

The *Apis-Bull* was the symbol *par excellence* for RE: Mostly sensed as a male energy, he ‹is› the power of the Sun renewed by ‹Egyptian VENUS› – HAT-HOR. In languages around the Mediterranean Sea, *Apis* became *a bee* (comp. finds in Merovingian graves: *golden bees*, i.e. Venus-Sun-symbols as ‹good spirits›). – The ancient Maya's as well associated bees and the ‹Bee-God› most closely with Venus, ♀, with the basics of Life, and with religious traditions accompanying Life: The main point of interest here always is solar energy (to which is also related *metallic gold* – as in *Gold-Horus*!); – and *Venus*: ♀ who has so many things in common with ☉, as shown on other occasions. ¹⁴⁻ᴮ

All these relations are – ‹at this point› of *Aquarius Genesis* – only just emerging from CHAOS which has hardly become alive, or *«begun to move»*, and which still is completely spiritual. – But even then, these *purely etheric* relations are already pre-shaped as distinct ideas – i.e. abstract, invisible spiritual images (see appendix. 4) – projecting in advance their concrete CHRISTIC LIGHT!

*3.) «Within the UNIVERSE OF PLENITUDE shone up now the LIGHT-CROSS ✕:
This is the Love Force of the CHRISTOS. – And thus was inspired a FIRST
PARADISE: ⊗. – There was just Spirit, Plenitude of potentialities, and Light.
It was the all-one Sphere of Existence – all Light, Goodness and Harmony.
No Evil dwelled therein, for no Evil existed yet; – and no Evil could
dwell outside of it either, for there was no outside yet. – All was One.
All was Spirit, Love and Light. God was in All, and All was in God.»*

The ‹Para-Diis› ⊗ – that means: «imitation of the multitude of
God's pure manifestations» – was illuminated by unity, brotherli-
ness and Love in the harmony of NUMBER, PROPORTION and GOOD
MEASURE – of LIGHT, TRUTH and LIFE in WELFARE and HOLINESS.

Unlimited Life, Light without Darkness filled the Paradise: No
shadow was there: nothing dark, no fear, no cupidity – and there-
fore no Death, either. The sacred Scripture of Persia – *Zend-
Avesta* – describes it like this: «*Ahura Mazdão spoke to Spitama
Zarathustra, saying: «First thing, I, Ahura Mazdão, created the
Kingdom of Light, dear to all that lives*».[15]

Thus, anon there were only spiritual light, spiritual harmony,
spiritual life. And until then, Paradise – the child born of the
harmony of the HEAVENLY FATHER – was entirely penetrated,
illuminated and animated by godliness.

– Question: How are we to understand: «*there was no inside and
no outside*», given that Paradise and God were two?

– Answer: There was no possibility of distinction yet, and thus
no God or Non-God either – no inside and no outside.

– And how could come up an ‹inside› and an ‹outside› in an Universe that *contained* all Spheres as one godly Paradise, which
knew no inside nor outside but was All in All, One with The One
– and therefore embraced All, as does HE?

– Answer: *Polarization* arising in Paradise produced a mixture
of free holy dynamics in harmony and unity on one side – and un-
holy dynamics creating disharmony on the other: A ‹malaise› like a
negative longing named anguish – a shadow image of the lightful
loving Godhead – urged for manifestation, just as LILITH, in a future
yet to be created, would become the gloomy shadow-image of
lightful EVE. – But still everything was mingled and united – without distinction, and thus there was *no inside and no outside*.

Every perception calls for an image and a counter-image; – every
movement calls for some force and its counter-force. – And all this
demands for divisibility and discernibility. The latter two are realized in *Thesis 4* of the *Aquarius Genesis*, their consequences
however only in *Thesis 6*: For: *still* this Paradise ⊗ was entirely
spiritual – *one divine Light-Universe, blissful in Oneness*.

Anon, the Paradise was *«one single, united sphere of existence –
all Light»*. – Nevertheless, Darkness and her ‹Evil› were *potentially*
contained also in the original, completely divine, paradisiac
Creation – And so it had to be. – For: in order that all creatures
might, ‹someday› ascend towards their Creator, obeying His will
in free devotion, unconsciousness had to turn into consciousness,
and dullness under natural laws had to turn into free will and
self-responsible discernment – and this through *experience*, i.e.,
through pain (see. *Appendix 3*). – Painful experience is the soil
on which can grow consciousness of the soul. Seen that way, ‹Evil›
has an entirely constructive and even absolutely necessary function
within the Universe. This fact is emphasized in *Faust* of J.W. v.
Gœthe, by the words of Mephistopheles: *«I am part of that power
that always intends Evil, but always achieves the Good ... – I am
part of that part that in The Beginning was All: a part of
Darkness that Light birthed for itself ... »*

Who birthed here whom, or what? – *Two ways on three planes*
of understanding are possible here. {In Gœthe's phrase, *«Darkness»*
can be understood as the subject or the object. – Remark by Trad.}

The first plane is the universally mythical one: Several creation
myths begin with some Darkness as *the Mother of all things*. – But
this is no darkness of Evil, as *«in the Beginning»* no Evil exists
yet at all; – it is the darkness of the womb of the Arch-Mother,
named also: *The sleeping God*: Thus the LIGHT can manifest itself
out of DARKNESS ... and will return to rest in Darkness again!

Second: The plane of words in partial truth by Mephistopheles –
this representative of all sly deception – deceiving whoever makes
a law of every loud word uttered by some ‹authority›: What in
realty is devilish in ‹the Devil› and in his essential insidiousness
is this: Each of his lies contains a spark of Truth, and every advantage he may advance contains some seed for the weeds of Evil and
distress. – But, as a proverb says: *«from damage we grow wise ... »*
– *«... eventually!»* we should add. – At any rate, there is no Evil
that *would not*, eventually, serve the highest, the sole Good!

The third plane, however, is *blunt lies*:
«Darkness that Light birthed for itself»: Who birthed whom?
Darkness can *engender no light from itself*, except ‹lights› of perversion and deception; – and certainly never THE LIGHT! – ‹Darkness›
is no absence of light either, but rather the latter's *invisibility* for
‹blinds›: To highest perception what ordinarily is named ‹light› – including sunlight unbearable for our eyes – is still darkness. For
natural creatures whose spectrum of visibility is outside of ours,

similar facts apply to ‹normal› daylight. – In view of the universal *All-in-All* however, there can exist no *Darkness as such* that *would not* contain at the same time LIGHT – SPIRIT – GODS BREATH. –

Darkness, thus, is only an inability to see – to perceive! Therefore, only ONE Light can exist that contains no darkness, and that is the Light of *unlimited Wisdom in Love*. – To this conclusion will unavoidably be led whoever deeply meditates these questions. The *lie* in Mephistopheles' words is the cunningly applied ambiguity of his speech: Who is unable *to distinguish* and to make a choice, will be led astray! This is *dazzling Darkness* birthing *Ignorance*! – That Gœthe was aware of this is beyond any doubt!

Therefore it is preferable to completely abandon the conception of ‹Evil› as such: Complete (so to speak perfect) Evil cannot exist in cosmic reality – no more than can perfect Goodness. ‹Good› and ‹Evil› are but opposing concepts and emotions within countless subjective relative realties demanding for an observing or experiencing EGO – thus they are completely human: «*I threw my shadow – I, Ahura Mainyu, who am all Death …*»[15-A]

On the other hand, the Ego, indispensable to acquire consciousness as it were, tends toward the Darkness of ignorance, and towards Death. – DEATH: is deepest ignorance; and ignorance fosters *discrimination of ‹Good› and ‹Evil›* in the largest sense of these words.

How is this to be understood again?

A *mineral* or *metal* never ‹judges›: It follows the rules of crystallization, transmutation and dissolution, obeying the *Laws of elemental worlds* – according to conditions for life in *its own* world: It knows not these conditions, but fulfills in a ‹neutral attitude› all-directing *cosmic laws* inherent in everything, «letting them work», as far as any kind of consciousness might be present here. –

A *plant*, regarding its growth, its timely blooming, its ripening of fruits, may ‹judge› given natural circumstances in which it was inserted: the spot where its seed dropped on the soil: A seed ‹knows› if, and when, it should germ on the place it fell on, and what etherically pre-shaped form it got to grow into; – but this is no real *judgment* – not even an *unconscious choice*: Plants follow *mineral laws* of sympathy and antipathy – of growth and order. –

Evenly, there cannot be spoken of any ‹judgment› in an animal – not even in one that would have achieved a certain extent of individuality through some kind of domestication – like for example a dog, a horse, or a cat: Indeed, it may chose the place where to feed, where to mate and raise its progeniture, and,

– adapted to its freedom of movement – even the place where to die; – but that is no conscious discernment: In all this the animal follows the laws of plants about structure, orientation and assimilation, without conscious judgment, and with no distinction of ‹Good› and ‹Evil›. – A dog-owner may well frown at his dog and say: *«Bad dog! – Bad dog!»*, because the latter followed his instincts or habits at an ‹unfit› place or moment, same as humans do. Instead, no dog would judge his master to be ‹evil›, but at the most incomprehensible, or threatening. – Distinction of ‹Good› and ‹Evil› has – *primarily* –nothing to do with fear: It is an exclusively human ‹attainment› – for it demands for an Ego living under the impression of being the navel of the world, and therefore of being allowed to make any judgment at all. –

Human egocentrism is generally said to be the immediate cause of the ‹Fall› – with the mythical expulsion of Man from a material Paradise, following an act stigmatized as ‹Evil› by some anthropomorphous god. – But this act was in fact inevitable and even necessary, should *originally divine but unconscious Man* become *all-conscious new divine Man* (see *Appendix 3-A*).

Following Jewish Gnosis, Man, as mentioned earlier, expelled God from Paradise and now seeks healing through the return of God into him – Man – himself[15-B]: Original divinity and purity Man has lost. – New divinity must be acquired on the painful path of physical experience *«with fear and trembling»*. This means to become conscious of one's own mineral, phytogenic, and animal nature – but also of one's human and divine responsibility – i.e. to *acquire ‹self-knowledge›*. – But what, really, is *this Self*?

Typical mass humans in their state of excessive egocentricity even lack consciousness of their low Ego as it were, living with no real consciousness about what so ever – and surely without the least understanding of Man's significance and responsibility within the Universe: – Man as a mass preferably follows the laws of a complex *brutish world of impulses and anxieties* within Clan Spirits and Race Spirits. Secondly, they follow an *ego-will* which they do not control at all. Therefore, so-called ‹reasonable› or ‹intelligent› average Man even lives *«beastlier than any beast»*, as says Mephistopheles, again in Gœthe's *Doctor Faustus*.

On such grounds, world-religions have stamped the image of an ‹evil›, a ‹vicious› or ‹sinful› Humanity, who must tremble before God, its Creator and ‹Judge of the world› – unworthy to look up to Him. The doctrine of such a pitiless divine judgment originates in the fact that those who spread said doctrine have themselves not yet digested the fruit, the one-time eating of which they call a perpetual hereditary guilt. For, even if it is true that Man – on the grounds of his existence already (as says the *Corpus Hermeticum*) – is half impure, and alienated from the Sole Good, he nevertheless is *neither* unworthy *nor* evil: *God loves all His creatures!* What human, then, may dare to reject whomsoever (beginning with himself!), when God loves all *with undivided Love?* – God wants us to look up to Him, joyfully! – He wants us to grow up to Him in Love! Already in the foundation of the first act of creating He prepared for all His creatures to return home, as soon as they would become conscious of being *part of* Him, and *in* Him – deeply enmeshed in matter as they were going to be! –

So: can there be any human bold enough to uphold that God made a mistake? – Who has a right to think of anger and punishment, where God is Love – and nothing but Love!?

On the *truly human* plane with clear human self-consciousness (consciousness of a Self) through self-acquaintance and self-acceptance, there now remains to discuss the differences between *examination, distinction, judgment,* and *conscious choice.* – In the present frame however, this would definitely lead too far.

But how does all this manifest itself on the *absolute plane* – the paradisiac plane ⊗ of *The Beginning*, where mineral, dog and God were still ONE, and where there neither was, nor could be, any Evil to be discriminated as such? – And one might as well argue: «But surely it cannot be affirmed that as soon as we don't use the terms of ‹good› or ‹evil› anymore, the Universe is in complete order and divine harmony again!?»

To this remark one might oppose that with respect to macrocosmic relations within the *eternal Universe*, everything is in harmony indeed, for, examined over time and all occurrences, the small deviations that worry so much our human hearts remain absolutely equilibrated by ‹DE›, or ‹KARMA›. – On the other hand – and seen in a more ‹scientific› way – these relations can be expressed in modern speech as follows, where planet Earth – *a tiny grain of sand on the strands of the Universe* – shall serve as an example:

Planet Earth – a live limb on the body of the World – is, like every animated living organism, composed of seven interacting bodies, overlapping and intensely interpenetrating each other (orbs are spheres!). Physical Earth, hence is – like the physical human body – ‹enveloped› resp. ‹penetrated› by her subtle bodies, namely by six concentric electromagnetic fields, each of them sustaining a specific, characteristic wave-band – corresponding to the consciousness, and therefore the vibrational properties of the carrier. If now an animated being lives in perfect harmony, all vibrations of its seven bodies are harmonized in perfect natural equilibrium, and together form a harmonious living unity. In so far, the original, virginal Earth as such – without a disturbing influence from either inside or outside – dwelled in perfect harmonious equilibrium of her seven bodies. And because the pure, original energy fields of the Macrocosmos determine generation and evolution of Planet Earth precisely as it is done for plants by *their* surrounding conditions – in harmony with the laws of the Universe and the One Law that rules it all – so *in* *«The Beginning»*, Earth and everything living on her and within her prospered in ‹paradisiac harmony› of higher and extraterrestrial energy fields surrounding them as well as of their own, the former expanding (so to speak) over the whole atmospheric Universe which, therefore, could really be denominated *«divine»* – or *«a god»* – in short: a Paradise.

The term *Paradise* – in ancient German: *Paradeis*, is, as mentioned before, to be understood as coming from the root *djaus / Zeus / deus* – as *para-deic*, or para-divine (*para-divus*) – hence: *similar to God*; – and this becomes quite obvious as the *Aquarius Genesis* teaches us that

«In the Beginning», the Earth was in perfect harmony, with her own individual as well as with the *common, all-enveloping, absolutely divine, supra-cosmic sevenfold field of vibrations.* – All together then, these 49 energy fields, or vibration bands, shaped the vibrant, shining Universe, and preserved it. Therefore, everything was *«perfectly good»* indeed – namely in perfect, *timeless,* absolutely divine harmony. – Not a single jarring note resonated in the World, nor outside of it; – for, as everything was still in Oneness, there *was no outside*; – and this view may be expanded beyond all thinkable (then inexistent) limitations.[15-C]

Now the most sublime vibration to be manifested in any microcosmos, World, or Universe is THE LOVE on the respective ‹octave› of said 49 vibrational planes. – God's Love however – God's own supracosmic vibration, so to speak – is the highest of them all! Therefore, the Cathars of the 12th and 13th century simply said: *«God is Love!»*. –

This eternal divine love-vibration now is of such a high frequency that its light would blind any human (hence would *appear black* to him); – and its heat should ‹scorch› him completely. Sacred Scripture sufficiently mentions this fact – especially in the Old Testament, in *Manichean Hymns*[16] in the *Corpus Hermeticum*, and in the gnostic text of *Pistis Sophia*[17].

In the *Corpus Hermeticum,* the Trismegistos says:

«Is it not really so that – as the beam of the Sun with its all too great splendor ruins the eye and blinds it – such also is the view of the Good? However, the light illuminates so much more, and increases for, the [human] eye, as somebody is able to seize more of the pouring splendor of Immortality.»

Therefore, the *Aquarius Genesis* quite rightly declares:

«All was One. – All was Love. – God was in all, and all was in God» – that is to say: one with the sublimest, absolutely divine love-vibration, and with all the 49 harmonious fields of vibration that envelop and protect the Universe and its Worlds – embracing and penetrating them with divine Love. Therefore, *«in the Beginning»* the World was indeed *«the sole, all-one Sphere of Existence – all Light, Goodness and Harmony»*!

4.) «Thirdly, God made the RHOMBUS ◊. *And with the* RHOMBUS *was created also the* CROSS ✛ *contained within the* RHOMBUS: ⬦. *– This is the spiritual potentiality of the* FOUR ELEMENTS.
In the RHOMBUS ◊ *the* TRIANGLE OF FIRE △ *and the* TRIANGLE OF WATER ▽ were still *united – but bare of consciousness. –* AIR *and* EARTH *instead were still dwelling in Secrecy. – This was the Plenitude of Possibilities within the wholly spiritual* FIRST PARADISE.*»*

To the Father-God and the Mother-Goddess (*Mother of Gods*) is added in every relevant Myth a God-Child to give a Triplet or Trinitas. The NUMBER FOUR then show up ‹much later›, as the fundament for physical Creation. It is connected to matter, motherhood and femininity – first as a cosmogonic, then as a cosmological widening of the NUMBER THREE. The latter is graphically represented by the TRIANGLE. – The Quaternary of the RHOMBUS as a feminine expression of spiritual *space for matter* is formed by *two Triangles* which, appearing like opposites, already indicate the dichotomy of universal physical Creation:

Firstly, a Triangle △ standing for the principles of Fire, Spirit and male energy in general – including the *Golden Triangle* of Hiram. Secondly – as the latter's counter-part – a triangle ▽ connected to the respective principles: Water, Soul, and feminine energy – including the *Silver Triangle* ▽ like the one worn by the Priestesses of *Atlantis*.

This separation between Silver and Gold, between Male and Female, between Above and Below, between ‹Good› and ‹Evil› a.s.f., could not yet be spoken of at all when «the RHOMBUS was created»: In the RHOMBUS, the Fiery Triangle and the Water Triangle were still united in perfectly harmonious *potentiality* of future physical manifestations – *undivided expression of the macrocosmic* TEN (the *macrocosmic* FATHER-MOTHER) – and of the NOW appearing *cosmic* TEN («so below as above»). Therefore they bore in themselves the potential THREE, FOUR and SEVEN – and hence also were an allegory for the future multiplicity of creative expression including human depravity (the ‹FALL›), viz. perfection (the ‹Path back to the Father›, through innumerous individual ways of struggling for spiritual evolution) ...

In other words: In the RHOMBUS there was already present the *plenitude in the Pleroma of all germs* for all Cosmogonies, all Anthropogonies, and for all creation myths including all hopes for redemption – like in a spiritual mother-field: From the *supracosmic primary fountain* ● poured forth as *macrocosmic* CHAOS, the RHOMBUS ◆: *Flamma – Materia – Mater –* and thereof the pure RHOMBUS or LOZENGE ◊ which as Spirit donned a *third veil,* became the spiritually elemental, cosmic ⊕. But ere the Elements mingled with each other, nothing could come into physical being. The cosmic ⊕ thus became – so to speak – the cosmic *Mother of all Mothers – Mother-Goddess*, and *Mother of Gods* . –

The RHOMBUS also appears in several ways in the ‹Star of Meta-tron›. SHE is the *Babylonian Mari* – and before that, the *mother-field* which, under the effect of the Holy Spirit, was to bring forth our physical Creation: ‹SHE› was there, ere even the slightest ‹thing› was created, according to the first antique traditions in East and West, like those quoted in the previous chapter. – Even biblical *Ruth* and the Old-Egyptian root *ruḏ – strength)* both are in a certain way *Arch-Mothers*, namely the ones of the later theo-logical concept of Jahwists: The first volume of the SOHAR dis-cusses the Mother-Goddess in a very satisfactory way !

As for this, we quote from the work of C. Meurant [18]:

«Hindu tradition associates the Icosahedron with PURUSHA {the Son, Prefiguration of the Christ}, the seed-image of BRAHMA, the supreme Creator. This image is the map of the Universe, and analogous to *Cosmic Man*» {comp. the ‹*Largest Human*› as described by Emanuel Swedenborg[12-B]}.

«The ICOSAHEDRON is appropriate for the first outer {physic-al} form, since all the other volumes arise naturally out of it. PURUSHA is envisioned as unmanifested and untouched by {manifest} Creation; just as in the construction the outer ICOSA-HEDRON is untouched by the other forms it contains.

«PURUSHA projects inwards the DODECAHEDRON of PRA-KRITI. This recognizes the primacy of these duals {DODECA-HEDRON and ICOSAHEDRON} with the highest, i.e. most sub-tle, *phi-relationship* associated with fivefold symmetry.[18-A] – The DODECAHEDRON is seen to be PRAKRITI, the feminine power of creation and manifestation, the Universal Mother, the quintessence of the natural {material} Universe. This DODECA-HEDRON touches all forms of Creation within her silent, observing partner. Within the dodecahedral Mother of Crea-tion, the CUBE of materiality arises, and naturally subdivides into interpenetrating positive and negative TETRAHEDRA, representing the fundamental dual oscillation of the created {material} Universe.

«The result of this harmonious interaction of opposites is the CUBE {→ ‹*incubation*›!} as *physical existence*. – At the heart of this CUBE is found the OCTAHEDRON as the adamantine

essence of matter. {Note by the Editor: The crystalline structure of the DIAMOND is the OCTAHEDRON}. –Within this essence, by sounding the sacred *phi-ratio* again, an innermost
ICOSAHEDRON of Spirit is revealed, realizing the *complete
octave*. The {*supra-cosmic*} FATHER OF BEYOND has generated the MOTHER OF CREATION through whom is incarnated
the spiritual SON. – In this concentric sequence, the various
dualities (complementary pairs of regular polyhedra) are arranged in their appropriate order. Their interrelationships respect the natural energetic structures of regular solids. – The
cosmological scheme and natural geometry are here in harmony, and thus at peace with one another.»

Thus far the quotation from R C. Meurants article which is so
surprisingly in harmony with text and commentaries of *Aquarius
Genesis*. – For this publication's complete text and pictures see:
http://rmeurant.com/its/harmony_files/ Ch-07-MythPerfectPlatonicSolids.pdf.)

The RHOMBUS ◊, or, when carrying the ‹CROSS of Matter› + in
it: ◊ (= 2 x 4 Tetrahedra), is thus the symbol of the (as yet entirely
spiritual) Four Elements *unmingled* and therefore *unmanifested,* in
perfect oneness of ‹Above› and ‹Below›. Even in today's World, the
RHOMBUS remains the foundation of every preserved, and preserving, motherly potential: almost an inversion of what will be said
about the SQUARE and the LIGHT-CROSS contained in it.

These relations, too, can be understood in the light of today's relations in our world: If in the *World of Shapes* the LIGHT-CROSS ✕ in □
forever shines forth from inside all manifested ‹things› as their core
and germ, the Cross of Matter + also forever remains enveloped by
the divine «*Above-as-Below*» of the hermetic RHOMBUS ◊, and thus
preserved as an eternally divine element. – There it is ‹floating›
amidst the animating stream of alchymical *Fire* △ and *Water* ▽
which, «*in the Beginning*», by their union as the «*Æsch-Majim*» –
Fiery Water – gave the RHOMBUS or LOZENGE ◊ its shape. –

Now Man was supposed to experience anew, and revive in himself, the Light-Cross ✕ within the frame of his etherically physical
paradise ⊕. But Man lacked consciousness and failed! – Today's
humans can do it thanks to consciousness gained through innumerous experiences in MALKUTH – *through Grace*. – If they understand and chose their *Path of Return*; their microcosmic sun will
rise – and thus «*Spirit can come into the flesh*». – Their souls as
yet cocooned within seven veils like the grub of a butterfly will be
set free, and see pure light floating around them again. And then,

the CROSS OF ELEMENTS inside the RHOMBUS will again envelop them as a pure Light Robe – as it was *«in the Beginning»* (pic.10). – This Light Garment formed by the RHOMBUS, or LOZENGE, expressed in consequent Symbolism appears as follows[18-B]:

Re-union of the Candidate with *primary pranic Waters* ▽ and with *primary pranic Fire* △ is what Sacred Language names *«re-birth through water and Fire»*. One might as well say: By successive psychic and spiritual baptism (*instillation*) with Æsch-Majīm – Fiery ether or Christic Fire – this Light Robe which at first appeared only as a RHOMBUS, grows in shape and volume, until presenting itself as an *octahedric crystal*. The latter *contains*, as its largest inner face, the SQUARE WITH THE LIGHT-CROSS. – *On the outside* it shows four RHOMBI resp. eight TETRAHEDRA (four Duals). Inside, it is (di-vision and de-cision!) vertically pierced by the fifth Element: the FIERY ETHER as an axis, so that the one common point of all eight TETRAHEDRA is the source or center of the axis towards the ABOVE and the BELOW. – If now said Crystal rotates around this vertical axis, the RHOMBUS apparently rotating in countersense within will appear as a SPINDLE, and at the same time as a glittering rotating Crystal of light, *girded with the Solar Orb* ☉!

This rotating SPINDLE corresponds to the *Mandorla* inside an Aura of golden ‹rays of glory›: This is the new astral Light-Robe which on many a tympanon surrounds the idol of ‹Mary› as an image of the MOTHER-SOUL – but also the image of the SON:

«And there appeared a great wonder in heaven: A woman clothed with the Sun, and the Moon under her feet, and upon her head a crown of twelve stars ... » – thus we read in *Apocalypse of John* (see Rev. 12:1; and pic.12).

Said *macrocosmic archetypal ‹woman›* stands in the center of an *apostolic Zodiac*. The latter envelops ‹the 10›: the FATHER-MOTHER that can also be represented by ☉ and ☽, viz. – as explained earlier – by ⌢ and ⌣ (see pic. 13). – Besides we may mention that numerous old Universities used to use a seal in the shape of an oval, or mandorla (vulva), corresponding exactly to their denomination as *«Alma Mater – Nurturing Mother»*!

Now one should remember that one of the uncountable names of the Great Mother-Goddess is that of VENUS who, among others, is also named the *Morning Star*. The Christ as well – as the SON – is, as the *Morning-Star*, linked to VENUS: «*I, Jesus, have sent my angel in order to testify onto you these things in the congregations (in ecclesiis). I am the root, and the kinship of David, the resplendent Morning-Star*» (Rev. 22:16). – Even the *Popol-Vuj* names these three in one breath: Venus, the Morning-Star and the ‹Messiah›.[19] –

Earlier in this book we alluded to the rune Ylhaz – ᛉ – with, a.o., the meaning of *Apotheosis*, and recalling the magical seal of VENUS. The latter glyph – ⚤ – is shown in its context by H.C. Agrippa a Nettesheim in his *Occulta Philosophia*. This representation of the SON as VENUS is reproduced also in the idol as macabre as it is pagan and magical, of ‹The Crucified› – a symbol the Church of Rome has made its ‹logo›, world-wide. – The depiction of THE SON inside the MANDORLA however is encountered in so many a tympanon since the Romanic church architecture, framed by the SQUARE of the Four Elements figured by the *Four Animals of Daniel* and the *Apocalypsis*, resp. biblical *Genesis* (see pic. 12) – and in the New Testament by *«the four Evangelists»*. – This MANDORLA – in fact a *Vulva inside the* SQUARE OF MATTER (all together a *six-pointed star*) – yields another Venus Seal. Nevertheless, this ensemble is *in general* interpreted as the SON functioning as the ‹*Judge of the World*›. That is what Jesus the Christ never said of Himself: He preached forgiveness under all circumstances but one. Only the Roman «Credo ... », edited much, much later, has stamped God as an unapproachable Judge. – As for how all this is to be understood in the context of *Aquarius Genesis*, the following paragraphs will give some further explanations:

Creation as prepared within the RHOMBUS ⬦ was still entirely *spiritually astral*. At the same time, it was a *multiplication of the Light Cross* ✕. In Heraldry this can be shown by an escucheon carrying *only one* RHOMBUS (resp., one *Cross of St Andrew*), *transmuted* into a shield evenly covered by a great number of lozenges – a so-called *lozengé*, thus showing a *reawakened heart in its full power and glory*. [19-A] – In addition, this is the escucheon showing the greatest number of facets, or *heraldic sections*.

. *Losange*ʹ

A lozengé may as well be seen – three-dimensionally – as a polished crystal, glittering with innumerous facets – or else as a *crucible* with the ᶜαλς χριστου – *hals Christou* – *salt of Christ*: a *flowing Light-Shape*, shimmering in thousand colours. — Similarly, the One Holy Spirit had to descend: first as an astral, then as an etheric Spirit-Fire ⚶, projecting itself forth, and down, until finally crystallizing in a physically condensed shape in *Malkuth*: This is SPIRIT condensing into MATTER. The latter – as compared to *«Light, Truth and Life»* – is rather accurately named «living Death». From there, then, can begin the new Light-Birth (Jesus/ Jesod, the Door): in the *renewed, awakened heart* (‹MARIA›, MANDORLA or ‹LOZANGEE›) up to alchymical Multiplication – *Multiplicatio* – of the Light and its power, *through mediation by the One* – *mediatione Unius* as says the *Tabula Smaragdina*:– the fire-born Son of God, that is ‹re-born› *Christ-Man* – fully impregnated with Fiery Ether.

Now are peacefully united: a Cross × specifically connected to Light and Spirit – and a Cross + very close to physical manifestation of the Spirit in Humanity. The *upright* CROSS + within the RHOMBUS instead – unlike the Light-Cross × ‹floating› through the divine, wholly spiritual World of Light – announces the future separation of the *potentially physical* FOUR ELEMENTS □ into FIRE △, AIR ⟁, WATER ▽ and EARTH ⩞, as today we experience them. Therefore, to ‹signal› the «fallen World» resulting from the projection of Spirit into Matter, appears the symbol ♁ : This is the World dominated by the physical Four Elements, and ‹separated› from Spirit. The Circle – O – is indeed another symbol for Spirit, and the Cross + another common symbol for the Four Elements which by their condensation into Matter have become *visible* and *palpable*, and can now be sensually *experienced*, and *consciously overcome*, thanks to the *Path of the Cross* in its numberless ways of human self-realization.

In this way the imports of Circle and Cross interpenetrate each other in the *Second (etheric) Paradise* ⊕, illustrating what says the text of *Aquarius Genesis*. Therefore, the ‹logo› for the WORLD crystallized in MATTER is the well-known *Earth-Symbol* ♁. Here Matter dominates Spirit – unlike the symbol of Venus: ♀, where Spirit dominates Matter. – All these symbols are polyvalent, and should always be meditated in their multidimensional, or multi-layer, spiritual and physical impacts.

Thus, the Earth Sign ♁ also reminds future overcoming of the physical world through *dematerialization* thanks to the *Fiery Ether* ⩚ – i.e. by the *Fire of Spirit*. – This is the return of physical Creation into the first Paradise ⊗ wherefrom it first ‹fell› – presently still falling, deeper and deeper, due to human ignorance. Said return – or salvation – occurs in the *sixth spiritual Dimension* (⟠), with the aid of the *fifth Dimension* (✶), thanks to the vertical ‹axis› piercing the ‹heart› of each of these symbols, whenever the cleaved microcosm Y is deeply immersed in the *Fiery Ether of the Christ-Force*, as it prepares for its elevation in Υ as a *divine Crystal*, or ‹Christ›.

Early christian iconography shows the Christ as ‹Lord of the World› – ‹Pantocrator›, holding in his Left the orb surmounted by the Cross, as a human misinterpretation of His mission on Earth: A Priest-King is no earthly Lord in the vulgarly human meaning, but a most excellent divine servant! —

How come that emperors, too, were depicted with the Earth symbol in or on their crown? – Wreaths and crowns – ○ – originally were attributes of a human awakened to solar consciousness: Mystes, Bacchants, spiritual ‹Kings›. – The mocking *Crown of Thorns* in judeo-christianic iconography for *Jesus the Christ* already appears with *Mithras as King of the World*: *Thorns* symbolize *Fire* (pic.13)! – The crown of today's English queen, with a Cross on top of the purple velvet vault is therefore an emperor's crown, really – hence a pretension for *World-Power...*!

Earlier in this book were indicated the four symbols of *light-consciousness* during the first four world periods: The Double-Helix, or double spire ◉ of the dark *Hyperborean* epoch – the solar *S* of the *Lemurian* epoch – the Triskell ⚛ of *Atlantis* – and the spiral Swastika ⊕ of the early Arian epoch. – Now that in *Thesis 4 of Aquarius Genesis* the Cross of the Four Elements has been introduced, we can refer to these symbols, starting from a new basis:

All these Light symbols, from the *Double-Helix* unto the *Swastika*, have one thing in common: They have a center, or *turning point.* In the Double-Helix, the (invisible) turning-point is more and more drawn inwards, like in a suction wake (pic. 2-4, 14 and 15-A). This shows the continuing degeneration and crystallization of the entire humankind: Lesser and lesser grows consciousness of THE LIGHT; while there dominates – in this view – complete darkness: dull, morose and unconscious unrest within the soft turbulence of «*Spirit floating above the Waters*». – Instead, in the solar *S* (see pic.15-B), as in the Triskell and the Swastika, the turning-point is clearly visible: Consciousness of THE LIGHT has begun *to unfold*; centripetal involutive movement and centrifugal evolution move as antiparallels, thus building up a tense equilibrium of Light and Darkness that more and more yields towards prevail of the Light (increasing number of ‹branches› or ‹rays› of above symbols; see pic. 16). The respective turning-point amidst a symbol however, always indicates also the *axis of ascent to the next dimension.*

The significance of the term *turning-point* is obvious: It means the *turn* from involution to evolution. From a psychological or mystic point of view, it is the *momentum of repentance*, and the *turn-about* of a human who re-awakens to the Light, then takes a new orientation, and starts on a new pathway: This is the turn from errant ways in the Nature of Death, to the *one but thousand-fold* «Path that leads to Life» (Mt.7:14). – But in *Aquarius Genesis* the latter will be mentioned only in *Thesis 11.*

With its *turning-point*, the Double-Spire is the simplest image for a *Labyrinth* – with all its implications (pic.11). – In the Labyrinth as an initiatic system, the *axis of ascent* was made visible in Antiquity by some typical symbol – preferably a golden circle or disk or another Sun Symbol at the point where the Candidate having attained the center of the Labyrinth *turns around*, in order to *leave it* again. – It says: Even in deepest obscuration of the microcosm: in complete lack of consciousness through human involvement, there still is present as a *turning-point* (albeit hardly recognizable): the *force of Ascent*; the live, vibrant *Christ-Force* (pic.21).

The *Lituus* (pic. 15-A) shows – besides the one, *basic* turningpoint – two other directive points *between Ascent and Fall*!

In other words: The Christ Force, the *Universal* CHRISTOS, exists from the very Beginning – *a Principio*: It is a *static presence* as the *Central Point* – and present also at every *Turning-Point* – no matter if consciously noticed, or not. – True: For low-level consciousness, the Christ Force remains latent and like inexistent. To this lack of consciousness corresponds the wholly *unreligious* (far from an *intimate bond* with God) imagination of an eternal sojourn in some Abyss *bare of hope* – so-called ‹Hell›: a vision really adapted to, and fastening, an involutive life on the wheel of the Double-Spire ⓔ:

In the *Corpus Hermeticum* ([20], loc. cit. viz. note 2 in present book), Hermes exclaims: *«Which fiery flame burns hotter than that of isolation from God?»* – And the commentator remarks:

«Who ... as a «victor in the competition» emerges from the Kratèr, alights from the non-divine state of ignorance and separation from God. This separation, it is true, is just another human illusion, for real separation from God is impossible: God is All-in-All. –

«Therefore, the impression of being completely abandoned by the Grace of God, must absolutely be relativated as a subjective, albeit real, hell-like sensation for whoever undergoes this experience: God's Grace remains inherent to every creature – even to the most obfuscated beastly ‹human› ... ».

In the solar *S* (Clothilde) and in the *Lituus*, the Turning-Point is not as clearly visible as in a typical intersection of lines. Here: a conscious perception and a formal *decision* to turn about. There: a fatal lapse, as shown in pic.15-A). – The positive decision pursued in fidelity leads to enlightenment and to elevation to a next spiritual Dimension, as in ♌, ♆, ✶ and ✿. – Thus is again demonstrated the effectiveness of the *Law of Number and Proportion* – in any purely spiritual domain and in concrete reality alike!

In the Double Spire with its central symmetry ⓔ the *turning point* is also the first criterion for the *Synthesis* of I and ○ to give the 10. –

The *sliding turning-point* of the solar *S* already hints at the appear-ance of the SON (Son = Sun), same as the specific symmetry of the *Triskell* prepares for the manifestation of the ‹Heliand› in the *Swas-tika*. – The spatial axis through the obvious center (intersection) of the Cross, opens up the *fifth Dimension of consciousness*, as soon as Candidates on their *Path of Return* (equally available to «*all humans of good will*»), enter a phase of concrete realization – through Grace, but in personal, auto-responsible effort.

Now the *fifth Element* – the *Fiery Ether* as the *Force of Ascent* – becomes visible, so to speak. And it is interesting that this same Symbolism can be recognized in the Etrurian representation of the *Sun-Wagon* with its wheels (sun-wheels I; pic.17): ⊗ stands for the all-embracing divine Heaven, ⊕ for the cosmic ‹Sun-Horse› – a Sun-symbol from China through Gaul – standing on one of the axes of the wagon, hence always wielded to the *Law* of the whole wagon as are the wheels of the latter – i.e. the cosmic ZODIAC, the central force of which appears to be the Fire-Ether ♐. – So much for the Quaternary and the Cross. —

In the *Pentagram*, the ‹axis› of the Cross has become the fifth ray of a star ★, and thus has become dynamic: A human in whom the five-pointed star has risen, has received a new and concrete *con-sciousness of the* LIGHT – and hence also gained a new access to, and become part of, the astral world – *world of stars*. – True: the six-pointed and seven pointed stars shine brighter than the Penta-gram; – but the decisive change occurs in that the Candidate of the Mysteries, from *elementic consumption* of the Light passes on to the dynamics of *spiritually emitting* Light as a Star! It is therefore easy to understand that throughout hermetic literature and prac-tice the *rise of ‹Bethlehem's Star›* ★ (mystically, magically or oper-ationally) is mentioned and experienced as a very special event.

In addition to both the *Pentagram* and the Celtic or Ancient Ger-manic *Sun-Wagon*, the *Number Six* is to be considered. This is a further evolution of ⊗ to yield the ⊕, interpreted by A. Schütze in his book *Mithras* as «*the rolling movement and creative life of the Sun-Wheel*» (see pic. 34). Schütze partly quotes R. Steiner[21], commenting the Sun-Wheel with its six ‹spikes› to which has been added the Moon ☽ – like so (here abbreviated in a few words):

Well known is the sign ✳, or ⊕, named ‹Chrisma› or ‹Christ-Monogram›. But this is only one of its exoteric meanings. The first Christians – as do today's Initiates into the CHRIST-MYSTERY, moreover recognize in the Chrisma *the cosmic nature of the Christ* as «*He in whom the Sun-Mystery and the Moon-Mystery are united»* {see Thesis 6 and pic.27}. – However, there is a third meaning as alluded to by Paul (Col.2:9): *«In Him* (Christ) *resides the Plenitude (Pleroma) of the Godhead, physically»*. – By the term of *Pleroma* in that era was also understood an assembly of spiritual beings (the *Exousiai*), known among the Jews as *Elohim*. – The teaching regarding the MYSTERY OF PLEROMA comprises this: Man lives on Earth in order to acquire the capacity of LOVE. On the Sun (which represents a higher level of existence), there dwell beings able to *enflame Love* and *infuse* it into other beings. By the fact that Earth receives the rays of the Sun, Love develops on her and within her[22]. – In R. Steiner's Words:

> *«There is, at the beginning of Earth's evolution, child-like Man who should have received* THE LOVE, *ready as he was to receive the Ego; – and on the other side, the Sun who split off [Earth], ascending to a higher level of existence. On this Sun, were able to develop seven directing Light Spirits who at the same time were the donating Spirits of Love. Only six of them made the Sun their dwelling ... six Elohim, as we find them in the Bible. One of them parted and took a separate course ...: He chose ... the Moon as his dwelling. And this ... is no other than the one that the Ancient Testament names* JAHVEH *or* JEHOVAH ... *».*[23]

The six solar Elohim are, in a way, PLEROMA; – JAHBEH, the Lunic God, is the seventh[24]. The *Sun Wheel* with its six spikes plus the sickle of the crescent Moon therefore clearly indicates the divine plenitude of the Christos as a Sun-Spirit – or, as R. Steiner says: *«an imagination frozen into a sign, and originating from the Wisdom of the Mysteries of primitive Christendom* (pic.37): That is the CHRISTOS as *the union of the seven cosmic* ELOHIM *«into one person»*. – And like *Aquarius Genesis* with its Scholia, Schütze moreover emphasizes:

> *«Pre-christian Mysteries, as far as they pointed at the essential Solar Being, finally are part and parcel of Christendom itself* {i.e. CHRISTIC}. *Christendom as such can be seized in its essential depth only if one acknowledges the physical incorporation of the Solar Spirit as its essential element»*. –

– So far the quotations from Schütze's book *Mithras*.

Thus, the modern, ‹enlightened› way of thinking is brought back to the arch-old *Star-Wisdom*, after having, since the start of the Christian era, been slandered by every dogmatic Church, and almost completely extinct by such Church Fathers as Origenes and

Augustinus – and after them, by the whole Western society. Tertullianus in his *Præscriptiones Contra Hæreseos, cap. XL,* writes:

«If I remember correctly, the Mithras[-Priest] there (in the Mithræum) signs his Disciple on the forehead ... » (see pic.18⁻ᴬ, 18⁻ᴮ and comments;[25]). – Secret, i.e. ‹occult› *Tradition of the Holy Grail* instead orally preserved the old wisdom until it was transmitted (for example, and in the most precious manner, albeit just in some eventual hints) in *Parzival* by Wolfram von Eschenbach.[26] —

But let us return to *Thesis 4* of the *Aquarius Genesis*, where no stars were manifest yet – neither physically nor even psychically, matter not being able to emerge before the Four Elements had become etheric, then would mingle and condense: In the Rhombus ⬦ as mentioned before only some preparations of physical Creation became ‹visible›, spiritually: The Elements ‹then› were contained only potentially – as *spiritual Virtues* (lat. *virtutes*). This means: Still there was not matter formed by condensation of ‹First Prana› into the four resp. five Elements, but only what is their essence: their potentiality – their *power* or *archetypal Virtue*: their *spiritual seed.* – Still everything was One: $^c εν το παν$ – *hen to pan: each One was the All*, as reads the *Chrysopoeia of Cleopatra* (pic. 28). – Here two examples to this:

WATER is linked, *in an astral way*, with the MOON, *etherically* with the SOUL, *as a physical metal* with SILVER, in the Kingdom of *humans*: with FEMININITY, in spiritual consciousness of humans: as ABEL, in individual self-consciousness: with the female EGO, and so forth. – Its ‹counter-poise›, FIRE is linked, *in an astral way,* with the SUN, *etherically* with SPIRIT, *as a physical metal* with GOLD, in the Kingdom of Humans: with MASCULINITY, in spiritual consciousness of humanity: with CAIN, in individual selfconsciousness: with the male EGO – and so forth ...

Fire and water ‹oppose› each other like the innumerable Duals of contraries: Night and day, active and passive, birth and decease a.s.f. – These Duals in their creative power-play fuel our split (or double-sided) World and its Wheel of birth, growth, fertility and decay. It is these Duals who keep in motion – and therefore alive – the whole Universe. Their union in the RHOMBUS ⬦ signals their origin and their role in the counter-play (counter-dance) of the Universe as well as in overcoming all this. –[27]

The Symbolism of the RHOMBUS – and of the CROSS contained in it – being really much richer, a short sum-up is required here: *In the Beginning,* when *«God made the* RHOMBUS*»,* and before the CROSS **+** appeared in it, Fire and Water, like all other Duals were not yet manifest. Still all was Oneness, divine and spiritual. The RHOMBUS ◊ therefore contained in itself all Duals, but anon just as potentialities – *each pair being a unit* that was one with the ONE, ‹slumbering› in perfect union and pure LOVE. This was an ‹arch-primitive› quietness in a perfect dynamic interplay of all spheres, powers, qualities and potencies: No physical inertia, without which Man of this World cannot imagine anything.– *And no time either*!

Earth ▽ and Air △ did not exist yet; – they only arose with said scission, condensation and materialization of the World ♁, *after* its separation from the ‹Second Paradise› ⊕ – *after* foundation of the KINGDOM OF WRATH ♂ by the ADVERSARY or DISTRACTOR. Evenly both first created Fire △ and Water ▽ that were created ‹much later›, were not at all physically present in the RHOMBUS the way we know them today, but only as pure, spiritual astral forces –*Star Forces*: *Star-Fire* and *Star-Water*. – Not even the water of the soul was there in the Beginning, for there still was no soul!

Instead, ‹in the Beginning›, Water and Fire were completely mingled: Not separated were they, but really one – as today inside our Planet elemental Fire and elemental Water still are mixed together as one, until they become physical in atmospheric Air and atmospheric Light (same as red blood is thickened from plasmatic to liquid only when it gets in touch with air and sun-light); – and so, in the divine World (divine kingdom) all spiritual elements (△) and all elements of the Soul (▽) are one.

This *wholly unconceivable* union of all ‹opposed principles› give, since centuries, a *splitting* head-egg, to Theologists and academic Scientists alike – especially since, by well-known reasons, biblical and natural ‹Sciences› were forcibly made to correspond, thus becoming implausible and untrustworthy, both of them.

While in the RHOMBUS ◊ – we repeat it – the Four Elements were completely One, their astral Virtues ‹virtually› existed: ◈ –but still united, notwithstanding that in Spirit they existed individually, *since the Beginning*. Their division, their separation in order to become the Tetrad of material Creation, was already indicated and induced by the Cross of Matter + as contained in the RHOMBUS – but yet in no way manifest, and void of consciousness.

5.) *«In the fourth place, God made the SQUARE – ever-maidenly mother of all material manifestations:* □. *And inside the SQUARE there again flashed up the CROSS always concealed within the Square:* ⊠ *– that is the LIGHT-CROSS* × *of the* CHRISTOS.*»*

To the AIYN-SOPH-AUR: ⊙~, the *supra-cosmic* origin of the first Numbers: **I**, O, 10 and ×, now correspond: the *macro-cosmic* △ (AIYN-SOPH of the Kabbalah – the HEART OF HEAVEN in the Popol Vuh); – and the *cosmic* ‹Sun-Eye› – the ☧ of Egyptian hieroglyphs: ATUM or ATON, i.e. AH-TAN – *the Great Lord.* This is also the *Great Sun*, or the *Great Name* – SHEM-ER, the veneration for whom gave its name to *Samaria (solar,* ‹Eloh-istic› Canaanite Tradition as opposed by *lunar,* Jahw-istic tradition of ‹Judah› since their seizure of Jerusalem, *returning from* their exile in Babylon.

The same steps of AIYN-SOPH-AUR, AIYN-SOPH, and AIYN mark the descent of *supra-cosmic Light* × (the SON, SUN LOGOS, or WORD) into Cosmos manifesting itself *macrocosmically* as the NINE of the DIVINE FIRST ADAM: **IX**, who *cosmically* – as the descended *Son of the Sun* – may also carry the symbol of ✳ (see comment to *Theses 4 and 12;* table of symbols, and pic.10). From the TEN (IO) *emerges* the *macrocosmic* SON **X**, following the will of the FATHER: **I** – and thanks to the motherly wisdom of the ZERO, O, out of which every sort of presence becomes manifest like from a hatched egg: I + O = **X**. – This **X** is the dynamics flowing out of the Ten: IO – and its *impact* in the **IX** of original divine Man, ‹ADAM PROTOGENOS› who could exist only as a *macrocosmic entity.*

In so far as on the highest plane the SON emerged from the Creation of NUMBER – as a NUMBER **(X)** himself, albeit as yet unmanifested; – and in so far as, none the less, through creation of the SQUARE containing the *Light-Cross* ⊠, His physical manifestation was a sublime and unconceivable realty, there was already prepared, within a still uncreated World where senses were not active yet, the possibility to sensually experience Him as a light-force. For: the SQUARE of Matter, □, carrying the Light-Cross, i.e. Spirit, ×, → ⊠, was, as mentioned earlier, contained already in the RHOMBUS ◈ when visioned as an OCTAHEDRON (see p. 72). And so it really was since the solely potential, entirely spiritual, presence of the Four Elements in their *pure astral virtue.* – The *macrocosmic* Trinity and the *macrocosmic* Tetrad (see comment.to *Thesis 1*) are evenly hinted at in C.W. Leadbeater's booklet about *The Astral World,* namely in its chapter speaking of *Deva's,* where he writes about the *Dhyan Chohans* who undoubtedly stand much closer to the Causal-Plane than to the physical world with its etheric and astral reflections and mirages (see note 8[-B]).

The Number NINE (9) obeys its own law: Seizable and yet unseizable, it is present and yet absent; – manifest and yet – depending of the will governing it and who's cipher the Nine is as well – latent and often ineffective, albeit at the same moment giving access to all multiplications: From ONE, ZERO and NINE, all further numbers arise: The NINE always leads the multitude of all other numbers back to their essence: – ONE plus NINE gives TEN – and One again: $1 + 9 = 10 = 1$ – a.s.f.!

Thus, *macrocosmic* NINE (IX) stands as a bridge between the Creator (I) and matter (⊠) – but none the less remains one with both. – Thus stands the SON at the brim of PLEROMA (within the OCTOAD): between *creative potentiality* and manifest *reality*!

All this is neither a speculative play with numbers, nor sophistic jugglery with terms, but just an unusual multidimensional calculus across several systems, whereby highest sacral relations become accessible to perception, expression and, so to speak, to communication. But nevertheless they remain entirely unthinkable, because the most profound essence of the highest Godhead remains inaccessible to the human mind: «*Dei Gloria Intacta – God's Glory is and remains intangible [for human reasoning]!*»

The dynamics created by the ‹very first›, *supra-cosmic* Triad or Trinity, from the *macrocosmic Sphere* down to the *cosmic plane*, is thus the NINE (IX ⇒ 9), so we saw. In our human language we say: ‹First Adam› – IX – is the anon unmanifested, *and therefore* perfect (immaculate) *celestial human ens*; but 9 is earthly Man attained to *new perfection* – an *ens* arisen to, and effectual through, union of the powers of all three ‹corners› of the *macrocosmic Fiery Triangle* – *thus,* the Divine Child of THE TRINITY, *after the World.* – Now that shall understand who can understand it.

First, there stood in *macrocosmic Space* the *Idea of Man* as a *divine thought* – an *astral* human IMAGE amidst creative consciousness of all three planes. This is the image the reflection of Man Yaldabaoth «*saw mirrored in the Waters*». – Anon, the *supracosmic* GOD-SON (the LIGHT ✗, the *supra-cosmic* WORD and subsequent macrocosmic LOGOS) – and the *macrocosmic divine Son of Man*, IX, were perfectly ONE. – Then, ✗ became the *macrocosmic Christ-Fire*: THE CHRISTOS who *in persona* «came into the World» (Jo.1:1-12) – and who, *microcosmically* as well, is «*coming into the flesh*».

What in the person of Jesus of the NT *uniquely occurred once* as the «*Mystery of Golgotha*» (R. Steiner), truly opened the door (JESOD) through which «*all humans of good will*» have access to the *Path towards Light, Truth* and *Life.* Similarly, every *newly conscious*

Son of Man – 9 – who on the path of Transfiguration has (so to speak) outgrown cosmic Creation, and in whose microcosmos the *omnipresent macrocosmic Christ-Spirit* has «*become flesh*» as the Gospel say, can become a divinely human **IX** again.

This indicates the function that Man is summoned to fulfill in *physical Creation*: To be the intermediate link – the Mediator – between Creation and Creator, as an elemental physical NINE in elemental MAN: (ADAM = אדמ = 45 = 9 = ט).[28] – These relations shall be commented on further down.

«*In the Beginning*», thus, GOD-SON **X** (who ‹later› as a human issued from LOGOS / DATH) — and the DIVINE SON OF MEN (Adamas, **IX**) existed only *potentially*, i.e. in the *potency* of the Father (**I**), resp. of the FATHER-MOTHER (10). – The SON as such was not just invisible, imperceptible, and unrecognizable, but even *unknowable*, same as GOD Himself. – But He was the *Core-Monad* within the *plan of Creation* on the highest *Devachanic plane* that at this point was known to GOD AL-ONE, and in no way ‹exhaled›. This is also named the «*Largest Divine Arch-Idea*» (see appendix 4). – As a universal impulse to existence expired from the divine Origin or ‹Zero-Point of Energy› ●, the latter *generates* the seven ‹waves of Life› of sevenfold Creation in the course of the «seven Days of Creation – *Hebdomas Hebdomadum*».

One might as well say: The divine arch-idea is the *Arch-Monad* splitting up into the seven sounds, the seven colours, the seven «Elohim before God's Throne». – But this «split-up» must be understood just as an allegory; for in reality it is the flawless sevenfold *Arch-Tone*, the sevenfold *Arch-Colour*, the all-healing *septuple metal*, the NAME composed of the *Seven Vowels*, the ONE who is named the *Sevenfold Spirit* in His (for manifested Creation) seven times sevenfold septuple manifestation on said three main planes of *absolutely divine harmony «in the Beginning»*!

In a cosmical view, these are: The ‹rainbow› of colours; – the musical ‹Octave› (its eighth tone already enters *another dimension*!); – the *united* heptad of all vibrations on all 49 planes of shapeless (‹arupa›) and shaped (‹rupa›) spiritual, etheric and physical forms of existence of a divine Day of Creation (‹Manvantara›). – In order to *at least sense* all these unseizable conceptions in a macrocosmic sense, it is necessary to become permeable to *spiritual Nature*, and free amidst (but not of!) terms and bonds of *ordinary Nature* and *ordinary Thought* (pic. 1).

The number Four – to turn back to it for one more moment – also in Mayan Tradition (in the *Popol Vuh*) is the basis for physical Creation: The four First Men, the four First Females – a Symbolism for the Four Elements with their two polarities: They «*were created and shaped from Tizé* (corn-flour mash) – hence from a substance of a plant primarily not belonging to our Earth; for *Maiz* – as says the Tradition of the *Hopi* – was brought *to humans of our Earth* by the ‹extraterrestrial Teachers› – namely from Planet Venus. [28-A],[29]

Following *Aquarius Genesis*, from the fourth act of Creation resulted the SQUARE with the LIGHT CROSS in it: ⊠ – and this means: The SQUARE – four-fold matter – is *the true vessel for Spirit*!

The SQUARE ⊠, therefore, at that point was still entirely divine: A Oneness *different* from the 10, *but not yet* separated from it (them). The path of evolution of this TETRAKTYS however was «*predestined*» already *since the Beginning*: In fact, he SQUARE □ itself also was a preliminary sign of the *Tetragrammaton* – יהוה (more about this further down) – and therefore also a first spiritual step towards ‹Separation›, ‹Fall› and ‹Redemption› (see *Thesis 6*). But when the Square of Matter is *illuminated by the Light-Cross*, then this ⊠ corresponds to יהשוה – i.e. the *manifested* SON: *Jehoshuah* (× = χ = ch = s = sh = ש, as explained earlier).

So: Already at the very Beginning – ‹long before› the descent of *etherically condensed Creation* ⊕ down into matter, in order to become ♁ ; – and indeed even before the first Creation and Paradise ⊗ were *conceived* by the macrocosmic plane (that is at the same time: *visioned, thought out* and *engendered*), the Path of *all matter* back into union with the wholly divine spiritual Kingdom was already established, fast and firm – including this union's *inner Light*, which – again – is the universal ‹SOLAR CHRIST-FIRE›, as on the cosmic plane it was going to be named. –

The universal LIGHT-CROSS × – we emphasize it once more – is the simplest possible symbol for radiating light: for stars and suns in view of conscious perception of the latter. For: the *Double Spire* ⑨ and the solar *S* – ‹unfolded form› of the Double-Spire – show ‹unconsciousness› regarding LIGHT; the *Triskell* ⚡ as a *three-fold*, and the *Swastika* ⊕ as a *fourfold Solar S* (both etherically ‹flamed›) are signs indicating ‹*half-consciousness*› regarding the LIGHT. – The ☆, on one hand, *issues directly from the Flaming Triangle*, and on the other hand, *indirectly*, from successive evolution of human consciousness regarding the LIGHT in the course of five Era's – resp. of their ‹embryonic recapitulation›[30]. – And this again explains the high significance and impact of the five-pointed ‹Flaming Star› (the *fivefold Solar S*) for cosmic consciousness of humans as well as for consciousness of the Universe (see number five in plants, and other shapes and movements in Nature, like orbiting Venus, or the infinite series of pentagrams inside the Fibonacci Curve, pic. 5). – This needs to promptly be explained further:

The Double-Spire ⊚ of *Hyperborea* shows profound, ‹death-like sleep› of the soul – full spiritual darkness, involution and degeneration. The *Sun-S of Lemuria* means a *first hazy unfolding* of the Double-Spire towards *«Separation of Light and Darkness»* in the human mind. ‹Atlantically› Druidic *Triskell* stands for dreamlike half-consciousness of the *Holy Trinity of Light*. – Follows the *Arian Swastika:* first idea of the redemption power of the PARACLET – i.e. macrocosmic CHRIST-FORCE (pic. 3). – Then, follow the magical initiation rites involving the etheric body, as symbolized in the *Pentagram* ✫ – fivefold soul-consciousness. – With the sixth, the *Salomonic Star,* ✧, we reach the highest step of physically human consciousness, if we exclude a seventh state: the actual Transfigured, i.e. ⊙, who have completely left behind human condition, as do Adepts of the *physical Philosopher's Stone* ✧ – beings able, for instance, to appear and disappear as did biblical Jesus. The last two symbols are the precursors of an eighth and ninth ‹dimension› of consciousness but which cannot be shown in matter anymore –in no plausible symbolic shape, that is.

In a mythical form, this Mystery is wonderfully described in a Bogomilian ‹Riddle from the East›:

«Seven daughters had the Snake. – The first sleeps like petrified; she doesn't see anything. – The second sleeps deeply: she sees colorful haze before her. – The third sees dreams and distant images. – The fourth sees everything around her. – The fifth sees the souls. – The sixths sees the gods. – The seventh sees the Sun. – Seven Daughters had the Snake.» [31]

As for the well-known tradition of Theogony – i.e. sequential manifestation of the One Godhead on the four planes: supracosmic, macrocosmic, cosmic and microcosmic – there is an analogy (to be understood *exclusively as an allegory*): The TURNING-POINT amidst the *Double-Helix* here corresponds to a ‹breathing-space of Brahma› – a night between two ‹days of Creation›. – But then: By the Turning-Point amidst the solar *S,* the Dual of the FATHER-MOTHER appears. – The *Triskell* represents the Trinity, including the SON (materially still unmanifested, but etherically quite real), presupposed as He was by some antique priests and prophets, and surrounded by the *Great Four* (pic. 5). – The *Arian Swastika* then already prepares manifestation of the Holy Spirit as the *Paraclet* (παράκλητος, the *«Consolator and Reassurer conjured against distress*»). – *Thesis 2* of *Aquarius Genesis* with its LIGHT-CROSS already symbolically evoked manifestation of THE SON as LIGHT.

The expression of LIGHT (Lux, like God LUG) means *Truth* in its essence (Jupiter virtue), potency manifest as *Knowledge* (Mercurial virtue) – and LOVE (the Light's solar dimension) – and LIFE (in its largest meaning). – In other words: Existence of LIGHT on one hand becomes *possible* thanks to that Trias: FATHER-MOTHER-SON – and, on the other, is a *live reality* only with matter as an intermediate. This fourth element – reality and effectiveness of the *SON as LIGHT in matter* (⊠) – is part of universal Creation in the sense of *Macrocosmos* or *manifested Universe*, i.e. the sum total of all Kosmoi (all galaxies, solar systems, etc. – including all microcosmoi populating the latter!

‹Supracosmic universal Creation› thus already as the sensually imperceptible ‹SQUARE› (no ‹senses› as such did *exist* yet at all!) was the first *Likeness* of the Number FOUR, □: Inside the latter, showed up the LIGHT-CROSS of the unmanifested SON: ⊠. – Thus: *Without* the LIGHT-CROSS – *without* the SON – no MATTER can be; – and likewise: *the LIGHT cannot manifest itself without matter reflecting it!* – So, «*since the Beginning*», the entire Creation was (and is) a universal divine *image in the likeness of God* – a true *Compendium* of HIS *universality and unlimited diversity of* ‹*facets*›. – Anon unmanifested, the Universe was already conceived *potentially* – i.e. within the *Power of the* One – *potentia Soli*. It is rewarding indeed to read in this context the first ‹book› of the *Corpus Hermeticum* (loc. cit.), where *Pymander* speaks of the *Wisdom and Power of God – de sapientia et potentia Dei.* —

Anon unmanifested Universe was an entirely fiery MOTHER-SUBSTANCE (MATER-EA – a macrocosmic *Root-Substance* – Buddhist ‹Prana› – «*concealed in the womb of the Godhead*», i.e. of SECOND CHAOS: ♦ – FLAMMA-MATERIA-MATER, corresponding to the Celtic Rune OTHALA which comprises matter and Spirit in one symbol: ᛟ. This ᛟ shows the potential primary 4 Elements inside the Rhombus: ⬦ – and ×, the Light-Cross of the SON, irradiated or embraced by both *wisdom and potency* of the FATHER: ∧.

Now the *efficacy* of the LIGHT was there present in a triple form as it were: Once through the supracosmic ONE «reposing in concealment», as LIGHT completely unmanifested. – Secondly, in the Trinity of FATHER-MOTHER-SON (1, O, IX), this Triplet, too, being an ‹invisible› *macrocosmic* FIERY TRIANGLE △ dwelling in concealment, but then descending, macrocosmically, as the AYN-SOPH △. And, thirdly, standing in the SQUARE of macrocosmic, but still perfectly chaotic Creation ♦ – the cosmic LIGHT-SON ✕, anon unmanifested Himself, and bound to manifest Himself only ‹later› in order to *microcosmically* penetrate in due course distinct humans prepared for this event (‹Illumination›).

Thus, if LIGHT as such was now created, there was, on the other hand, nobody to see it; – and so it was as if still no light had been present at all. For, as nobody was there to *consciously perceive it* – on whatever level or plane – it evenly was *not true yet* – no *true reality!*[31-A]

At the same time, and because the LIGHT-CROSS ✕ stands – and must stand – amidst the SQUARE, there appeared the *Fifth Element*: the central point of the *Crossed Square* – the focal point of physical Creation and Light, resp. the ascending axis inside the *Pyramid* (half an Octahedron !). – And it must be remembered that still nothing had come forward and stepped into being as an objective reality – and that everything still really was in *spiritual Oneness*: The pure eternal and ever remaining One divine Spirit thus had donned only its *second Veil* on its way ‹down› into some physical or even material Creation as we ‹know› it today (pure energy and ethers are physical, but not material).

One more word now concerning the *central point,* or *vertex,* amidst mentioned light-symbols: It always also indicates the *vector* up to the next dimension. In the Double-Spire, it is the *point of return*: the first ‹step› from Darkness and deathlike sleep in unconsciousness regarding the LIGHT – *towards spiritual evolution.* In all other cases, the vertex appears as the *de-cisive point of orientation*: *decision* and *turn-around* in one. It also signifies the spark of the CHRIST FORCE ✕ in the core of each and every creature, dynamizing them from the inside, and setting them in motion on their path: ‹inwards, upwards, outwards› – from force to force.

Modern Symbolism expresses this fact by the *Rosicross* – here to be understood as MAN standing in the physical world as a Latin Cross: On the latter's crossing – heraldically: its ‹heart› –blooms the Christ-Force, as a rose tinged in the colour of each humans state of consciousness: black, white, red, silver, or golden.[31-B]

The central point, or focus, of the ⊠ as the *matrix* of the FIVE therefore is, «*in the Beginning*», pure, anon unmanifested Man **IX**. Agrippa of Nettesheim in his *Occulta Philosophia* shows him like the ‹Vitruvian› Man› (see pic.6). There he stands as an ANCH *under the One Eye* ‹⊙›: ☥ – a symbol of *conscious Life.*[32] One with the One, original Man already in the *potentiality of the Universe* was its *Compendium* – as its *abstract* and *coronation,* and as an *image* *in likeness* of God: first cause and last goal of Creation; –*pre-figuration* of physical manifestation of the WORD which was to become perceptible only ‹much later›. – Thus Man was, *from the Beginning* – *«a Principio»* – predestined to become a SON, and as such *propagate himself* LIGHT and *universal eternal bliss*, for every creature to recognize itself as being a child of God!

Trinity and Quintet are what Man expresses when standing as an ✝ inside the macrocosmic *Square* – being the only creature posses-sing – *yet unconsciously* – a divinely perfect ability of Thought: Standing as an ✝ inside the Square, Man could not yet say : «*I am*»; – and even less could he say: «*I think*». – For, anon he *was not*, and least of all was he an EGO, not even unconsciously. – But in his *not yet physically manifested*, still entirely divine potential shape, as a *pure divine idea of Man*, besides his four extremities of an animal nature he was already equipped with a fifth, very particular ‹ex-tremity›: the future upright and *really thinking* head as the feature meant to essentially distinguish him from beasts: ✶.

Already now – standing in the Square as an ✝ – original, anon non-physical Man pointed to the «way back after the Fall», when *New divine Man* as a new Tetraktys ⅄ will fully unfold to become a perfect *Pentagram* ✶ *inside the Pentacle* ●, and at the same time inside the Circle ○ of the actual World: a ✪ – as staged by the *Cathars* in their Initiation rite as a *Parfait* (pic.7).

The symbol ⅄ – the Rune YLHAZ – stands for *Elevation, Transfigu-ration* and *Apotheosis* – and from there, probably, comes the para-doxical figure of the ‹*Crucifixus*› as shown by the iconography of ecclesiastic Christianism. – The five-pointed star ✶ (pentagram) thus displays the fully awakened *Vitruvian Soul-Man* inside the pentacle: an image for *union of the Four Elements with the Fifth* – the *Fire-Ether*. Here, the SQUARE breaks open and is elevated by the Spirit to reach a higher octave: the level of *soul linked to Spirit*. Thus *«God has come down»*, resp. has lifted his *fourth Veil* (mythic-ally displayed by the *dove descending upon Jesus*.[32-A]

However: Before *any* physical manifestation bestowed with Spirit became possible (one gifted with *individual spiritual consciousness of Light*), *some* physical manifestation at all was to appear first. – And it *did appear*, given that divine Spirit (so to speak) des-cended some octaves deeper, still, and on top of the first two veils «donned» two more, then three more again: that makes a total of seven veils! – On these ‹veils›, the *Aquarius Genesis* comments in its *Theses 6, 7, and 8.*

So, in its elevation, the SQUARE became a PENTACLE; – or: As soon as (so to speak) a PENTACLE had been formed *as a vessel for it*, the

LIGHT-CROSS was elevated to a higher octave in the Rune Υ, thus transforming itself into a PENTAGRAM. The language of Mysteries names said vessel *The Holy Grail*; and it therefore is quite irrelevant what physical shape one might ascribe to this symbol – a stone, a chalice, a human, or THE WORD: It always means the first definitive ‹shape› a manifestation of the LIGHT might acquire, reflect, and in a certain way: *multiply*. – That is why in the Round-Table of the *Grail* – in that spiritually live Community truly dedicated to the LIGHT, united with it, and protecting it – «*all are allowed and invited to drink from the Grail's chalice the Light of perfection and salvation, and are enjoined to proffer it to others*». Another expression for this enhancement and sanctification is given by the formula: «*The Grail is composed of seven metals*».

And so over time – i.e. in the course of evolution of human consciousness of the LIGHT – from the Double-Helix ◎ was roused the *Pentagram* ⚝, thus producing the symbol of the so-called *witch's tread* (a goose foot!) as a testimony for wakened mystical consciousness, and at the same time a promise for magical fulfillment!

This transformation of the Double-Spire into the Pentagram now is no mystical invention: In fact, the fifth dimension of consciousness – the birth of a Candidate's «new soul» projects itself from the first dimension of consciousness – numbness in the Double-Spire or Double-Helix ◎ – by mediation of the FIERY TRIANGLE.

Picture 8-A shows in a most impressing way that this «*coming forth from the Light*», resp. «*entering into the Light*», as the ancient Egyptian expressed it, is a process following strict spiritual laws – an evolution based on the GREAT LAW OF NUMBER and PROPORTIONS, as made visible by the well-known curve resulting from the *Fibonacci*-Series of Numbers. — The latter is an immense, absolutely incomprehensible wonder, reinforced moreover by the fact that both follow the same law of formation: 1° the *Fibonacci-Series*, and 2° the *Jacob's Clam* so closely linked to the operative procedure that in the alchemical labOratory allegorically corresponds to the birth of Jesus (and of the ‹Regulus›), (pic. 8-B).

At the same time it is impressing to recognize how deeply anchored in all humans – including the most evolved – the heritage of basest Hyperborean unconsciousness is (*pic.9* and comments to it) – and how inconceivably great the Grace that gives to every being – even the ones sunk into deepest spiritual unconsciousness – the opportunity – and the ‹potency› – to become carriers of pure divine LIGHT again: «*children of God*», as says the Gospel (Jo 1:12).

How come that the Pentagram has such a high sacral significance? – Because the dynamics of its *pentagonal line* conceals a *sixth element!* – And how come that in late christianistic normality the Pentagram got aliased as a devilish, black-magical tool of witch-craft? – Because the leaders of established structures of world-power *are afraid* of the soul-liberating power of the Pentagram! Who sincerely stands amidst the Pentagram; – who's ‹five spiritual extremities› are truly fixed to the five points of the Pentacle – as a manifestation and re-diffusion of LIGHT by the GRAIL – such a one is *freed* from the bonds of this world, even if he or she in their every-day's life are subdued to the constraints of the systems in which they live.

Said sixth element is a great Mystery – more so than that of the Grail. All *Christic* oriented humans of today – as well as pre-christian and non-christian individuals who in past centuries were living in CHRISTIC LIGHT and LOVE – may be aware of the sub-stance of this Mystery: It consists in the *human manifestation* of the CHRIST-LIGHT, of the CHRIST-FORCE, of LIFE manifest in the SON – and in what the Community of the CHRISTOS emanates as the LOVE of sublime VENUS-VIRTUE! – This is the true power that is «*not bringing peace*», but thrusts the sword into the ‹heart› of the earthly physical existence of the Disciple or Apostle: The outstretched (unfolded) position of Man who with his entire being stands in the pentacle, is his and her testimony that they are ready to receive this sword – unconditionally, relentlessly, with all consequences this may, and will, entail.[32-B]

Not that ‹in the Pentagram› this CHRIST LOVE were fully realized and could already have *manifested itself as flawless reality.* – But the Love Force is contained, and manifests itself *progressively*, in the ‹Vitruvian man› thus spread out, ready for self-sacrifice: He who stands *as a rising star inside the Pentacle* which, as a vessel, *envelops him: the Pentagram.* –

Thanks to radiant new soul-consciousness, the Candidate has, from his fixation to the Elemental Cross, «*come forth into the Light*» as One special and new, and as One bound up with the spiritual world rather than with matter. He has perceptibly become a *Star in its Vessel*, from who's *Center* can shine the Love-Force of the CHRISTOS: Testimony of eternal Divine Light in the World: a Holy Grail! — One might say as well: He has truly become a live link between the manifest world of cycles and contraries – and that other world: perfect, ‹immutable› and divine! –

Pymander comments in *Corpus Hermeticum* (loc. cit. supra):

«*The World is the first animate being; Man is the second animate being, after the World – but the first among all others ... – And Man is not only good, but also bad; That's why he is found mortal ... –*

Even the Good Demon names the gods immortal Men – but Men he names mortal gods ... – Thus there are three: God-Father: the Good – and the World – and Man ... »

Thus, in ‹five-fold Man› the CHRISTOS has not yet *«appeared in the clouds of heaven»*; but He stands in Man's core (same root as lat. *cor, cordis* – *heart*): invisible, and yet *factually*, i.e. *effectually:* The LIGHT OF TRUE LIFE – wanting to grow, as Light and Love ever and everywhere vibrate in this urge to radiate, to spread out, and to become *manifest and effectual.* And it cannot be otherwise: This urge must and will succeed. Potential Christ Force in such a human *will become manifest,* and *«come forth by day»*, visibly and perceivably exerting its influence upon the world – even if the world rejects it (Jo. 1: 8-12)!

That's how rises the *vital six-pointed star,* the so-called «Seal of Solomon» ✡ that in the Western World has become a symbol for attained wisdom – GNOSIS. Adding its focus or central axis ✡, it becomes the star of the CHRISTOS in its absolute perfection: Love, justice, absolute health, and unlimited ‹power through freedom›. – The same seal stands for the physical Philosophers Stone. And both also stand for a macrocosmic impact of the tenant (pic.10).

This exactly is why the power system of *official Christianism* has a.o. named *«devilish»* the Pentagram which covers yet more Mysteries: Who as *Renewed Man* physically stands inside the Pentacle (as a Pentagram), is about to strip off the fifth of the seven Veils: the second one donned by the Light in its descent. The same Light now leads back Man who fell into ‹Sleeping Death›: up and back to his or her Origin, their true homeland. This is the fifth step of their *«return to the Fathers House»* as chanted by ancient Bards in their teachings about redemption – the highest goal for Man of olden times to aspire to: Two more steps – and the ‹Crown of Creation› has returned, *«glowing again on the head of the Creator»* – yet this time not wrought of gold alone, but also ornate with the precious stones of consciousness, as a living spirit-soul ripened through stepwise experience – and through pain – returning into the perfect Harmony of the ‹seven colours› ... !

Hermes Trismegistos says:

«This is the only salvation for Man: Knowledge of God; – this ascent to the Olymp {the realm of gods}. Exactly for this reason a soul becomes good. Until then, however, it is not only good, but also occasionally evil – depending of circumstances». —

In the six fold seal of Wisdom ✡, hence, a *seventh element* is inherent. Out of it, an *eighth,* and yet a *ninth* seal will grow: be it a nine fold star composed of three flaming triangles of the three planes: microcosmos, Cosmos and Macrocosmos – be it as a perfect *Enneagram.* – This is the symbol of utmost divine perfection of the *newly divine* SON OF MAN **IX**. For the *tenfold star* can rise and exist only in one instance, and for a short moment only: «*at the End of all Days*» – when all opposed Duals *coincide*, i.e. *collapse*, into the perfect IO of *original macrocosmic Creation* – equivalent to the whole Universe melting back into the ‹bosom of God› I [32-C]

This *pro-gnosis* is an anticipation of what in *Aquarius Genesis* needs to happen first: Birth and lifetime of a Universe to be created yet; so we resume the state of Creation after *Thesis 5*:

The anon completely spiritual World with its Square of Matter (in its ‹abstract› state as divine idea in a spiritual shape) will yet have to condense, first etherically then physically, by the increasing number of veils enveloping Spirit in HIS self-sacrifice, which indeed makes up HIS true inner essence and purpose: – Spirit will have to become manifest physically, and lastly in matter itself – «*in the flesh*»!

But simultaneously there will appear the opportunity of the PATH BACK for all creatures ready to seize THE LIGHT, and to step forward in the power and the Grace of the CHRISTOS – i.e. in the glory of the macrocosmic GOD-SON × !

6,) «*Within the harmony of primary paradisiac occurrences a* FIRST SEPARATION *happened: The Elohim of the archaic Trinity* △ *created* EVE, *and with her they engendered* CAIN AND NORIYA *(a cosmic Triangle* △*!). The* ELOHIM OF THE TETRAD □ *instead formed* ADAM *in their image. When The One of them ordered* ADAM *to mate with* EVE, *sprang up for him* ABEL ▽. – CAIN *was a son of the* ELOHIM OF FIRE*: divine.* ABEL *instead was engendered (at the directive of the Seventh –* ⟨*The One*⟩*), as a son of* ADAM *and* EVE *as it were: an earthling – still spiritual, but elemental after the* ⬦. *– And this elemental separation entailed the* FIRST FALL».

Esoteric Science is known to speak of «*Seven Spirits before the Throne of God*». – If now the above conception is developed further, seven times seven fields of vibration are engendered. – These 49 fields of vibration are emanated by the above mentioned macrocosmic primary source of all energies and vibrations in the Universe: by that ⟨Zero Point of energy⟩, AIYN-SOPH – or ● – that macrocosmic Sun which is ⟨black⟩, as ancient Initiates said; and they brought forth every creature, every microcosmic ⟨heart⟩, every atomic nucleus, so that they should vibrate in tune – as living beings. These 49 electromagnetic fields of vibration now are standing – using mythological expression – before the Throne of God, like guardians or messengers – like seven ⟨Spirits⟩ or ⟨Gods⟩. «*Lords serving Him*» is what Pymander calls them in the *Corpus Hermeticum*. – Hence they are, quite literally, *standing waves* of highest frequencies: on one side, in dynamically opposed, i.e. ⟨*androgyne*⟩ *binary* amplitudes; – and on the other, eternally static at their ⟨knots⟩ (see. pic. 36). –

These forty-nine fields of vibration ⟨stand⟩ in harmonious reciprocal action, having as a center the ●; and they transmit their ⟨call⟩, their ⟨message⟩, over all distances – and to all worlds!

Let us now adopt and develop further the image transmitted to us since olden times, and renewed in our time by H.P. Blavatsky[33], M. Heindel, C.W. Leadbeater and R: Steiner – an image which nowadays is confirmed by modern Quantum Philosophy – Also let us consider more in-depth said «*seven Spirits before the Throne of God*» – these «*seven Elohim*» ⌂ – as being seven fields of vibration. Then can be seen as a modern interpretation of the old myths what follows:

The *collective* expression of ELOHIM is a plural form from Semitic Arabian. If the Arabian word *Allah* , *Ilah* or *Lahu* stands for *one god*, the term of ELOHIM (read as *Allahim*) may be interpreted simply as *the gods*. Biblical tradition gives us no specific number; – the *Aquarius Genesis* however gives way to such an interpretation:

The NUMBER THREE was shown to be linked to the macrocosmic triangle of FATHER, MOTHER and SON; the NUMBER FOUR (elemental

Cross inside the Rhombus, or the Square) with the FOUR ELEMENTS: +, or ⊕ – as being linked to elemental MATTER. – The ordering (ordaining and organizing) spiritual force for the macrocosmic triangle △ in the FIRST PARADISE ⊗ was the ×. The principle ‹EVE› (הוה) correspondingly was ordained› by the macrocosmic FATHER, י, or ⌒. – The ordaining force for the elemental but not yet physical Universe was the + in the ⊕. That is how *purely spiritual* FIRST PARADISE ⊗ became the *etheric* SECOND PARADISE ⊕.

Now it can be said that EVE was *cosmically* created by the *fiery virtues* of the *Three Elohim of the* elemental Fiery Triangle, △. Thus, EVA is the feminine form of the *descended solar spirit*, who in Hellenic (‹Eleusinian›) Mysteries was named Εϋος – EVOS – resp. DIONYSOS (*ovoς – onos* = a young ass!). This is an allonym for BACCHOS (celt. *baccou/vacou* – *The Little One*, Roman LIBER), – that is the famous *descended* (solar) *divine child*: prefiguration of the cosmic CHRISTOS as shown in ancient Mysteries.

ADAM instead was created by the four *elemental Elohim* of the ‹Tetragrammaton› יהוה: by the etherically elemental Virtues (lat. *virtutes*) of *Matter and Shape* – the virtues of the Four Elements □. To these *materially physical* virtues – the Four Elements – had to be *insufflated* as a fifth *etheric* Element the fire of Spirit, ⚥: The ש in יהשוה, and × in ⊠ are homologous. Only in that way an astral elemental Creation could be *called into live being*. – Thus, what is known as the *schism of genders* amidst the paradisiac Oneness, was already predetermined in the ⊕, viz. the ‹First Fall› as already prepared in the ⊗. For: Where there is *differentiation*, there also is *judgment and division*! – Indeed: the THREE (△) and the FOUR (□) already were TWO – given the duality of divine Oneness in the ◇. Now – to cut a long process short – CAIN was ‹engendered› out of the Will of the FATHER-GOD ⌒, through union of the Spirit with ‹fiery› EVA, the *feminine form* of solar Evos: ⊙ + △ = ◉ – Together this makes FOUR as well, and thereby a physical (etherically astral) manifestation.

Therefore CAIN – besides the central Spirit ⊗ – was also connected to the tetrad of Matter +, thus forming the ⊕ – but dominating both, and therefore he was a true «Son of God». As such he also was directly connected to the «Father-Mother» of the △, hence with ⌒ and ⌣. – That is why CAIN is directly linked to the SON *since the Beginning*: to macrocosmic *Sun-Wisdom* ⊙ – and also to the cosmic CHRIST. – And this – in a certain sense – is still true for all «Sons of Cain» today: humans simultaneously linked to the revealing force of the SECOND CHAOS ◆ and also to the primary creative Fiery Force △. – Therefore they carry the ‹Seal of Cain, ⊗ on their forehead. As live testimonies, they carry this *double fire* throughout the visible world – as an offering and a sacrifice with all the positive and negative aspects and consequences thereof: This makes ‹TWELVE› in all, and thus, lastly, THREE again: the *New Fiery Triangle* of fundamental creative renewal – *Vulcanus*!

The Christic Mystery expresses these facts by the inscription above the head of Christ crucified: *INRI – Igne Natura Renovetur Integra: By the Fire, Nature shall be renewed to integrity* – «*as it was in the Beginning*». – But this is still a long way to go!

‹Only then› ABEL was engendered – out of the will of the *Tetragrammaton*, of יהוה in the □ – by ADAM and EVE: terrestrial, i.e. elemental, ‹First Parents› as baroque theosophical literature names them: mating and multiplying according to the rules of the Four Elements. Now Abel is, in all respects, an oppositely polarized reflection of CAIN as shall be demonstrated soon; – because the twelve virtues of each, ABEL and CAIN, are so to speak contrarily polarized, same as *male* and *female*, or EVE and ADAM. – Thus ABEL and CAIN together make the *twenty-four cosmic forces* as mentioned by Theosophy as well as by the Popol-Vuj (III.9).

However that may be: As soon as ADAM and EVE, CAIN and ABEL «were created», the harmony of the original divine Paradise ⊗ was disturbed. And thus it had to be, lest the Universe could never have evolved further (see appendix 3-A). – But this disturbance developed its own dynamics – the dynamics of *judgment and guilt* – and from this astral dynamics again sprung up a separate being: The *Aquarius Genesis* calls it the ADVERSARY, or Great DISTRACTOR. – That's how a SECOND SEPARATION occurred.

Thus, the famous ‹FALL› is no ‹*fall through sin*›, and its primary cause is not the ‹ego-will› as is commonly taught: The Fall was absolutely necessary as an impulse for Mankind to evolve: It was the inherent *imperative consequence* of the First Separation in Paradise since ADAM and EVE. For, the seven Elohim □ who in the Beginning had collaborated in oneness – so very united that the authors of biblical Genesis generally just name them «*God*», or others: «*Sevenfold Spirit*» – these Seven had split up: Not in oneness of the Septuple Spirit did they work anymore, but in groups. –

Pymander explains this fact to Hermes like this:

«*But those cannot possibly cooperate peacefully without the ability of one who unites them into a team ... So it is not possible that there could be two or more Creators, nor that a common arrangement could stabilize itself among many. For, naturally, the weakest of them would envy the most potent one, whence then disputes would arise among them ...»*

Three of the seven Spirits before the Throne of God, △, «created» Eve», says the *Aquarius Genesis*; the other four, □, under the direction of the יהוה «created Adam». Thus the separation of genders was indeed «created» – and thereby the first etheric, i.e. physical and almost material, Dual of contraries: The kinfolk of Eve and Cain (through creation by the Three Spirits △) could at first still be named a *divinely spiritual and fiery primal race*, namely the race of *Titans* (comp. the *Book of Enoch*). —The *slyly slow humid kinfolk of Giants* of the prime race of Abel however – engendered by Adam and Eve after the will of the Tetrad named JHVH – was *a cloudy kin*, slowly condensing into a terrestrial shape (→ Germanic ‹Nifelheim› is the ‹Land of fog›!). – All this is meant to be understood *as mythical language*!

The kin of ABEL remained strongly linked to the feminine, watery virtue even during its definitive descent into matter: This might explain why (Jahwistic Abelian) rabbinic tradition never names Abel, or femininity as a whole. Similarly, Jewish Christendom after Peter and Paul was shaped according to both intrinsic and explicit antifeminism, and remain so until today.

An exception to this is ‹King Salomon› (*Sal Ammon* of Alchemy, and *Sol Ammon* = *Sun of Jupiter Ammon*) – linked to solar tradition. Equally, the fiery male descent of Cain can explain why the ‹Sons of Cain› always remained connected to Fire – revering in their religious cults Fierce Femininity (Great Mother) – be it in their cult of the Arch-Mother as *Ninti-Mama-Mari-Astaroth-Isis-Ceres-Venus-Dana* etc. – or be it in the mystic ‹Person› of *Sophia*; – or again, through the symbolic ‹Cour d'Amour› of the *Minstrels of the Middle-Ages*, singing for their ‹Dame›. –

Celtic mythology names the kin of Cain TUATHA DE DANAAN: TITANS and divine sons of DANA, Mother-Goddess of the Celts. They were ‹humans› – but myths tell us that occasionally they blew sparks from their nostrils, eyes, hairs and even from their hands. Thus chanted Babylonian myths along with hymns of the *Edda*. The *Essene gospel* says so about Jesus, and some sagas and pictures of the Middle-Ages tell the same thing (pic. 29 & note 34).

All gnostic movements as well were rooted in a double worship of God as Fire, as Sun, as Light, as a creative fiery Light-Force – and as VENUS: the *Morning-Star*. – Why, of all those, Freemasons make an exception here, R. Steiner explains in his excellent book: *The Temple Legend and the Golden Legend.*

It also goes without saying that the claim of JAHVEH, to be the *One Lord – Jehw Wahw –* already presupposes a discrimination of *oneness* and *division –* and, in other words, already this claim defines and definitely seals plurality, separation, conflicts, judgment, sense of guilt and the FALL! The first commandment of the AT: *«Thou shallest adore no Gods besides me»* in fact presumes an existing (macrocosmic) *plurality from the Beginning. –* The same goes for ALLAH of Islam: *«Allahw akbar – Allah is the greatest»* clearly hints at an unnamed plurality of *unequal gods. –* All this confirms tacitly that the tetrad of Elohim created *«ADAMU»* (interpreted by some authors as ‹*the Earth-born*) *with an un-outspoken aim* ...

But ADAMAS also means the *steely –* and: *«He who cannot be damaged»* (lat. *incorruptibilis,* Greek αδαμας *– a-damas). –* Therefore, in later times, resistant, non-corrosive iron *– i.e. steel –* was named *adamas. –* Opposed to this stands *Dami-ourgos – He who creates ephemere, corruptible things* !

By the way: *Non-corrosive steel* was made since Antiquity by adding to iron some materials named after gods, or with divine properties, among which also metallic elements of primarily extra-terrestrial origin and *completely unknown to modern science!* –

Coming back to the image given in modern terms regarding the seven fields of energy and vibrations: △, what has been said above can also be formulated like this: The original *unique macrocosmic* field named *«Father-Mother» –* due to the bipolarity inherent to every field of energy – was divided into two spheres or vibrations, bipolar themselves: male △ and female ◊ – both with THE SON as the solar focal point, kernel or axis in their center (the upper tip of the RHOMBUS coincides with the upper tip of the TRIANGLE). – From them splits off again the ‹double› or ‹divided› filial field the biblical myth *primarily* names ADAM and EVE – but *secondarily*: CAIN and ABEL.

Direct consequences entailed by this relation, the further inevitable process as described by the Bible, and the significance of all this for *today's Mankind,* have been commented on elsewhere[35]. At present let us only state that the field of Cain *eclipsed* the field of Abel, *«slaying it».* But an energy field can only be disturbed or neutralized, not annihilated, and hence *«as a replacement for ABEL»* a field *«ABEL-SETH»* had to spring up, as indeed it did ...

Thus, the originally united force of the ‹Seven Lords› was split up and, as a consequence of Abel's ‹death›, Cain's energy and Abel's energy were separated even sharper, and polarized even stronger: Cain thereby even more pronouncedly became ‹solar›, as shows the so-called *Elias-Tradition* of North-Canaan: Male, solar, fiery, and innovatively creative; pioneer-like, combative, and ‹*magically intelligent*›. – The lunic *Abel-Seth energy* instead is feminine, watery, formally traditionalistic and in a *mystically magical way* conservative (through ‹laws› and rituals), and ‹*sly*›.[36]

Evenly, JHVH himself as Lord of the Moon Angels is often interpreted as feminine. This corresponds to his being linked to the NUMBER FOUR, to the Sephira BINAH and to the androgyne nature of the Tetragrammaton: י for IAO (the Lord) – הוה for (H)EVE.

Abel-Seth then was seen as ‹*lunar*› or ‹*lunic*› as well: This is made evident by the original cultual traditions of South-Canaan with its worship of the Mother-Goddess: ASHERA, or ASTARTE, or ISHTAR (‹DIANA OF EPHESUS› so bitterly loathed by PAUL) – and its Yahwistic religion so clearly focused on Hebron viz. Jebus/Jerusalem.[37] –

But here a short excursion into the history of religion recommends itself:

Babylonian *Christic* religion worshipped ENKI (son of FATHER ANU) as the Son of Heaven. – Another Babylonian strain adored his brother ENLIL. – Later *biblical Genesis* names only ENLIL-JHVH the Lord of Humankind and initiator of the Big Flood. – Babylonian *Hebrew* religion around ENLIL-YALDABAOTH was named much later after its devotees: ‹Jewish›, from JEHW. It then suppressed the original lunar Mother-Goddess, supplanting her by their allegedly purely male god who, as shown above, is nevertheless linked to feminine energy: ‹*lunic*› JHVH-EL-SHADDAI.

This intrinsic contradiction is reinforced by the well-known *fight of solar Šams-son against lunar Philistines* (SHAMS-ER against ISET-ER again), and by that other fight of *solar David*, father of *Sun-King,* Ophite and Baal-worshipper *Solomon* (comp. 1 Ki.3:2-4) against the Philistines, devotees of ISHTAR – whence the name *Phil-Ishtar.*

David himself was anointed as king by *solar Samuel,* in order to replace *solar Saul.* The Old Testament constantly mixes up in its books the *solar culture* of *historically ascertained* original tribes of *North Canaan* with its predominant kingdom of autochthone Canaanite *Yezreel* (the cities of Jezreel, Megiddo, and Yebus) – and the intentionally *constructed heroic myth* of the insignificant nomadic tribe of shepherds later named ‹Judah›, living in the *southern* mountains near Hebron. – Both of them together are mixed with Semitic Traditions around *lunic Yaldabaoth-JHVH-Enlil.* – And all this while the mythic patriarch of the Semites – SEM – is a sun-hero himself: SHAMS or SHEM(S) = *Sun.* – But *Shem(s)* later on became the Semitic root for both *sem-,* and *izm*

– i.e. ‹name› in a vulgar sense, and so the original sacral notion of «*Sun = God*» went lost.

Thus, to sum it up, there were mixed three elements; and the resulting mix was recast between 500 b. C. and ca. 100 a.c. (actually since the return from Exile), to become the basic construct of Jahwistic rabbinic anti-history of the so-called «People of Isr-ha-El»: That is the period when the three super-powers of the Middle East definitively crumbled: Omrides (‹Syria› and ‹Turkey›), Babylon (Sumer) and Egypt (through Roman invasion). Thanks to Syro-Babylonians retreating northward, it could happen that said insignificant nomad tribe could become a political power in the lands of Canaan. Definitive conversion to the cult for JHVH-Enlil apparently was sparked under the above-mentioned influence of esoteric doctrines of Cushites and Chaldeans, during the Babylonian Exile.[38]

The same goes for the quadratic alphabet *adopted* from Pelasgian Cushites for Hebrew writing: ‹Ivrit›, the script of the ‹Immigrants› – *Ibirw*. At the *alleged* time of construction of the *so-called* first *Temple of Salomon*, no Hebrew writing, no Jewish architect nor Davidic Salomon existed.[39] – So much for ‹biblical History›.

Remains to give as a short synopsis of what A. Schütze, in his book *Mithras* again, quotes from Rudolf Steiner, regarding antique initiation modes:

«*Among various methods of pre-christian initiation systems we should distinguish two main groups: One strain adhered to by Nordic peoples attempted to gain, through their Mysteries, some knowledge of the Divine concealed behind exoteric, cosmic natural phenomena. The other strain adhered to by people dwelling more in the South, endeavoured to find God on the path of inner mystical experience by diving into the depths of their own soul ... These two orientations were named: Ascent to the upper, and Descent to the lower gods ... The (solar) path to the upper gods turned out to be a dangerous one because seekers were opposed by the appearance of Ahriman: the dark adversary of bright solar beings. – The path down to the lower Gods instead was deemed to be even much more dangerous. Here the danger consisted in that the Myste could be seduced and dazzled by Luciferic spirits, and entangled within a world of delusions ... Cosmic initiation then led to experiencing the solar gods (Ahura Mazdão, Marduk, Apollo a.s.f.). Mystical initiation led to the lunar gods (Hermes, Ishtar a.o.)... The Persians preferred the outer (exoteric) Path, while in Egypt there was preferably fostered the inner, mystical path ... The higher union of both strains was yet found during the Indian Era when the all-embracing*

Divinity of Brahma was experienced ... Among Persians there was still present a memory of this ... »[40]

Said cultic separation of North- and South Canaan stamped – however indistinctly – Levitic resp. rabbinic Judaism, namely through the separation of solar, so-called Elias-Tradition and Jahwistic Tradition[41], when the primary Jewish *moon-religion* was forced to distinguish itself from then new *solar Christendom*: This facilitated, nay, was positively decisive for, a theocratic union of the whole land of Canaan under the sole regime of the tribe of Judah. These are the real background conditions for the connection of Jahvistic ‹Jewish› religion – and therefore JHVH himself – with the *Moon* and the lunic watery feminine powers. – *Equally lunic* are the anthropomorphic properties postulated by JHVH for himself: Microcosmically, both anger and jealousy can be explained by the five somatic *fluids*: Blood, lymph, bile, sperm, nerve fluid. The heraldic pair of ★☽ means the *Unio Mystica* of SUN and MOON – VENUS and JHVH.

The Dual of ‹solar North› and ‹lunar South› of Canaan reminds the fact that antique Egyptians positioned their god of Light (the ‹Good›) in the South, and the adversary of Light, (Seth, ‹Evil›) in the North. This ancient Egyptian orientation however stems from *before the great inversion of the Poles* when, according to many Traditions, North Pole and South Pole changed their places by 180 degrees. For above concept, the question of orientation has to be taken into consideration accordingly.

The Symbolism of the two *Hostile Brothers* – CAIN and ABEL – is anticipated already by the hostility between the two divine brothers: ENKI and ENLIL of the Babylonian-Assyrian Pantheon: ENKI as the Lord of Light (Xi) – ENLIL as the Lord of earthly humankind (Lulu). En-Lil, as mentioned before, is also identified as JHVH-ZABAOTH, i.e. YALDABAOTH). Sacred literature of late Babylon shows beforehand how he more and more pushed to the foreground. He then dominates, resp. furthers more and more, not just all day-to-day business – and not just that of ordinary people, but also that of the kings who then became «*Sons of Enlil*». At the same time instead, his brother: *Father of the Gods and of humans* – EN-KI, and the *Mother of Gods* – INANNA, are elevated to far-away high places, thus withdrawing them, so to speak, from the Babylonian Pantheon. Jahwistic religion emerging precisely then, reflects these facts, as stated earlier ... [42]

The very old story of two hostile brothers is repeated by the fight between SETH (Lord of Darkness) and OSIRIS (Lord of Light), and mirrored in that of HORUS, son of OSIRIS, against SETH. – HORUS corresponds to the solar GOD-SON and thus is the Egyptian prefiguration of the CHRIST, same as MARDUK was the prefiguration of the CHRIST in Assyria. At the time where the books of *Exodus* and *Deuteronomy* are placed, Egyptians also were the lords of Canaan as part of the immense empire between Nubia in the South and today's Turkey in the North – and from the Mediterranean isles in the West to the Indus in the East. This once more shows the very dubious historical value of the book of ‹*Exodus*›: an otherwise sacred text forcibly back-dating the claim for a prosperous land abused by barbaric invasion and brutal bloodshed until today.

Mythological enmity of *two hostile brothers* (naming always first the lunar, then the solar one: ABEL against CAIN, SEM against CHAM, ISAAK against ISMAEL, JACOB against ESAU, ADONIAS against SALOMO etc.) continues throughout the whole Pentateuch. It still goes on in today's war in Palestine (Isaakites against Ismaelites; Jacobites against Esauites, Sephardim against Ashkenazim, and all against the MisraimCanaan's sons. – It is interesting to see that most of those mythic brothers are half-brothers: born from the same (lunar) father, but of different mothers: Spiritual (magic) heritage was always transferred by maternal genes, but the royal dignity by the father's status (or an uncle's for that matter; but that is another story). – In historical JESUS (following the Gospels) these two lineages joined inside the Levitic descent. – Most remarkable in this story is the fact that according to the Bible the one of the two featured as the somehow rejected genuine heir – since Cain – *always had red hair!* Red is the color of solar Fire. – Possibly even the pair of Jesus and Judas partakes in this Symbolism … —

If now the most famous pair of ‹hostile brothers› – Cain and Abel – have been engendered before or after the second ‹Fall›, the book of *Genesis* does not explicitly say; and it is difficult (but not necessary) to definitively decide this question: In either case their never-ending conflict is *the actual result* of the ‹*First Fall*›!

7.) «*From separation into a spiritual and an elemental Creation there re-sulted contrarieties between the Light Creatures among them, and inside themselves as well. And thereof arose as a ruling spirit the GREAT DIS-TRACTOR – alienated from paradisiac harmony of the divine World of Love, albeit yet united with it. For, from the separation into ADAM and EVE, CAIN and ABEL, the World experienced envy and gloating, anger and sufferings, violence and Death. This was the SECOND SEPARATION – the SECOND FALL. – Thus, the FIRST PARADISE ⊗ inside the all-one, divine spiritual Light-World was transformed into an etherically elemental SECOND PARADISE ⊕.*»

As a consequence of the ‹First Separation› – the split-up of the ‹Seven Spirits before the Throne of God› – emerged, and indeed *had to* emerge: thoughts, emotions, desires, and actions expres-sing and even reinforcing this same separation (see p. 95: quotation from the *Corpus Hermeticum*). From these thoughts, emotions and desires then issued *independent thought-beings, desire-beings* and so forth – and these increasingly disturbed, and finally destroyed, the original harmony: They were not part of the original harmonious Creation in Oneness of the ‹First Paradise›; and therefore nobody was there to direct and dominate them. – Now, the harmony of the original Paradise being deranged, and said derangements developing their own dynamics, there emerged, like an etheric sum of all these disturbances, another individual being – a separate Æon. – The *Aquarius Genesis* names him the DISTRACTOR.

The expression: «*Counter-creation*» reminds us of the creation myth in the *Zend-Avesta*: There, as mentioned above, AHURA MAINYU or AHRIMAN – the Lord of the abodes of Darkness who is also named ANGRA MAINYU – opposed to each act of creation by AHURA MAZDÃO (the Father of Light) an act of creation of Darkness – i.e. ignorance, negation, lack of love and consciousness. Thus was caused the ‹SECOND FALL›.

Following both the *Midrashim*[43] and the clairvoyant reports by Dr. Rudolf Steiner[44], one easily understands why the *Four Elohim* on one side created for themselves ADAM.

(By the way:It should be clear throughout this whole book that mythical happenings and their effects never are exclusive alter-natives, but can combine in multiple layers.)

As shown before, the word *Eloh* – singular form of *Elohim* – is analogous to ALLAH, EL and ILLU. The Quaternary is expressed by the *Tetragrammaton* יהוה. – ELOH-JEHOVAH, better known as EL-SHADDAI, corresponds to EN-LIL – ‹*Lord of earth's humankind*›. He is the Lord of the Moon-Angels, and therefore also the Lord of the cosmic Reign of material shapes: EARTH. For it is known that it was the Moon-Angels who shaped all material bodies – through (or «into», as R. Steiner says) etheric forms –. According to Babylonian mythology, the name for humans created by the *Nephilim* – namely LULU – is in harmony with above interpretation of the name of ENLIL read as EN-LULU – *Lord of Earthlings*.

ENLIL-JEHOVAH is, following some, analogous to ADONAI – and thus with JHVH (יהוה). The Sumero-Babylonian pantheon as well as the Talmud and the Midrashim, teach us that CAIN was a son of EVE (HAVA or HEBE, הוה) with ENKI. – And ENKI was also named SAMAEL, or THE SNAKE: That is the *Snake of Light* (like QUETZAL-COATL resp. CUCULCAN): This snake is – mythologically – linked closely to the SUN ☉ and VENUS ♀ [45]. – Thence one understands that the Serpent in the shape of the OUROBOROS *embraces the Cosmic Egg* and thus is, so to speak, *the solar guardian of the World*.

That ENKI, the Snake, encouraged Adam and Eve so that they «at from the tree of knowledge of Good and Evil» is less surprising if one understands, on one side, the mythic rivalry between ENKI and his rebellious brother ENLIL in their courting their half-sister NINTI, sovereign mistress of life – and on the other: the mythological identification of this tree with the pair of ‹ENLIL and LILITH: EVE is – following this myth – a granddaughter of ANU. – Seen that way, LILITH – albeit ‹elder› than EVE in the Babylonian genealogy of gods and half-gods – appears one rung lower than her.

So CAIN was the son of EVE, engendered by the Sun-Angels. ABEL instead was a son of EVE, with ADAM as his father. The latter fact became the basis of *physical Humankind* who, as shown, developed from the NUMBER FOUR and of the SQUARE, the sovereign of which consequently appears to be JAHVEH-ENLIL. – Or, taking into consideration the Babylonian version as the source of biblical *Genesis*: ENKI made EVE, and with her engendered CAIN, the *Son of Fire as a* SON OF HEAVEN. – JAHVEH-ENLIL instead made ADAM: *«From moist lime he made him»* – earthen. Today's Sohar equally says: *«Biblical EVE in Genesis I is not the same female as the one in Genesis II»*! – Unlike the creatures issued from the Quaternary, EVE and CAIN materialized following the laws of the *Fiery Triangle*, and later on engendered the lineage of half-gods – so-called ‹divine humans›. – CAIN means: *The strong one* (see Celtic *khèn*; French *chêne* for *oak-tree* – lat. *quercus robur* – a sacred tree standing for *vigor*, and highly revered throughout the AT !)

Divine Man Cain, the ‹Man of Fire› is linked directly to divine *Fire of Spirit*. – One might also say: the Three Elohim of the *cosmic* Fiery Triangle △ formed EVE pouring *macrocosmical female* (i.e. *positively polarized*) *Fire of Spirit* into a (negatively polarized) female physical shape ‹loaded› with fiery male Spirit. – KYBELE (riding a Lion, like Hindu Goddess Durga!), mythologically linked to whatever Earth brings forth, is a personification of this *female solar force* giving birth to everything; – It therefore seems quite coherent that CAIN offers – as the product of his work – orchard fruits and *spikes of cereals* from the field (CERES!), as is still the custom today – under the ecclesiastic name of *«Thanksgiving»*. – CAIN, himself divine, and sealed between his brows with the divine hallmark (‹Cain's Sign›, ⊗), is linked to the fiery, spiritually solar Goddess – ♀ – as Her Son.

YALDABAOTH instead had a different aim in mind. ADAM, the «earthling» created *from Water* ▽ *and Earth* ▽ («mud») was bound to earthly Elements. He therefore had to find the cosmic fire of cosmic female energy *outside himself.* – Not linked to macrocosmic Fire of Spirit like CAIN – ♀ – was Adam, nor ‹loaded› with the fire of enthusiasm, but with the cosmically brooding mother elements of Water ▽ and Earth ▽. – That is why God had to inflate to ADAM some kind of Spirit: «breath». And so besides Earth, Water and Fire, physical Creation, was given also the ETHER OF LIFE ♀ *as a fourth Element* – a volatile mediator between Matter and Spirit. When Creation was separated from (the second) Paradise – i.e. when EARTH was expelled from the MOON, (equivalent to a THIRD SEPARATION, the THIRD FALL), – *only then* a fifth Element appeared, due to *scission of the fourth Element*: The Element of *Life-Ether* split in two; and so was generated AIR, △ – life-giving Element for known physical nature below the ‹Firmament› – and on the other side: FIRE-ETHER ♀ as the life-giving Element for *macrocosmic spiritual beings* beyond the ‹Firmament› – angels, spirits and gods.

Since then, Creation consists of *five Elements*. Two pairs of them are – in a large sense – of the same kind: elemental Fire and Fire-Ether, resp. elemental Air and Fire-Ether ♀. – The symbol of the most subtle Element of all – ♀ – very clearly indicates the active impact of *godly human* spiritual fire as the *Force of Elevation* («redemption») – ☺ – out of the world of matter +. – Therefore, while ordinary humans feed only from earthly substances, individuals in the process of *transformation and Transfiguration* more and more directly breathe and feed life-force from *Fire-Ether.* – Thus, temporarily they live *out of all five Elements*!

The so-called Earth-sign ♂ has several significations, and in the present context especially these two:

Firstly, the Four Elements + ‹dominate› (prevail over) original, purely spiritual Creation O: This O becomes ⊗, then ⊕, and finally ♂. This is the so-called ‹Triple Fall›. –

Secondly: the *presence of* the fifth Element named *Fire of Spirit,* or *Fire-Ether* – ♀: This is when the physical elements + can be overcome by Spirit ✕ (the two symbols superposed form a Sun: ✳), and when the Force of Elevation with the same symbol ♀ prevails. The Earth symbol ♁ must then be seen, for a moment, as *three-dimensional*: Here the *two* ‹lateral arms› of + correspond to the *four arms of the Cross of the Four Elements on top of* the ⊕, while the *upper vertical arm* of the ♁ represents the *fifth Element,* the *Force of Elevation,* or the CHRIST FORCE experienced in the physical World. – If the *lower vertical arm* of the Cross on top of the Earth symbol ♁ had to be given a name, too, then it would without any doubt be MAN who – in spite of his fallen state of existence – remains the *eternal intercessor and* MEDIATOR between *worldly Nature* of physical Creation, and *spiritually divine Nature.* – That is how the *cosmic Christ-Force* envelops and penetrates Earth; and thus the Fire-Ether ♀ works in order to lovingly penetrate and impregnate every microcosm in the Universe, as the *«incarnate» Love-Force of God»*!

Alchemy represents all this by the ♀ inside the symbol of *Baphomet* described and transfiguristically explained by Fulcanelli in his *Dwellings of the Adepts.*[45-A]

That is how ADAM emerged: born from the Square of Matter. EVE instead as a creature of the (cosmic) Fiery Triangle; – and CAIN as a triple, semi-divine Man of Fire △; but ABEL as an earthling mixed from Water, Fire and Earth: earthly son of an earthly father and – since the pungency of CAIN's great fire fell down on him as a ‹ploughshare› (see appendix 3) – linked to Spirit in so-called ‹negative›, ‹passive› polarization: Here ‹matter dominates Spirit›: ♁.

Following Jahwistic mythology as adopted also by Christianism and Islam, it was the Great DISTRACTOR who motivated ADAM and EVE to ‹eat from the Tree›, disregarding the ban by JAHVEH-ENLIL, *Lord of this World* who's Elements, *in a spiritual sense,* precisely are *Earth* ♁ and *Water* ☽: ♀. – Following Babylonian Mythology instead, it was ‹EN-KI›, Lord of the *Ether of Life* (*En = Lord;* χ = Khi = Light and Life). – This ambiguity also applies to the ‹Serpent›.

Accordingly, the *Essene Book of Creation* says: *«The Law – the creator gods – said: «See there, Man is not like one of us anymore – for he distinguishes between Good and Evil, and now he cannot stretch out his hand and eat from the Tree of Life as well, and have eternal life!»*[46].

Now this helps to understand why the Snake coiled around the *Tree of Discrimination* is repeatedly represented with the horns of a ram: The Ram is a sign of Fire and of Sun. Both mythical and

Alchemistic iconography show the Dual of *Water Snake* and *Fire Snake* – combined in the *«fight between the Two Natures»*. The myth of how HERMES got his Caduceus explicitly says that! – It is the fight between the creeping earthly *Water-Snake*, ENLIL-☽ and the flying airy *Fire-Dragon*, ENKI-☉. This fight will finally end in peaceful harmonious *mating of the two*, thus generating *«double Mercury»* ☿ – see pic. 19. – From this fight between ‹fire› △ and ‹water› ▽ then issues – thanks to the penetrating potency of the ‹Christ Salt› – the Star of Wisdom ✡, and from it, sealed in Love and Knowlegde, the all-effecting Salomonic harmony of the physical *Philosophers Stone*: ✡ – in transfiguristic lore: ◉.

In *Thesis 7* of *Aquarius Genesis* however, this peaceful union is yet far from reach: Not only was Man expelled from Paradise (or as Jewish gnostic Kabbalah sees it: expelled God from it): According to *Aquarius Genesis*, Man expelled himself, thus falling into slavery in the World of shapes ☄, as was the aim of YALDABAOTH, the GREAT DISTRACTOR who «fell, together with Man and the whole Creation».

That is how the FIRST and SECOND SEPARATION came to pass among all creatures, while for the time being they still lived inside Paradise, against all odds. – Only in a THIRD SEPARATION there appeared an *outside* as well: a *sphere› of space and time outside Paradise*: Here lived the creatures that had separated, or rather *alienated themselves* from original harmony. The three ‹SEPARATIONS› along with ‹exclusion from Paradise›, are regarded as a blood-heritage of all living humans alike. That is why this ‹separation› must and will be reversed one day (one lifetime) by every individual human alike, as the *Aquarius Genesis explains in its* further Theses hereafter. To this end, Man needs to free himself from the laws ruling Earth and Moon. Only then will he grow up to solar freedom under the one commandment given by Jesus the Christ: unconditional Love for *All and everything in our Universe*!

The Lord of this lower World instead, who is named *the One Lord – Jehw Wahw –* (the other six Elohim remaining in Paradise) persisted in bondage with the Moon and the World of Shapes. Thus lacking the *solar Fire*, he depended on Life-Ether, the fourth primal Element as his nutrition: But that only creatures with red blood could offer him. All sorts of etheric offerings are what JAHVEH demanded from ‹his People›: Fumigations and vapours from oil and wine and blood – much blood! – Blood ethers from ‹pure› beasts in immense numbers according to the relevant prescriptions in the Pentateuch: Oxen, rams, he-goats, kid goats, lambs, pigeons – all *exclusively of male gender* – and even humans! The female energy remained again excluded from *official* Judeo-Christiano-Islamic religious practice (and thus also from original Freemasonry); – excluded completely! Today still, lowest Black Magick fosters to the extreme: offerings of blood, sperm, and lowest life-ethers of all kind (e.g. from greed and from fear of, or while, dying), in most cruelly perverted rituals ... —

What JAHVEH of the AT demanded was male fire-ether: This is a *light-force surrogate* especially released by *warm red blood* of dying beings. Under this scope, it is understandable that JHVH accepted with pleasure Abel's *blood-offerings*, while despising Cain's offering: crops ripened through solar power: Spikes are sun-rays of KYBELE/CERES! – These facts are most impressively described in the ‹hymns of repentance› of *Pistis Sophia*, where we read:

«*But all the material emanations of Authades surrounded her, and the great lion-faced Archon devoured all the light-powers of Sophia, and her matter was thrust into the chaos; ... a lion-faced ruler ... , of which one half is fire and the other darkness; that is Yaldabaoth, of whom I* {Jesus} *have spoken unto you many times.*»[47]

By *Authades* one should not exoterically understand the Hellenic Underworld – ‹Hades›. This text really speaks of the cosmic Æon of the physical Universe which indeed, as compared to Paradise, must be named a ‹Hell›. Microcosmically however, *Authades* is the personal Hell, self-made from thoughts, words, and actions of each individual. In both of these ‹worlds› there govern forces and ‹gods› imitating the Christ-Force: Macrocosmic ‹Great Chariot-eer› of Mithraism – cosmic *Yaldabaoth* – but microcosmically,: everybody's personal Karma built up from causes set by each of them: This is *Aut-Hades* – the *Self-Hell* of every individual human – without an exception (see pic. 28 and 30). —

The text of *Pistis Sophia* (loc. cit.) goes on saying:

«*And all the Archons of the Æons and the Archons of Fate, and tho-se of the Sphere* {of the Universe} *turned towards the refusals of their matter* {which, loc. cit., should have been «*wrought into souls for humans, animals, reptiles, wild beasts and birds*»}, *and devoured it. – They did not allow anymore that it might be wrought into souls for the World. They now devoured their matter* {i.e. their ethers of soul-fire}, *in order not to be weakened themselves ... in order that their own regions might continue to prosper ... and that the time un-til the fulfillment of the number of perfect souls that dwell in the treasure-vault of Light-souls, might be delayed as long as possible, and thus they might spend a long time as rulers, still ...* »[48]

8.) « The DISTRACTOR – arisen out of negative thoughts, emotions and desires of elemental creatures – now generated himself negative thoughts, emotions and desires. In him arose the lust of power. – And so ‹EVIL› was born. – In order to establish his own kingdom, he misled the dwellers in Paradise to follow his will: So, from the ⊕ came forward – in a THIRD SEPARATION – the physical World ⚲ with its well-known properties. This was the so-called EXPULSION FROM (etheric) PARADISE – the THIRD FALL.

Physical creatures as well as the DISTRACTOR were expelled from Paradise; and thus the DISTRACTOR got his own kingdom ‹outside› of the paradisiac divine world: This became the dark Kingdom of Anger and ignorance – the KINGDOM OF WRATH.»

Foregoing *Thesis 7* explained how inside of purely spiritual Paradise the FIRST SEPARATION of ◊ occurred – the FIRST FALL.

The still paradisiac Dual of △▽ now split into *four* ◈, then into *five Elements.* This field of energies, radiations and vibrations still in tune with the divine harmony of the elemental Tetrad ◈ began to condense, and became an etherically paradisiac world of Creation: This was the SECOND SEPARATION – the SECOND FALL.

From interferences of the Tetrad with the fifth Element there arouse a field of alienation from the original, divinely harmonious Field of Spirit. Thus developed a field opposed to the former one, soon usurping all potencies, and proving ‹fertile› according to *its own nature.* This pernicious fertility through further condensation produced the dense world of Matter – thereby causing further separations, and thus the THIRD FALL.

True: the will of the AIYN-SOPH-AUR is that *all creatures* should – in freedom and Love – grow up towards IT, so that ‹one day› they might reunite with IT as newly divine beings: *Igne Natura Regeneretur Integra – By Fire intact (i.e. flawlessly divine) Nature shall be entirely re-established!».* – The will of the forces of the Tetrad instead was precisely to impede Man to ever re-become divine; and this explains both the interdiction of ‹eating from the Tree of Knowledge, and the comment by *biblical Elohim* when this prohibition had been transgressed:

« ... so that he may not eat from the Tree of Life as well, thus becoming like one of Us!» (1 Mo. 3:22).

Therefore, precisely *three Separations* can be identified – *three levels of the ‹FALL›* : The FIRST FALL was separation of one perfectly spiritual ADAM-EVE (*«male and female, i.e. androgynous, created He them»*) into ‹opposed› ADAM and EVE. – The SECOND FALL was the division of entirely spiritual Creation into *four* resp. *five ethers*: Thus resulted both judgment and choice. – Only in a *«Third Fall»* the World condensed and crystallized in Matter. –

All too clearly one understands: Who discriminates ‹good› and ‹evil› without at the same time being ‹*dwelling under the Tree of Life*› – i.e. under the tree of universal Love – will be deprived of his or her harmonious union with Paradise – the ‹Divine World›. Such a one will be welded – «*three octaves deeper*» – to the World of Darkness with its manifestations in Matter: obscure denseness, emotions and desires (i.e. unqualified, unintelligent expressions of an egocentric will). Thereby he or she become *strangers*, ‹separated from the Light› which, nevertheless, embraces them *always and forever*, even if they live in deep ignorance and blindness, and fully unaware of *the Living Spirit*!

Thus is lifted the veil of Mysteries enfolding ENKI and ENLIL – the bias towards ‹SNAKE› and ‹DISTRACTOR› as promulgated by the biblical texts: *Man lost Paradise* because he *did not ‹eat› of the Tree of Life* (or else he would have become a true god); and the DISTRACTOR *was excluded from it*, because he diverted Man from ‹eating of the Tree of Life›. – And such is his doing until today!

That is how ‹outside of Paradise› – ‹outside› of the triple Sphere resting in God, with the ‹Good God in its core› – emerged a Universe alienated from God, with its own Prince as a ruler. And thus from now on there were three kingdoms:

1° a purely divine spiritual realm ⊗ – *a paradisiac Universe* in perfect oneness and harmony with the supracosmic Trinity: Here purely spiritual creatures lived in Oneness, Love and veneration of the One Light – but *in unconsciousness*.

2° a first physical but just etheric paradisiac world ⊕, polarized into the 4 + 1 Elements: ⬦ + ⬦. – And

3° there was now a ‹*kingdom outside of Paradise*›: a *physical Universe* filled with material manifestations: Heavens, Earths, stars and living beings, dense or volatile: of creatures divided in themselves, lacking knowledge of God – i.e. in ignorance regarding Light and Love – but in their blindness, obtuseness and darkness nevertheless destined to choose the *Path leading ‹upwards*› – *to God* – some day!

The DISTRACTOR as well lived in this ‹outer sphere›: The former oneness of the RHOMBUS ◊ organized itself in four spiritual, then physical, and lastly material *Elements:* ⬦ and – after the THIRD FALL – in a Universe of innumerable pairs of Duals symbolized by △ and ▽, △ and ▽̵, a.s.f. (see pic. 23 and image on p. 221).

The *forces of negation* now developed into stronger and stronger *beings*, because they were nourished by humans living in this World: through their thoughts, emotions, desires and fears of Separation. The driving force to all this is the *Ego-Will* – in physical and spiritual beings alike! – Thus appeared, besides all humanities, such beings as antique Greeks named *Demons* and *Archons*. – Today, such Spirits are also named Æons. – These Æons and Demons even today still reinforce a continuation of FALL and SEPARATION. –

In said ‹outside› after Separation from Paradise thus, the once divinely spiritual but now etheric physical Quaternary of *Elements* of Nature – ⬦ – became materially manifest. Divine Life, divine Fire-Ether as the fifth Element was withdrawn from physical Creation ♂. Who entirely lived in this Nature of Matter outside of Paradise, had *fallen into unconsciousness* of the divine Fire-Ether – and therefore was left without a possible access to it. But even now ADAM's Children stayed connected to the paradisiacal kingdom of Divine Spirit – ⊗, so that ‹one day› they might ascend to Him again and unite with Him anew; – namely through the sublime heavenly Love-Force of VENUS-OURANIA: ♀ or ⵚ.

‹Earthly Man› ♂ on his *way back to the Father* therefore evenly needs – as below, so above, and on a small scale like on the big one – to be crowned and surmounted by the spiritual Cross in ♂ and ♀, then dowsed with Fire-Ether ♀ and filled with Light by it – then *turn around* to face ♀ – i.e. *Venus-Columba*: That is the alchemistic ‹Eagle› ⵚ that appeared to Constantinus: *«In hoc signo vincas – under this sign shallest thou overcome!»*. – Then, *donned with the fiery Purple Cloak of Priest-Kings*, and presenting in his *Senestre* the Orb ♂ as the sign of ‹Ruler of the Earth› – Man will «eternally be sitting at the Right of the Father». – But beforehand …

Opposed Duals had turned into strife and anger; and the latter produced the KINGDOM OF WRATH with its Sovereign – the PRINCE OF THE KINGDOM OF WRATH. This Reign of Wrath successively accumulated all other kinds of etheric and astral creatures as well: shady reflections of Light-Beings in Paradise, along with their monstrous phantoms. The Prince of the Reign of Wrath became also the Prince of the reign of Death; and because he had abandoned the Sphere of Light (i.e. consciousness), he also was named ‹PRINCE OF DARKNESS› (i.e. IGNORANCE). – Here now becomes clearly visible ANGRA MAINYU trying to slip a shadow over every entity belonging to eternally paradisiac Light-Nature.

The whole completely mystic situation can be described still more in depth in today's symbolic language:

The First Reign is the triple Sphere of highest harmony in its original seven times sevenfold plenitude of radiations: ⬜ – these are the ‹Seven Spirits before the Throne of God› resplendent in purity of the original divine Universe ○. This is the Reign the vibrations of which continually renew themselves from the supracosmic sevenfold Light of absolute purity and Love. The ‹Seven Spirits›, or fundamental radiations issuing from the Throne of God are immutably one with the One, and therefore revered as ‹the immutable Kingdom›: ◉. – While physical Creation separated from Paradise, the *macrocosmic* Fiery Triangle △ did not descend as far as the material World: It remained concealed, ‹motionless›, in the ‹center› of the Macrocosmos – as its invisible, eternally divine LIGHT SOURCE: as a ‹*Vulcanic, black, central sun*› ● emanating all Light and all Love into the Universe. In the *visible Cosmos,* this fiery divine Eye △ – the *macrocosmic Aiyn-Soph* – is represented as THE SUN ☉ and, as mentioned earlier, also as divine Trinity of ⌢, ⌣ and ×, or *cosmic* FATHER, MOTHER and SON.

The same is expressed by the glyph ♄ in the hieroglyphic sacred scripture of Ancient Egypt. This is the Sphere of sublime perfection resting in itself, emanating from itself, and reaching out to Universal Space as if with a thousand helping hands. This was repeatedly represented by *Ach-n-Aton*: It is the Sphere *«the center of which is everywhere, and the periphery nowhere».* The Egyptian glyph for *«eye»* may be read as both *Aiyn* and (like in today's Berber language) as *Anu.* – This is the supra-cosmic Arch-Father-God of Sumer – Egyptian ATUM, or ATEN. – But A-NW may also be understood as *the Great Waters,* hence, the Prime Source whence everything springs up – hieroglyphically read as: ᶜ3-Nw – 𓀠𓈗𓏤.

Here we should remember the above statement saying that Arab *Aiyn* – ع – originally means all these: *eye, navel,* and *source;* — also that it is linked to *black colour* (Arab ‹*kohl*›) – and finally, that in Western Symbolism this same eye is tacitly united to, and identified with, *the New Sun* ☉ (HORUS' EYE). One should also remember what Fulcanelli writes in his *Mystery of the Cathedrals*:

«Immediately before he was to pass the initiatic trials in the temples of Egypt, the Candidate was approached by a priest who whispered into his ear the mysterious phrase: «Never forget that OSIRIS is a black God!» [49]

The *fourth or earthly Kingdom* ♁ is the one of the *quadruple sphere of continuous changes* with its *seven Spirits of Darkness* – the servants and underlings of ‹AHURA MAINIYU›: AHRIMAN stands for a band of vibrations progressively slackening down, due to fear, rigidity and *condensation,* until reaching *crystallization.* –

According to the laws of the Universe, this is a growing and deepening DEATH also named *Sheol* (a fire!) – or *Abyss* (comp. Jes.14:15). That is the dark alternative as opposed to the *real Path to perfect* LIFE!

In the course of TIME, more and more such ‹Death-vibrations› split off the four sevenfold vibrations of the REIGN OF WRATH, forming new Æons, meaning that Earth and Humankind were more and more encircled and enveloped by vibrations and spheres of Death: The latter's frequencies are so much inferior to those of the Immutable Kingdom, that by right this world may be denominated as HELL – utterly immersed into Ignorance and ‹Death›.

The ‹FALL› according to biblical myths is depicted in a very colourful way by the well-known *tale of Snow-White*: The *pure but unconscious* soul unable to distinguish Good and Evil is seduced to take a bite of an APPLE, thus falling into *a death-like sleep* of which – like the ‹Sleeping Beauty› – she can be awakened only *«by Love's first kiss»*. – She is accompanied by seven clearly differentiated ‹Spirits›, or levels of consciousness, here represented as seven dwarfs (the jelly-bag caps correspond to the *Liberia* of antique Persian Initiates). This is to emphasize once more: *The only real dynamics to redemption is to possess full discernment in absolute, unconditional Love!...* – [50]

Now one should not assume the mentioned ‹first›, ‹second›, ‹third› and ‹fourth› kingdoms (Spheres) to exist, so to speak, as *four isolated spaces*: No, all energy fields and their vibrations are interwoven and interpenetrate each other. So-called ‹inside› and ‹outside› are only realities of a consciousness and its evolution over aforementioned seven steps – meaning: On the basis of Jewish Gnosis stating that ADAM expelled God from Paradise, and not the inverse, the Candidate, first thing, perceives his or her alienation from God; – then, thanks to the ‹new-born soul, his *etheric bond with Him* in the ‹third kingdom› $\oplus$; – and finally, when all mental fictions (fixations) and all veils have gone, eternal reciprocal presence of God in Man, and of Man in God. – However: the more ‹fallen› fields of vibration there arise from thoughts and hopes, from desires and passions, from hate, anger and ignorance, from joy and tears of Man – the more they build up new Æons: *microcosmically* in and around every single creature, but *macrocosmically* in and beyond Earth's atmosphere and throughout the whole Universe. – Thus, the top veil of obtuseness and unconsciousness regarding the Light becomes still denser; – and so vagary, confusion, discord and desperation are spreading more and more. Hence, realization of the One Path becomes still more difficult for individuals, for groups of individuals, for all Humankinds, and therefore for the whole Universe!

For all these reasons it would be quite inadequate to see the *«Fight between Light and Darkness»* – like in a fairy-tale – as a combat of hosts of Angels cloaked in white, and with golden wings, against swarms of filthy black, sooty nude devils with dreadful horns: Those are primitive pictures from an ancient vision of natural magic, unfit for today's sober, objective state of mind. Indeed, such war-like imaginations lead still further away from salvation by the Light: Relieve from this war will become possible only when the *astral soul-image of fight itself becomes extinct* – like by itself; but not as long as war is fought as such, not even in the best of humanistic intentions, like by ‹leagues for peace›!

A better way to picture the contest between ‹Good› and ‹Evil› is to imagine it as a mixture of parallelisms and disarrays in two fundamentally opposed fields of vibrations – or ‹Natures›:

One ‹Nature› is the system of vibrations of divine purity, of unimaginably high frequencies and lucidity, ‹formed›, or emanated, by the harmonious sevenfold radiation of *Aiyn Soph* △ – the permanent macrocosmic radiation of the Sevenfold Spirit before God's Throne: ◹ in divine love, wisdom and impact. This is the universal radiation of Love, conceived as THE CHRISTOS, sacrificing Himself by «taking upon Himself» the mentioned seven veils – and thus penetrating the central heart of Cosmos and of every single microcosm.

The other Nature is a completely opposed field of vibrations: the extremely impure muddle of radiations and vibrations within the KINGDOM OF WRATH with its opaque, obstinate, obtuse vibrations. And there are the states in between: All together, this is what creates the situation described by esoteric Science as the *Dichotomy of the Universe,* usually denominated as a *«competition, or fight, between Light and Darkness».*

This fight between the «two kingdoms» can be described in a very plausible way by the following sound-image:

When two disharmonic bands of vibrations are stricken up with all their overtones and undertones, a so-called *jamming interference* arises between them – i.e. a *disorder* of sounds building up and growing until it becomes unbearable; – then ebbing away again until it becomes inaudible; – then building up and shrinking back again … – a phenomenon very suited to reflect the uninterrupted up and down so overly typical for our World of Duals. The same vision also allows imagining – to a certain extent at least – what hardship, pain and immeasurable sacrifice it must be for the *Brotherhood of the Spheres of divine Purity* with their unchanged divinely harmonious vibrations since *The Beginning*, to remain present amidst this mess of interferences created by Man – until finally – oh, finally! – the Brotherhood proves victorious after all. – This image also reflects the amount of inner force required of Candidates, to neutralize as well as possible – through «*Love higher than every reason*» – the raging storm in and beyond Earth's atmosphere, inside and outside of their microcosmic Lipika. – The same goes for planets and Kosmoi – and also for highest entities (‹Lords›) harmonizing the Universe and thus keeping viable the One Path, ‹*back to the Father*›, for «*all humans of good will*» – in strength and devotion!

The situation of Darkness continually growing while the World is accompanied in infinite patience and love by the Light stooping deeper and deeper down to matter, is visualized again by the symbol of the *Double-Helix* ◎ : While the spire of *involution* contracts itself more and more, there also remains inherent – as long as possible – the *turning-point* where the movement of involution and crystallization shall turn into evolution and spiritualization. This (invisible) turning-point is the Redemptor: The CHRISTOS ! – Moving thus ‹inwards›, the Element of Earth ▽ gets heavier and heavier, until the elemental fire △ in SHEOL is kindled at its highest possible level. Instead redemption by the Fire of Spirit × becomes quite impossible. – On the other hand, opposed dynamics boost the vibration frequency of Earth: Thanks to spiritual evolution and sublimation it climbs higher and higher until the Universe begins to glow and shine, and until the *Fire-Ether of Spirit* ⊕ predominates all, entirely: This is spiritualization of matter, and redemption through *Transfiguration* – ♈.

As a parenthesis let us notice how *even language* accompanies the movement of said continuous fall – from perfect cosmic health down into the deepest state of sickness of today's world: The originally harmonious cosmic *melody* (the Greek word *melos* is linked to the harmonious loving heart) has become a *melady* (Greek *melas* = *black*); – as an expression of deep Darkness; – and this finally became a *malady: illness*, or *plague* – an expression of how deep disharmony has penetrated into matter, today shortly named «*Evil*» – in French: *le Mal*.

Not that the inner vibrational harmony of the ‹Immutable Kingdom› could be weakened that way, or even destroyed: The old Rosicrucian slogan: «*Dei Gloria Intacta!*» will eternally remain valid; and so will the Symbolism of the eternally maidenly pregnant *Mother-Goddess – Venus-Isis-Kybele* ... – pure sacred ‹NATURE›! Macrocosmically it is her who was, and is, and always will be, revered under countless names since the beginning of times. Her center is the ‹*Navel of the Universe*› – *Aiyn* – ε, thought by ancient cultures to be *Planet Venus*: ⚥. – But it might come a moment where these sacred, pure vibrations *must retire*!

The holy field of this «ever maidenly mother-vibration» is nurtured by the eternally pure Harmony of the electromagnetic mother-field, whence all other vibrations are issued: the macrocosmic ‹black› zero-point of energy ●. – This electromagnetic mother-field is in turn sustained out of the *supracosmic Tetrad* of One, Zero, 10 and ×, according to the will of the *supracosmic Unique Father* ‹👁›: «the First and the Last» – the *absolute* zero-point of energy – AIYN-SOPH-AUR – perfect inner plenitude and outer fulfillment at the same time; the *absolute* ‹*Central Sun*› – cause of all causes – which was there before there was anything at all – and which will still be there when all what now is will have passed away. – It is *the One with the unspeakable name* – yet named: «GOD», «LIGHT», «MONAS», «the SOLE GOOD» – and: «FATHER».

But what will be the reaction to these vibrations and radiations by blindfolded humanity amidst its global delusion and idleness – in its darkness of ignorance so cunningly upheld by the GREAT ADVERSARY – the Prince of Darkness and Wrath with all his servants and ministers especially in the Reign of humans? – And what hope remains for the Brotherhood of liberated souls to keep up their beacon-fire of redemption throughout this sick world? –

This question will be discussed in the next Scholion.

9,) « *The dwellers in the* KINGDOM OF WRATH *were completely subdued and dominated by the latter's Lord. They were separated from the Sole Good like he, in quarrel and anger like he, in Darkness and Death like he. – In one thing however they differed from him: Abel's sons as well as Cain's sons preserved – hidden in the innermost core of their hearts, but more and more unconsciously – and imperceptible for most of them – a divine core-vibration issued from the Kingdom of Light and Love.*
This divine core-vibration the Lord of the Kingdom of Wrath did not have, him being of no divine origin but emerged as a consequence of division – from negative thoughts, emotions and acts by the creatures within his reign as well as by himself.».

Thus, inside the kingdom of anger, divine dynamics of the paradisiac occurrences of the Beginning – this absolutely harmonious circular movement reposing in itself and issuing from itself – turned into a spire of involution leading «inwards» and «downwards»: a spiral of densification and crystallization as explained before and which is named DEATH. – This contrariety as outlined in previous chapters illustrates the *double nature of the Double-Helix* ⑨ as an *arch-ontic, i.e. arch-essential twin dynamic* of involution and evolution. This is extensively described in a scroll named: *«Hypóstasis of the Archons»* (i.e. *«The Real Essence Of Celestial Powers»*) – and similar very old text fragments also discovered in Nag-Hamadi, only mid of last century.[51]

In the *fifth hymn of repentance of Pistis Sophia* this state of matters is expressed in these words:
«MY POWER is filled with darkness, and my LIGHT has sunk into Chaos ... I have become a physical body that no-one in Heaven wants to save. I have become like one of those physical beings who's POWER has been taken away from them, so that they are now cast off into Chaos».

And in her *Thirteenth Hymn of Repentance* we even read:
«I have turned into sinful MATTER. I am whirled hither and thither like an Air Spirit. MY POWER has ceased because I have lost the Mystery of Salvation. And my light substance has waned because those have taken away my LIGHT. – And they mock me; and waving at me they look down on me ...».

As an image this could be expressed like this:
Ouróboros – the live Sun-force, or sun-like life force, was the blazing «*εν το παν*» – *One is also All* (pic. 28) – corresponding to the *Light-Force* of Hermetic Harmony: *«on a small scale as on the big one – as above, so below».* Microcosmically, the original shining serpent-power of *Ouróboros –* that means: *He who carries*

the Universe (or else: *the Light* or *Fire*) 52– turned his movement inwards, curling up around a yet invisible central point or Sun, thereby *projecting* something like an EGO. Hence not only differentiation and separation came into the world: There also arouse an (unconscious!) EGO capable of *becoming aware of, and consciously experiencing,* differences and separations. But since every EGO perceives divergences and separations differently, at the same time also came into the world discord and anger. This was the turning-point, away from permanent harmonious circular movement (immortality) to the spire of involution – of ignorance, crystallization and Death. – For, where there is anger, there Love is lacking; and where there is lacking Love, there is Death!

Forgetting their union with the Seven Spirits before God's Throne, and their harmony with the seven sacred primal vibrations of the Universe, the dwellers in the Kingdom of Wrath sunk deeper and deeper into disharmony and sluggishness of matter. Slower and slower became the core-vibration of all creatures. That's how they ‹fell› and became separated from the Oneness of the Universe – from the most-inner *source* that is the nurturing mother of all vibrations: No longer were they nourished as before from immediate oneness in love, wisdom and power; and so it was unavoidable that all creatures – along with general abasement of their vibration frequencies – became more and more inert, more and more dense: First fell the ‹Crown of Creation›: Man; and then, – through fundamental resonance of the whole Creation with Man – all other creatures ‹fell› as well.

Instead of consciously transmitting vibrations of absolute Love to his co-creatures and thus lead them upwards to the Throne of God, Man even lost his own bindings with the divine Love-Fire, becoming thus sluggish like Matter, dense like Matter, plummeting into brutish unconsciousness, into plant-like immobility, into mineral hardness and coldness, into arch-elemental shapelessness and disorder – like into an impure terminal CHAOS. Thus falling, Man dragged down with him the whole Cosmos ... – and all of them plunged into the now forming World of dense Matter.

One might complete this view from a third point of view:

The original world of *paradisiac Spirit* ⊗ was transformed into the World of *paradisiac ethers* ⊕. The etherically physical World that had been thriving in the abode of pure Light-Force, *pushed itself off* the latter and now stood outside of it: ♂. – The four Elements +, which originally had harmoniously filled the world ⊕ in tune with the Fire of Spirit ♃ – these physical Elements fell out of said Oneness and *began to rule the World.* – Much more still could yet be said about all these occurrences!

However that may be:

Further and further away drifted Man from the pure dwellings of the Beginning; – more and more he took after the monstrous beings birthed by his own thoughts, emotions, desires, fears and passions that are his creatures by the fatherhood of the GREAT DIS-TRACTOR. – More and more original divine heavenly Man became an entity of Earth – earthly!

The DISTRACTOR, too, as the PRINCE OF DARKNESS and of now un-godly Creation, was banned from Paradise. In said ‹outside› that developed through him, he built his own kingdom, ruling it as the central dynamic of the Spire of involution – as macrocosmic EGO-WILL, so to speak. And by means of fear, anguish and sorrows he continued this separating sway. This is the well-known ‹Ahrimanic› dynamics of the GREAT ADVERSARY or DISTRACTOR.

Simultaneously came to pass *physical separation of all Life* into two ‹genders›. – This was not just a spiritual bipolarity any more, but a contrariety that could be experienced physically: Hence came the *longing for salvation*: the desire of the separated parts to reunite (→ *Appendix 3*). And from the lack of harmony and love experienced because of this separation, *envy* was born.

Alienation from God grew so strong that humans, in their abys-mal ignorance began to distrust God Himself: «For» – thus thought they, bound in their illusion of real separation as they were – «an absolutely good God couldn't possibly create, nor tolerate, any evil, harm, wrath or pain!». – However, it has already been explained earlier, why and how ‹Evil› arouse, how separation from The Father occurred; – and how the DISTRACTOR, whom our text also names YALDABAOTH, founded his kingdom on Earth.

Now: talking about this ‹Fall into Separation›, while at the same time stating *Separation to be an illusion*, we need to emphasize that the latter statement is incorrect on the microcosmic, subjec-tive level – but correct to the greatest extent on the cosmic and macrocosmic planes – and absolutely correct on the supra-cosmic plane – same as the *Dichotomy of the Universe is a cosmic reality*, while on the supra-cosmic plane it is an illusion: Never ever can any creature entirely ‹fall› out of its oneness with God; for God is everywhere, in all and every one – and all and everything are in Him. *Lack of consciousness alone* effects humans to sense and experience, feel and suffer, a separation from God and from His field of vibrations – having ‹fallen› so deep that ordinary people have forgotten the *experience* of being immutably one with God – along with the relative sensation of joy and gratitude about this fact. Low vibration frequency, unconsciousness, inertia of matter, and Death, are equally bound together as are high vibration frequency, wake consciousness and conscious dynamics of true *Life in the Spirit.*

The hidden divine *kernel of remembrance* in every microcosm however mirrors the two movements of *Fall and Salvation* – of *death and resurrection,* as demonstrates the macrocosmic Double-Helix with its *turning-point* ⑨ (→ pic. 21 & its legend): As soon as the microcosmic kernel of an animated being is stricken and enflamed by said *Love-Impulse of the Fire Ether* ♀, the focal point of it's heart becomes the turning-point – the point of return for the so touched human. – This corresponds to the *awakening* from ‹Snow-white's› Hyperborean ‹Sleeping Death›.

Is, then, Evil nothing but an illusion as well?

Yes and no: Evil is experienced in the World as *a smart.* – Painful experience is the daily bread of ego-centric humans in this World; for smart and disappointment are the overripe fruits of the EGO! – But the sting of smart is precisely a gift out of the love of God who wants to awaken His creatures: from numbness and darkness to intelligent empathy, and to the longing of the soul to meet the Light! – It is *smart* that births those well-known questions of the seeker: «*Whence comes all this? What for is all this? How to get out of this muddle with all its pains and tears?*» – Very few are they who, from birth, so to speak, bear a wake remembrance of the *path of return to the Light* – of this unique but multiple pilgrimage back to God!

Through this dilemma – amidst these painful questions – man immerged in deep ignorance and unconsciousness is touched by the love-radiations beaming forward from the divine world. Extreme separation thus at the same time becomes the *apogee* of the orbit on which unconscious Man feels himself hurled out into Space, as if no return were possible any more, just as *Pistis Sophia* expresses it in her hymn of repentance quoted before. And so Evil itself turns into an expression of the «Good Law» – for from disappointment and smart grow the dynamics of *Self-salvation in Freedom of the Will.* – Delusion is the wound through which the light beam of salvation may penetrate into the innermost heart! It was Gœthe again who thanks to his deep insight and universal view let Mephistopheles – personification of Evil and the Great Adversary in *Dr. Faustus* – pronounce the shortest definition of himself: «*I am part of the one force that always aims at working Evil, but always achieves the Good*».

Indeed: Humanity seems lost in the ‹apogee› of the Spire on which – ascending or descending – it circles around God as does a

Planet around the Sun. – But God *«drops not the works of His hands»*: His Love which is the all-one, all-embracing, all-driving power and dynamics in the Universe, is at the same time the source, the womb, the envelope and the life sphere of whatever exists. God's Love eternally is the utmost sublime vibration radiating in all directions, from a Center that *«is everywhere»*; – and as a vibration that universally IS!

This universally effective, boundlessly blazing, divine love vibration is absolute freedom – and at the same time an absolute haven. It penetrates into the deepest depths of the Kingdom of Wrath, sacrificing itself in this abyss, and lifting everything up to its own height. – It is the power and ever present impulsion named the *universal Christ-Impulse* – no matter what time, place and cultural environment: This is the true royal *Power of the Anointed* – the *Messias-Power*, which wants to sanctify everything, and save everyone. – Some also name this power: THE HOLY GRAIL.

«To all ready to receive Him, will be given the power to become Sons of God again», says the Gospel of John; and this means: Whoever awakens to consciousness of the ever living presence of the universal Christ-Force – consciously *receiving its impulsions* – is *at the same moment* also received in its haven as a *Living Soul – as a new-born child of God*!

Now this is the clearly positive answer to the apparently clumsy question of Nikodemos in Jo. 3:4 – *«How can a man be born again, when he is old? Lest he could enter his mother's womb for a second time, and be born anew?»* – Original Divine Man – the divine «Son of Man» **IX** – has really come forth through the creative will of the FATHER, and from the revealing womb of the MOTHER. – This **IX** is the DEED meant by Gœthe who perfectly knew the tree of the Sephiroth, when he let *Faustus* exclaim as a kabbalistically phonetic pun through his regional Saxon vernacular:

«In the Beginning, there was DATH!»

‹Fallen› Man instead, in order *«to be reborn from Water, Spirit and Fire»* must turn around *and face* the power to which, «long ago», he *turned his back*– and thus become one with it again.

Salvation of cosmic Nature from the Nadīr of its mortality – this universally redeeming dynamic is represented here by the Rune Ylhaz – Y – now resulting from the Power of the FATHER – ! – plunging into the Dichotomy of the Universe **Y**, and becoming ‹flesh› therein: Y – This, finally, is the *«ex Deo nascimur»* of classical

Rosicrucians; – expressed microcosmically as an *immersion of the Holy Ghost* – ' – into the orphaned and by its nature ‹divided›, or ‹split› human, **Y**, thus elevating him: Ϋ (pic. 38). – The *Corpus Hermeticum* comments the same in the following words:

«*Thus the World is really an accumulation of evils, but God instead [is the accumulation] of the Good ... – Therefore one may dare to say that earthly Man is, so to speak, a mortal god – while a celestial god is an immortal Man*» (see note [12-A] here-before.)

Divine Love-Force is the reality that – superseding all religious dogmata, and unprejudiced by any belief, creed or dispute about them – simply IS and works for every creature alike: Who opens himself to said elevating force and tunes in with this eternally loving vibration, thus ‹becoming an YLHAZ› – and then «*follows*» this ‹key of vibration›, will by the forces of natural laws be *elevated* from the depths of Darkness in Ignorance into the Light of Knowledge in The Light, thus becoming a participant of the Light: This is what «*Imitation of Christ*» is about; but it must be born from conscious free will, and through autonomous endeavour of each creature. Such is «*redemption from the Kingdom of Wrath and Death*» – for: where there is Love, anger cannot be. – *This* is *Man's true resuscitation from his grave* through Self-initiation and self-healing: Wherever the Kingdom of Wrath is overcome, there will awaken: *eternally greening joyful Life* !

All chronicles in the World are full of stories about bloody battles for power and fake missionary expeditions for discovery, as far back in time as one might look or think. Questioning the motivations for all these attempts to fasten the Power of the Few at the costs of the Many, one will find the answers always woven into the background of pseudo-religious power-play in real power-politics. This is true for the great war-expedition of Alexander the Great and the destruction of Troja, for the campaigns of Julius Cesar and Charlemagne – and quite as well for the invasion of both America's – masked as a «new discovery» *in the name of Christ!* – The same goes for the Persian Magi killing Mani as an attempt to delete his competing religion (a typical case of preconceived judgment in an act of fake justice) – or the Pharisees hiding behind Roman law to kill Jesus. – Again and again lust of power is the motive for brutally killing peaceful ‹civilians› out of their quiet pious life – in every epoch: In France of the 13th, 14th and 16th century; – in North America from the end of 15th century until today; – in Iran, Syria, Afghanistan, Vietnam and Palestine since 1945 until today: War and repression, marginalization and violation will go on in this poor World as long as egotism and megalomania govern, and as long as dim-witted Masses sheepishly obey ... —

True religiosity instead achieves peaceful steadfastness towards the outside, and inner victory of each human over his or her own microcosmic fiend. – Here there is no question of a war: Who might want to defeat Evil with earthly means – with *«the will of the flesh»* – would only get enmeshed deeper into discrimination of ‹Good› and ‹Evil›, hence wielding themselves to ‹Low Nature›, faster than ever before: *«Truly overcomes who does not fight!»*, says a typical Daoist book of wisdom [53].

Almost all exponents in human society who entered World History thanks to their «strength of persuasion» (whatever kind), or who already while living entered the pantheon of ‹heroes› (by whatever right), believe(d) or pretend(ed) to have acted out of their own will and virtue, and for a specific human goal (whatever their criterion). – Instead, they truly all act(ed) under some æonic spell to the advantage of the GREAT DISTRACTOR, the ‹Lord of this World›: Devotedly they serve HIM who wants to defend and expand his Kingdom of Darkness and Wrath. – This also is his positive macrocosmic reason of existence within the ‹Plan› of the sole Good God who is all Love and wants His creatures to turn towards him – again: *consciously and in free will* – in this (if looked at it sharply) most perfect of all possible Universes, with all their worlds habitable for whatever sort of humans!

But before such Love can *consciously be experienced,* and answered in the sole adequate way, *«the dwellers in the* KINGDOM OF WRATH *were completely subdued and dominated by its Lord».*

– And the decisive way out: *what indeed* does it look like?

10) *«Those others however, albeit being immersed completely in Darkness of Ignorance, were touched from time to time by the luminous, fiery love-vibrations issued from the pure divine world ⊗ that irradiate and penetrate the Kingdom of Wrath, anytime. Whenever such a beacon of Love-Light hit upon one of said kernels of remembrance, it flamed up – for a short instant or longer. – In human hearts this flare-up of a reminiscence of the original Light-World kindled an undefined LONGING to return to the original KINGDOM OF ONENESS».*

«God never abandons the works of His hands». – His ‹hands›, i.e. His ‹*Seven fundamental Vibrations*› – the Seven Spirits before His Throne, the seven sevenfold beacons of Light. These broke through all Spheres, moving even the lowest depths of Darkness: the Abyss of the Kingdom of Wrath – the kingdom where dwells the entire enslaved Creation. But not in their essential power and purity did these beacons hit the lower planes, for the World and its creatures would have been incapable to face the fire of these radiations due to without being «burnt to ashes» by them due to their inconceivably high frequency. That is why the Seven Spirits – the seven sevenfold beacons of Light – hovered down in a strength and impact the world and humanity were just about able to cope with. – To pursue the image of waves and vibrations (and this may be the reason why Angels are mostly represented with wings) these Spirits had tuned in with the few individuals *able to react with them at all,* so that the latter could build up a positive resonance and, meeting minimum conditions, in their darkness *experience the* LIGHT, look up to It and even ascend to It: From their ‹infernal cacophony of interferences› in the so-called *Dialectic World of Dichotomy* they were awakened by their own surprising resonance with the harmonious waves and radiations of the Angels of Light who had come forth from the Kingdom of Light, in order to meet Humanity!

The seven times sevenfold vibration thus did not descend in its unbearable fiery, blinding plenitude: Descending from the highest spheres that are its dwelling, it donned – as says Mythology – *«seven veils»* : one veil after the other. And with each ‹veil› its frequency was lowered, its fiery radiation lessened, and the difference from its original purity and unspeakable luminosity, augmented. – But its *Essence* remained the same!

This is what the *«descent of the Sun-God»* as articulated by myths and fairy tales is all about; – It is the *«Arrival of the Savior»*, the *«return of Quetzalcoatl»* so fervently waited for by the Maya's. – And it is the unspeakable sacrifice of the universal, sublimely pure Love-Light of the ‹Messiah› who took upon Himself to endure sluggishness of matter and hardships of earthly spheres, until earthly humankind finally κατέλαβεν αυτόν – *grasped Him, received Him,* and thereby could *«become Sons of God again».* This is the healing of the soul, step by step, from the ignorance enveloping it, the reality behind the *«Seven Veils of the Mysteries»* – Judith's famous *«Dance of the Seven Veils»* which, as Scripture says, cost John the Baptist his head (see pic. 11 &comment) ... –

Once more we quote from the *Corpus Hermeticum* (loc. cit.) as illustration to the mentioned facts in Antiquity:

«But first of all it is necessary that you depose the wrapping in which you linger around: this garment of ignorance; – this fundament of dissolution; – these fetters of depravity; – this thick hide; – this Living Death; – this sensual corpse;– this dancing tomb; – this villainous servant ...!»

So that is how the pure divine radiance of Love pierces all obstacles, like an appeal: A call to awaken creatures from their slumber of ignorance – and particularly those humans who, as a consequence of their state of evolution, are pre-destined to *become aware of* the Christ-Vibration, to *answer it* positively , and *to «follow»* this fiery appeal as its loyal *‹Disciples›.*

This has no longer to do what so ever with any mystical dogma or specific doctrine in the East or West: It is the way to hear with *ears that understand* – to see with *eyes that can distinguish* by themselves. – And it is why not a single human mediator – no priest, magician, shaman or Saint, is able to confer any of this redemption to any other human, nor to withhold it from him or her: Whoever receives HIM – thus promises the *Euangelion (ευαγγέλιον–* the *Good Tiding)* –will be given the power to become a participant in the everlasting Kingdom of Love again:

«... Those who believe in His Name; – they who are reborn not of blood-magick, nor through sacrifices of the flesh, nor by the will of Man» (Jo.1:13).

It therefore essentially is the immediate task of the Candidate himself to qualify for his or her redemption. – And indeed there always appeared some individuals who, knowing THE LIGHT from their own experience while daily following THE PATH, were liberated during this life already and «taken away» – or remained in the flesh, helping their brothers and sisters to find certain ‹keys› that open a first door, then others, in the *«House Sancti Spiritūs».*

So, even in deepest distress and darkness Humanity remains – Creation remains – in communion with the immutable KINGDOM OF THE LIGHT – of God, Whose love never abandons His creatures.

«When distress is at its worst, help is most close as well!», thus says Sacred Language. — At the apogee of its orbit — when it appeared to be the farthest away from Light and Love, humanity also became the most inclined to receive the salutary Light, and to find the turning-point to redemption — *Praise be to God!*

The schism of the Elohim was the immediate cause for the ‹First Fall›. — One might say as well: The schism of the Elohim *became the pulse generator* for Separation and Fall, *setting in motion* the dynamic *alienation* of creatures from the One God Who, nevertheless, remained their immutable ‹focus›. Without this alienation, Man — petted in ever preserving and ever preserved divine harmony and oneness — would never have developed his positive *auto-dynamics*: *«Who never leaves home, will never return!»* as goes an old saying. And that is true also for Man in Paradise: *«He would»* — as says the text in *Appendix 3-A*— *«have remained drowsing under his tree, forever!»*.[54]

Thus Man would have remained incapable for all eternity to *discriminate* what so ever (e.g. ‹good› and ‹evil›), *to choose* things or behaviours in self-consciousness and auto-responsibility — let alone *to form*, or — *«at the End of Days»* — even *create* in autonomous initiative, things or thoughts. — This was a serious obstacle to the evolution towards true perfection of Creation. — The latter will be achieved only when all creatures will have wakened to the One Life — and become Creators for themselves! —

The 13th hymn of repentance of Pistis Sophia expresses these facts as follows:

«Among the Invisible Ones in whose dwelling I was staying, {namely in the Light-Paradise ⊗ of divine *Oneness of All with the One*, as says our text} *I have all by myself committed the transgression, so that Your commandment be fulfilled ... »*[55]

The ‹Fall› of divine Man is generally ascribed to the evolution of an Ego. But this is only semi-correct: Without the existence or conception of an Ego, never could be pronounced the great word: *«I am!»*. — The EGO is as crucial for spiritual evolution as is JUDAS for the Passion of Jesus! Accepting this insight as a truth — and that is hardly avoidable — one promptly will have to face the question: *«What now?!* — Where indeed is the difference? — Why is it that all teachers of Wisdom unanimously name self-abandonment and *«annihilation»* of the Ego the first-and most important precondition for any progress on the *«Path back to The Father»?»*

The word: «*I am who I am*» undeniably presupposes a double individuality: «*I*» – and a reflecting «*Self*». *Self-consciousness* is, therefore, not just acknowledgement of the outer personality – «*I*» – but the discovery of one's *inner Self.* – On the basis of *this* Self will develop comprehension of the significance of this Self within and for the whole Universe, as well as the purpose it is meant to fulfill in it, *self-consciously* and in *self-responsibility*. –

The word: «*I am Who I am!*» is commonly ascribed to biblical JHVH. – The difference between a pure, *originally divine*, but completely unconscious *‹Man in Paradise without an Ego›* — and *New Divine Man* who has *overcome* this Ego through letting go of all passions and desires, is precisely this consciousness: While he or *she* now can say in full self-consciousness: «*I am Who I am – and I know who I am!*», the mass of Humanity keeps erring through the World, uttering the well-known crucial questions: «*Who am I? – Whence might I come? – Whereto am I headig? – What is (if any) the good in all these sufferings?*» –

Who then in full consciousness can say: «*I am who I am*», has indeed become super-human in wisdom and power. – But who can utter this «*I am who I am – and I know who I am*» on the grounds of *perfect Love*, has outdone all earthly dimensions, all Lunic separations, and become a DIVINE SON OF MAN – **IX** – and therefore, like Jesus the Christ, may declare: «I and the FATHER are ONE!»

These comments answer the question, why already the initiation schools of Antiquity – in one way or another – charged their pupils with the task: «*Know Thyne Self!*» – So it is easy to understand why in innumerous fairy-tales the protagonist is confronted with what may be seen as a *mirror image*. – And they all tell the same story: The awakening from a death-like sleep as in *Sleeping Beauty*, or a transformation as in the *Frog-King*; or in *Puss in Boots*; if *one set out to learn to know fear*, to answer *three riddles*, undo some *obstacle* or a curse, or to pass some super-human tests in order to find «*the Golden Feather*» or conquer the (ill or captured) Princess ... – if all such tasks appear in India (*Baghavad Ghita*), in Persia (*1001 Nights*), or in the *folk tales of western Europe*: They all emphasize a process of attaining *self-consciousness* and *self-realization* on the «*path back to the Father*». *Self-consciousness* and Knowledge of the inner Self thus are important intermediate steps on The Path. – But on the other hand, many myths, saga's, fairy-tales and hymns depict the Ego in a most impressively colorful way as the (microcosmic) *Great Adversary* on the Path!

Now, Religions and folk wisdom throughout the World have stamped for the Adversary a most vivid picture of an evil Demon with many names: To the imaginative consciousness of primeval humanity who had not yet acquired today's analytical intellect, such images were very suitable to generate an inner under-standing – a ‹knowledge of the Mind› – and project it into a person's soul. – On the other hand, such horrific images adorned with all attributes of Evil were (and in places still are) apt to streng-then adherence to the dogmata of the Establishment. [56]

Those abhorring mirages of a «Devil» in the shape of an *intri-guing person* were quite useful for a long time, but differ from reality as much as does the old Father-God depicted with a flow-ing silver-beard: If it were true that *«the Devil walketh about as a roaring lion …»* (1 Pet 5:8), even today nobody would be blind enough, nor stupid enough, to throw themselves between his jaws and thus help populate the KINGDOM OF WRATH.

No, reality is much subtler, more artful, more refined: Just as everything throughout the Universe carries in itself its duality of ‹good› and ‹evil› from the first breath of its existence to the last, so every human, throughout all his and her births and deaths, carry their personal Great Adversary *within themselves* … – First Theosophist Valentin Weigel in his *Book about Praying* (authored around 1570) expresses this issue like this:

«That everybody must preserve themselves from the Devil and from the World – this is well known to everybody; – but that one must be on one's guards against oneself more than against the Devil, this is astonishing and hard to believe for the inexperienced. – But god-wise people sense it quite well that Man has no greater fiend than himself; and whoever comes to know himself has to attest alike: Nothing is as difficult as overcoming one-self.» [57]

Meanwhile, every human development in culture, economy, Reli-gion and Science – and therefore also every chance for a secure pilgrimage on *The Path Back* – carries in itself already the germ of abuse, of errors and distractions causing even deeper ignor-ance: The higher a human may climb on the rungs of spiritual evolution, the subtler become invitations and seductions by the Adversary. – The more temptations from the World will diminish, the more subtle will become approaches to the candidate by his or her inner Tempter. Who then loses clear positive orientation, or, – like Orpheus of the myth – «looks back» on his trail, will very easily loose this – or that – or all: *«One cannot at the same time be who one is and who one was! – One cannot have at the same time what one has and what one had!»* – thus teaches the alle-goric *Story of the Soldier* so ingeniously put into music by the Russian composer Igor Stravinsky.

As soon as a human thinks to successfully step out on his path;
– as soon as he or she deem to have left their Ego far behind, having
denied and destroyed it in the most exemplary way, yet another,
sublimely shimmering Ego stands at their side – one much more
difficult to let go of than the gross, uncultivated old one. Whoever
wants to rid themselves of their Ego by an excellent *act of good
will,* will chain themselves up to it as fast as to their own shadow.
Already a slight relent of pressing pains can make people light-
headed, and receptive for forces opposed to Light and Redemption,
issued from their own inner Adversary.

In the *Seventh Hymn of Repentance* of Pistis Sophia, we read
accordingly:

*«When I (Jesus) had brought her (Pistis Sophia) to a somewhat
more open space in Chaos, the creatures of Authades stopped
entirely to harass her, expecting her to be lead out of Chaos completely. But when the creatures of Authades realized that Pistis
Sophia was not [entirely] led out of Chaos [yet], they immediately
turned around in order to assault her again in the most ghastly
way. Therefore she expressed her eighth Hymn of Repentance, because those others didn't stop waylaying her, pressing her to the
extreme ...»*[58]

If the Adversary fails to catch a strong or sublime Ego in his
snares, he may use, as his subtlest means, the forces that charac-
terize his own essence. – His essence however is *negation.* – a
fact shown most typically by the words of *Mephistopheles* in
Gœthe's *Faust,* stating: *«I am the Spirit who always negates!».*

Negation however does not just mean any clear No by an individual; – it already lives in each *doubt,* and even in every intellectually critical *analysis* looking out for contradictions only: As soon
as a clear YES – the undivided, positive orientation – is missing, the
path of negation and error is open. – Thus we easily understand the
significance of the words of the Master: *«Your speech shall be
yes, yes – or no, no – all beyond this is of Evil!».*

But this YES has to come out of the candidate's new will, and not
out of blind *faith,* nor from even blinder *credulity or orthodoxy!*

Doubt and negation never were looked upon as good virtues,
really. It was the ‹privilege› of famous Enlightener *René Descartes*
to define the movement of ‹Enlightenment› with his proud phrase:
*«Dubito, ergo cogito, ergo sum – I doubt, therefore I think, there-
fore I am* (understand: *a human)».* – Is it then not true that precisely this new and so-called scientific state of mind in critical doubt
has cemented for our modern times the discrimination of ‹Good›

and ‹Evil› so severely punished by the God of the Bible? – And is it not precisely critical doubt that has precipitated Humanity still deeper into blind error, pompous arrogance and gloomy forlornness – deeper than ever before?

Modern sciences prove it every day, with one ‹progress› chasing the other, and constant ‹reorientations› driving Humanity further and further away from inner *Truth, Light and Life* of all things! – Such at least is the opinion of such humans as know how doubt activates negative processes, and how much stronger hate, deception and guilt bind individuals together, than does passionate Love.

Therefore the GREAT DISTRACTOR is ‹in an evil position› face to humans who on the basis of a pure heart and with a clear spiritual orientation keep up a strong conviction – named «faith» – rooted in inner and outer perception and experience – GNOSIS: What proves to be good in practical reality will not easily be drowned out. *Lao Dse* in his 54th lesson says it his way:

«A man well instructed will not be misled. – Who hangs on with strength will not be thrown down ... ». [58-A] —

The most successful instrument of the Great Distractor is *perversion.* This must not be understood as a gross inversion of facts, nor as direct lies and fraud. Those indeed are part of his instruments when subtly and artfully they are interwoven and well dissimulated by truths. – No, what is meant here is *perversion* resulting from *perfidious exaggeration,* from *overstated confirmation* of some fact or conviction: Whatever stops flowing, will soon be the victim of Death; – whatever excels too much over the harmony of the Whole, will soon separate from it and fall ... – (see *Appendix 3-C*).

The same is true for the way humans see their own personality: Too much devoutness will turn into pietism; too much conviction will generate intolerance. – Where the YES for one thing becomes all too exclusive, it will tend to become a NO for everything else. That is why intolerance, exclusiveness and perversion are as important instruments in the service of the GREAT DISTRACTOR and of his Kingdom of Wrath, as is any human's misdeed: – From intolerance spring forth persecution and oppression, and thence: violence, blood and tears. As a consequence, fear, terror and hate may arise – the preferred weapons of Darkness. All aggressiveness among humans – observed in an overall view, not just over a few years – serves *no human* but only the Archons of this World and their vassals. And because humans then seek for a possibility to live in relative peace – or because otherwise they would not be let survive at all – the end-result will be compromise, forgetfulness, and finally: complete ignorance regarding original Wisdom, Strength and Beauty.

Subsequent results will then be decrease and even disappearance of true knowledge from collective human consciousness: from the systems of education and of culture as well as from *folk-lore, folk-knowledge,* and *popular beliefs* – and lastly from human blood: Whatever is not sustained regularly, must die! – There is only one single alternative really: YES or NO – thriving or vanishing – Life or Death ...[59]

Lies and perversion, anxiousness, fear and sorrow expand throughout the world as it pleases the Prince of his World – today more so than ever. But nevertheless: the call from the *Kingdom of Light not of this World* penetrates deep into the hearts of Humanity. There it resounds in the tiny indestructible remainder of remembrance of human communion with God: This ‹core consciousness›, this ‹core-vibration› works like a *Consolator* who never will abandon Man – not even in their deepest state of ‹sleeping Death› (see pic. 21 and its legend).

Coming back to the image of the sevenfold fundamental vibration of the Kingdom of Light and its seven sevenfold powers working into this World, one might say also: In every animated creature – from an electron to a Galaxy – there always lives, on and on, a minimal, immortal divine *core-vibration* that must – and will as a consequence of natural laws – react on each irradiation from the divine realms, in a resonance which therefore resembles to some kind of a memory.

Memory, in fact, is nothing else than some resonance of an individual with a thought, a feeling, an emotion from the ‹outside›, somehow corresponding to some element of the ‹inside›. If now this resonance produces a *positive* thought, a *positive* feeling, a *positive* emotion, this will promptly produce the wish to *repeat* the corresponding emotion, feeling or thought, and thus *renew or prolong* said resonance. – In daily life, one speaks of an *urge* to renew sensations of happiness (avoiding sensations of pain) in an attempt to fix the former in a *lasting Present.*

Resonance and longing will then produce the dilemma – and thereby also the task – of *differentiating* what belongs to this earthly, ephemeral World, and what partakes in that other, spiritual and immutable World. In its reaction to the call of said vibrations of the Seven Spirits before God's Throne letting resound its eternal core-vibration, the human microcosmos, from its very first resonance, is confronted with, and depends on, *the decisions* made by the Ego carrying it: At first, this human yet ignores the significance of said call, or where it comes from. But out of his dull, mineral Hyperborean night he or she pass over to Lemurian twilight of a first insight: They somehow experience light and warmth, even while ignoring their cause and essence – as does some snail or worm.

Thus awakens the unseizable *longing for the Light*, and simultaneously also ‹repentance› – this vague pain enhanced by a conscious incapability to adequately answer the call which will be sensed both as an encouragement and an indefinable urge of ‹the heart›. – This so to speak *animal* ache of repentance has nothing in common with any ‹consciousness of guilt› – and even less with any positive spiritual consciousness at all. – But it is, at the same moment, the first positive answer to the eternal call sent out by the divine Solar Æons (see pic. 22).

This first stirring of an answer suffices to spark the fiery process of Redemption, for: Promptly the saps begin to flow from the microcosmic primary soil, or rather from its Prime Foundation – or ‹Non-Foundation› (see p. 41 here-before) – in which the mentioned central atom of the heart is rooting: Up to the newly formed flower-bud the saps ascend. This is, so to speak, the Atlantean phase of half-conscious dreaming. – Will now this microcosm, called to half-consciousness as it is, awaken to real human consciousness? Will the flower-bud also open itself and bloom in full glory? Will the respective human make the positive decision to take up his or her pilgrimage – *under a new will* – setting foot on the Path that leads to LIGHT, TRUTH and LIFE?–

These crucial questions will be discussed in the frame of the next Thesis of the *Aquarius Genesis*. —

11.) «This LONGING produced the REPENTANCE of the lost Paradise. That is the ardent pain consciously felt because of the ignorance relative to the ‹Path of Return›. – REPENTANCE became the turning-point: the point of conversion from the dynamics of Death to the dynamics of Life. – Whoever faithfully follows this dynamic born from INSIGHT, LONGING and FREE WILL, will finally be allowed to return to the Kingdom of PURITY, WISDOM and LOVE, as a child and brother of God – a God himself.»

Thesis 10 spoke of the *flare-up of* REMEMBRANCE – a memory incapable of relating itself to any specific issue in particular; for no real remembrance of the Paradise and its relations to the original divine Kingdom – no clear memory of Harmony, Oneness and Love – had been spared from oblivion. This precisely is the essence of Darkness, Ignorance and Death, contrary to Light, Wisdom and Life. — Only a primitive ‹seed› of remembrance – said divine *core-vibration* as a resonance to the seven fundamental vibrations issuing from the original divine Kingdom – was left. But due to resonance of this nuclear memory sparked by the vibrations reaching the human heart from the innermost heart of the divine realms – through *macrocosmic* △, then transferred by the *cosmic* Eye of the Sun (☉ or ♃) – and together with the solar force of the *intercosmic* CHRISTOS ✕ – arose this vague but growingly clear *longing* – this wish to vibrate in harmony with the original divine ‹standing waves› again.

That the world of illusions and painful experience cannot be the true aim of Creation, and therefore can be no true reality – this feeling is clearly etched into every human's heart. In Truth it may be said: In every cell of every creature – animated or not – slumbers a memory of the original divine Love-Vibration – as if in the belly of a musical instrument some tone had fallen asleep, ready to tune in again with the old Harmony, at the first original «sound of the Trumpet».

Indeed: the Lord of this World and his vassals do whatever they can in order to keep Humanity separated from the Light, and bind them forever to the *wheel of unintelligent experiences* – this wheel onto which everyone is chained every day anew, as a consequence of our appurtenance to the Kingdom of Wrath: *«Faster and thicker the thorny sprouts clung and clustered around the walls and pinnacles of the enchanted castle»*, as says the tale of *Sleeping Beauty*. – Nevertheless, the mentioned grain of remembrance of the original vibrations survives amidst the wildly spreading thorns, albeit *«deeply asleep»*. –

The *spindle* however remained on the floor ... !

This is what the *Aquarius Genesis* means by said *immersion into Sleeping Death* of profoundest ignorance. – But once – or even repeatedly – the flow of Love from the World of divine Paradise is perceived by the human heart, and sensed as light and warmth: The seed of remembrance is revived; – the tightly closed flower bud awakes, yet its petals are completely curled inwards so that the Light can hardly penetrate. The sepals expand into free space; – the subtle vessels of the petals start to swell; – an indefinable urging pressure penetrates the whole bud, and slowly it begins to open without even knowing it. – If now the blossom thus awakened from its deathly sleep swells up in search of space for *the blossom's crown,* then the irradiated WORD – the divine call from Eternity – resounds in the soul as an aching pain; and the whole personality resents kind of a shock: the impulse to open; the pain of still not being able to do so – *this* is the REPENTANCE of the wakening human!

Now there are two possibilities to react on said longing and repentance (see Dao-De-Ging, loc. cit. N° 41):
One is: to turn around, *towards the light* that emits these vibrations like a call. This *conversion* may express itself as a wish – and occasionally even as real greed – to unite with the origin – the source of said burning fire. – But soon the Candidate thus flamed by divine vibrations will become aware of how far his actual state of being is from the spheres whence those calling waves are reaching him. He becomes aware of his incapability to *understand* what he only vaguely *perceives:* – to walk towards the source of which he or she have an unclear idea only – and on a trail that *yet they ignore.* So the alternative is to droop in a complex of unworthiness, and turn away ...
Thus is the complex dilemma resented by new Candidates – in their soul, in their mind, and even in their physical body:
They have been flamed – now they are burning in their new desire. – But how to transform this desire into positive action? Through said *«short or even longer flare-up of the memory from the original Kingdom of Light»,* as says the text, they feel a burning pain: a pain consisting in the resentment of complete disharmony between pure divine irradiation and the poor resonance of the microcosmos trapped in its usual vibrational pattern.

The question is now: Will they react as an ABEL, fleeing from pain in order to turn towards the next ‹zone of comfort›? – Or will they become active, accepting pain, and courageously setting foot on the path their heart indicates to them – and follow their longing desire to approach the Light?

This conflict does not only exist on a goodly humanistic level, but also on the level of the universal Law of Cause and Effects: Of course, no sane human being would ever intentionally harm or cause pain to any other being; and this has – especially in the Orient – led to some most extreme behaviours. Truly: Who could dare to conclusively define the limit between what is tolerable and what is irresponsible?

In the meantime it seems necessary however that a human positively oriented towards the supreme aim of the ‹Path of spiritual Evolution› – i.e. Gnostic Transfiguration – will not only be challenged to make some sacrifices, but in certain circumstances also cannot avoid to cause sacrifices and pain to other beings, in order to be able to continue his own path – the path of consciousness in the Universe. – And it is quite obvious that this human also takes the responsibility for causing pain that way. –

This is what shows the biblical myth of CAIN, the *Son of Fire* – or *Son of the Sun* who on his cosmic path *«is obliged to slay»* his brother: ABEL – the *watery Son of the Moon* (see *Appendix 3-B*). The sacrifice of CAIN lays precisely in that he accepts to become guilty in order to foster realization of the supreme aim of the entire Universe: The warrior-like, revolutionary aspect in MAN – in order to definitely progress – is bound to *«slaying»* the sluggish, conservative aspect in himself, which, undeniably, lives from the ‹blood› of others as does ABEL. – On one side then, the blood sacrifice of ABEL is «accepted» by his God – the God of the Quaternary – but he gets nothing in return. CAIN instead – in return of his sacrifice causing guilt and responsibility – receives on his forehead the seal of the Son of God ($\otimes$; see pic.18-A to C and comments). This is the glyph of the Christ-Force *in the Universe* – and the sign for its *«incarnation»* in a human microcosmos.

It is not just by some whim that the *Order of the Knight Templars* chose this sign $\oplus$ as their seal: that is sanctification of earthly existence of the Four Elements by the Spirit descending and enveloping them. – *«Et VERBUM CARO factum est!»* – the WORD illuminates the material personality (French: CARREAU = □). –

The solution to aforementioned dilemma with regard to guilt may seem hard to understand to cultivated, goodly humans who live following the norms and criteria of the *Ancient Testament*. But the solution comes from the *New Testament* – and it says: *«Love your enemies! – Love those who hate you! – Love yourself!»*

Hate is a category from the World of Wrath and Darkness. ‹Fiends›, then, are but obstacles on the Path – expressions of the *Great Adversary* who wishes to detract humans from the Path.

Those humans instead who really follow the trail of growth of the soul, growing in knowledge and in their capacity to love, see their fiends as their brethren as much as those who (through too goodly a human intention) try so terribly hard to further them according to their own criteria: In supra-personal compassion born of his *new nature* the Candidate feels solidary to all these— even when in an allegorical sense he *«has to slay them»*.

For: the Candidate has no right to let himself be damaged either, lest he should inevitably be charged also with the guilt of those who hamper him. This then is the last consequence of the words by Jesus: *«Be clever as the snakes, and soft as the doves!»*. The Greek expression ακεραιοι – *akéraioi* in Mt.10:16 is often misunderstood as meaning *simple*. – A meaning closer to the original root of the word would be: *without horns*, i.e. *unaggressive*!

This *«cleverness of the snakes»* has nothing in common with proverbial *«Atlantean slyness»*, but means: *«intelligent awareness in Love»*. One should remember also that – following Gnostic Tradition of *Ophites*, (or *Naasseans*) to whose cult Jesus was initiated, too – the SNAKE is a symbol of wisdom closely linked to VENUS. *Jesus himself,* faithful to esoteric Symbolism, linked himself to both the SNAKE and to VENUS (the *Morning-star*), as we may read in the New Testament, and also in the *Apocalypse of John* (see note 19).

Mt.10:16 therefore sees no *inner contradiction* between SNAKE and DOVE – although ordinarily interpreted that way: The two are each other's *complement* rather, as are ‹Yin› and ‹Yang›!

The narrowness of The Path thus becomes quite obvious: While the Candidate on his quest tries to avoid whatever might trigger him into causing pain and therefore guilt, he is not allowed to let himself be abused on the grounds of his kindness, humility and indulgence, nor may he deviate from his trail: In the first instance he would render himself as guilty as those who impair him; in the second instance he would become a traitor, clasped in the claws of the Great Adversary!

Meanwhile – thank God – decisions don't always have to be taken by the Pilgrim himself: When the right moment arrives – when qualifications meet requirements – there often arise situations that let occur the necessary steps spontaneously – out of natural dynamic. If nothing of this happens, but the Candidate still refuses to err from the One Path, he will – as typical esoteric teachings of primitive societies like to say – become a ‹warrior›. – This is a CAIN'S SON who *in Love without fear, and in full self-consciousness and awareness of others,* pursues the One Path without a compromise – because *by his new Nature he cannot be, nor do, otherwise!*

So this is one possibility to face said sensations of *longing and repentance*: Courageously orientated towards the Light, *accepting in free will* the inevitable pain as a consequence to this conversion: «*I have not come to bring peace but the sword!*», said the Master. – This is the «*path towards crucifixion*» as depicted by the Gospels on account of the *Passion of Jesus the Christ*. A path not meant to be reserved to a single Jesus, but to become a reality *for all humans*: «*To whoever will receive Him ...*», namely «*all humans of good will ...*» – thus promises the Gospel – redemption will assuredly be granted (see pic. 24 and its comment).

The other possible reaction is *to decline pain*. This is the way of ordinary human life, where impulses and influences are *shunned and evinced* because they signify that the usual zones of comfort have to be relinquished, new experiences and mistakes to be made, and a new equilibrium to be acquired – thus inevitably causing toil and fights – and occasionally also pain. And there is no big difference if this pain is lived by the respective human himself in the way of changes – or if, by the inner development of the same human, pain is caused to another creature – plant, beast or man – thus also accepting guilt – for:

Changes are often linked to pain, but pain *always* causes progress on the Path – even if both change and pain at first sight look like a detour. – True: At first, Neophytes lack discernment to make the good choice. Even the most enthusiastic beginner will often be driven by ‹ordinary human› animal consciousness – and therefore will experience illusion, delusion, and pain linked to them, like before. The *proven Candidate, however, will always continue his strife* – imperturbably!

Who instead choses to shun the pains of *the Path to the Cross* by simply avoiding them, will *fall behind*. – However: every creature in the Universe is lastly destined «*to return to the house of the Father and sit at His right hand*» – some ‹day›, even if this takes an inconceivably long ‹time›. This ‹day› will be the end of the *Path to the Cross of the whole Universe*, and it is basically the same for all creatures. Therefore, as a ‹day of manifestation of Brahma› progresses, the universal call of divine Love-vibrations becomes more and more intense. Delusions and pains of those who stay behind will become nastier, and surrounding conditions more hostile, too. As a last way out of the agony, before complete annihilation of the individual, he or she might finally – out of sheer pain – chose the described path of self-redemption: as the minor pain of the two: «*Don't postpone it from one day to the next, nor from one circuit {i.e. incarnation} to the next!*», said Jesus.

PAIN is known to be a particularly typical expression of all forms of LIFE in this World. If only an EGO is capable of suffering pain and fear *consciously*, it is always pain and fear that set an Ego in motion: What the call of Love radiations – this divine Light Power that is entirely Love – was unable to trigger through the pain of *humble longing*, will finally be achieved through the pain of *the Ego being crushed* – Thus, illusion and delusion will finally be dissolved. Where insight and repentance were insufficient, the assail of a great pain, or an existential crisis with no issue, might do the job: When a hesitating person is so fed-up with delusion and pain that they will accept any way out available, they will finally prove ‹ripe› to follow the beacon of Light shining through the Narrow Door; – this ‹eye of a needle› the over-busy, over-individualized ‹man of the world› on his «Broad Way» had shunned for so long.

This forced turn of course is not quite equal to positive orientation towards the Light; – but doubts *about,* and aversion *from* the Light may at once turn into doubts and aversion *about* and *from the World.* And so a *suffering* human turns to become a *seeker.* – And to every seeker who really opens himself to the universal CHRISTOS and to His cosmic Light of Redemption, salvation is firmly granted – as promised by *Aquarius Genesis* and the *Gospels* alike:

«*Whoever faithfully follows this dynamic born from INSIGHT, LONGING and FREE WILL, will finally be allowed to return to the Kingdom of PURITY, WISDOM and LOVE, as a child and brother of God – a God himself.*»

What in this situation positively *needs to* happen – and therefore finally *will* happen, too – is quite obvious: Every evolution or change in this world – from the beginning of time until the «*End of all days*» when the illusion named «*Time*» will be completely extinct – happens to no other purpose than that those humans who in their soul experience the described development, should undergo the mentioned *awakening shock,* and the pains of *longing* and *ruefulness* it entails, then take *the one decision* and thus find their individual w*ay back home.*

On the other hand, it is the character and real essence of the Great Adversary to call in question again and again exactly this decision, wishing to jeopardize the path of the Candidate in such a way that the latter should – if possible – abandon it. For: every entity finding reunion with the Light is lost to the kingdom of Darkness – *His kingdom*! Therefore, the ADVERSARY, the GREAT DISTRACTOR will quite naturally do whatever he can in order to prevent such losses: Whenever a microcosmos keeps trying to achieve resonance with the divine vibrations of the Seven Spirits before the Throne of God, the ADVERSARY, or GREAT DISTRACTOR attempts again and again to drown out this resonance by his own fields of vibration and – if possible – to paralyze them, and be it only in the absolutely last moment of evolution of the highly initiated Adept! This is typically illustrated, again and again, in the already quoted *Mysteries of Pistis Sophia* – including the last chapters of that text; – and it can readily be observed in our physical reality!

It is the situation addressed by the *Aquarius Genesis* stating: «*Whoever faithfully follows this dynamic born from INSIGHT, LONGING and FREE WILL, will finally be allowed to return to the Kingdom of PURITY, WISDOM and LOVE ... »* –

And this is precisely the meaning of said return to original divine Harmony: the return to the full harmonious chord of the *Flaming Triangle* – *Trigonum Igneum* – of *Freedom, Brotherhood and Love.* – Therefore, the text of the Aquarius Genesis addresses here the *faithfulness* of the Candidate on the Path – i.e. his *imperturbable steadfastness.*

This *steadfastness* that the Great Adversary tries to jeopardize again and again is achieved by each Candidate holding fast to his *unshakable faith.* This is the first grace received, and the first acquired «virtue» he absolutely needs to hold on to – in the beginning, in the middle and at the end: It is the first fire that he must *lighten* and always carefully *keep burning* on his altar – as was the symbolic usage of the Antique Zoroastrians: Without faith, *nothing* is possible – *thanks to* faith, *everything* can happen!

«*As much faith as a mustard seed ...»* – Here the Master not only indicates a minimal requirement, but also the *fiery character* of faith: Whenever and wherever the Candidate on his pilgrimage might stumble, or fear to have gone astray: As soon as he goes back to the *Corner Stone* of his *first faith, Jesus The Christ,* he will fall in step again and, remembering anew where he stands, can courageously stride forward again. Thus, the Pilgrim progresses on his path, undisturbed – «*from power to power ... ».*

In exactly these words Sacred Language (2 Petr.1:5-8) gives its clear indications for this luminous trail:

« ... *Giving all diligence, add to your faith virtue; and to virtue knowledge* (literally: *Gnosis*), *and to knowledge steadfastness; and to steadfastness patience; and to patience godliness; and to godliness brotherly love; and to brotherly love,* {finally!} *Love. For if these [latter two] things are in you in abundance, they effect [that you shall] neither [be] lazy nor barren in the imitation of our Lord Jesus Christ!»* –

In other words: Who ever on the basis of strong faith and inner knowledge (Gnosis) follows the Path, will be given the *outer strength* (i.e. «virtue» and capacity) and the *inner, divine plenitude* to continue this quest until reaching harmony and oneness with God who is LOVE. – Then the Pilgrim – the Pilgrimess – will be home again, sitting «TODAY» as a son (or sun) of God at the right of the Father again (Lk 23:43) – *as it was in the Beginning»*!

Again then, *«I, Angra Mainyu»* – the Ego that *«is all Death»*, will himself have induced the End of what he so eagerly strived to perpetuate: The doubts he sowed will finally turn against himself. – When we say *«his eager strife»*, then this is valid only for his – the Adversary's – first consciousness. His *overall usefulness* within the perfect plan of the ‹Good God› however becomes evident from the final deployment of Light in the Universe – at the *phase-out* of the «fight between Light and Darkness»:

The Hyperborean *Double-helix* ⑨ in which *transmutation and evolution* had shrunk into the center of the Spire of *involution*, opens up to form the Lemurian *solar-S*: – Now the crucial *turning-point* lies open – and doubtful considerations find their ways! – Then begins the *burgeoning* of triple discrimination as shown by the Celtic Triskell ♌. – At the beginning of the Arian epoch of consciousness of the Candidate, the four branches of the Swastika ⊕ unfold until reaching the fully deployed Cross of the CHRISTOS. – Now opens the starry flower of the *Pentagram* ✬ – signaling transition from passive resonance of the newly born soul to active eradiation of the message of Light and Love *as a Grail.* – And already there shine up the first signs of the star of Salomon ✡ – of the seal of Spirit, reached during the Arian Period by a few pioneers only: This will turn into the sign or symbol of the Alchemists' Adepate of the physical Philosopher's Stone ✡ in its hidden *Heptavalence.* – And evenly shines up on the mystical gnostic path, the signal that only some very rare Elect attained during life-time – the seal of *absolute reunion* with God: ⊚ – i.e. the seal of achieved *Transfiguration,* and *union with the One!*

The ✡ is the state of consciousness donated to the «Columns in the Temple» of the coming: the ‹Neo-Celtic› race – the *Neo-Galatians.* Here all contraries are dissolved – collapsed into the One that is all Light, Harmony and Love. To this corresponds the Number Six – 6 standing for elevated *Venus-consciousness* – ♀ or ⚲. From here can be made the decisive last step of «Apotheosis» –

ascent into the macrocosmic *Fiery Triangle* △, where dwells the ‹Universal Brotherhood› of the Redeemed[60]: – This then is the famed re-union with the oneness of the ‹Seven Spirits … ›, at Whitsuntide – *pentèkostós, πεντηκοστός* – and with the Throne of God itself. – Who thus has come back home can by right be named «*Son and Brother of God – and a god himself*!

– Why «*a god himself*»? –
This will be explained by the commentary to the last, the *twelfth Thesis* of the *Aquarius Genesis*.

The *twelfth Thesis* stands, on one hand, for *our* world on *our* cosmic plane; but for *other* worlds on *their* cosmic plane – and therefore *for all worlds together* on the *macrocosmic plane*. – But fundamentally it is directed towards the *supra-cosmic plane* and the *Prime Source* ● (the absolute zero-point of energy), from which «*in the Beginning*» All comes forth, and into which «*at the End of days*» All will return

This Prime Source or *Arch-Cause* is the *Prime Foundation*, or, as Jacob Bœhme put it, the *Non-Foundation* which cannot be expressed by any symbol, really. – Thus the *Aquarius Genesis* in its *twelfth Thesis* returns – or curbs itself back cyclically – to its *first one*: When *All in All* – passing from 1– 2 – 3 … over the *Ennead* to the *Decade* – has returned to original *Oneness* (10 = 1), then, and at the same moment, is reached the starting point for a new ‹Day of Brahma› (i.e. another ‹Manvantara›, each of those equaling ca. 300 million years). —

Thus the end of one cycle marks also the beginning of a new one … – until reaching a last … ? … ? … ?

12) «Thus on one hand became true the curse uttered by JHVH in Paradise: «Whoever will eat from this tree will die by Death!» – But on the other hand, the promise by the SNAKE: «You shall be like the gods!» has – through the grace of the FATHER himself – become a reality: While the entire Creation fell into Death, the GREAT DISTRACTOR was lashed in his own nooses. For, the Light came down ... until reaching the deepest Darkness. And thanks to POWER, WISDOM and LOVE from above – and through pain, longing and repentance from below – the Path was laid free, and the doors opened for elevation into the Light, so that all humans might regain the pure, entirely spiritual Kingdom of Love: ⊗ – in oneness with the FATHER: Through GRACE – but BY INDIVIDUAL EFFORT – and into greater power and splendor than ever before!»

Said «curse» is actually a ‹Geis› in true Celtic tradition[61]: When the ‹Lord of Darkness› made himself the ruler of this World, sowing the seeds of the great Illusion of Separation, negation and perversion as well as regarding the antagonism of ‹Good› and ‹Evil›, he at the same time made himself the cause of his own perdition. For, if the entire Creation dominated by him had to experience the spire of involution, crystallization, doubts and Death, there nevertheless remained in every creature said immortal seed of remembrance: As long as this seed remained sealed down in ‹Sleeping Death›, the respective creature remained chained to the reign dominated by the GREAT DISTRACTOR «who is all Death». – But as soon as this kernel of remembrance awakened, doubt and negation of earthly humans affected the Kingdom of Wrath the same way they before had affected the reign of Light: And this triggered as a first dilemma the human urge for *differentiation* – but now not just in the infernally degenerated world of dichotomy Y anymore, but regarding perfectly divine Nature as well – and then a second dilemma: the increasingly pressing choice between Light and Darkness. That is how humans became seekers of Truth.

What an unconceivable wonder is it indeed that even the slightest resonance of the vibrations issuing from the divine Kingdom within the innermost core of a microcosmos can activate the *turning-point* – the source for evolution, for *«Rebirth from Water and Spirit»*! – Thanks to *doubt and negation along with awakening insight* into true spiritual interactions, the immortal nuclear vibration in the heart was reactivated, and thus the twin illusion of Separation and Death overcome. –

This happened thanks to the gift of discernment acquired by *«eating from the Tree of Knowledge»* – and notwithstanding the dazzling tricks of the Great Adversary. True insight into the essence of *illusion and self-delusion,* and a new understanding of the ever inseparable communion of all creatures with the FATHER, made the *Path of Return* an accessible reality!

True: The Great Adversary absolutely controls all dwellers in the Kingdom of Wrath; but he will rule only until these – enflamed by the flare of longing and repentance – decide to follow the Path back to the original Kingdom of Light, and also *follow it in deed*: – This is the «*factual proof*» by Man as the highest evolved animated being on Earth – the proof he *must furnish* in order to rise from slavery in the Kingdom of Death, ignorance and Darkness. *Through Grace*, every human receives «the call»: The penetrating vibration coming from the Seven Spirits before Gods Throne and its flow of Love inspire the *heart of the Macrocosmos*. From there its rays penetrate the *heart of the cosmos* with its cosmic Central Sun, and through it attain the center of the *heart of every microcosmos*:

Thus *through Grace* receptive humans are «enflamed». – Through individual determination – i.e. *discernment and faith* – they put their foot onto the Path. – Through individual effort, they acquire knowledge, and through steadfastness in their *hope* they remain faithful to the Path. – And thanks to the Love of the CHRISTOS within them – i.e. through growth in growing *love capacity* – they are ‹redeemed› and ‹exempted› *by themselves*!

This may be expressed in another way, still: When an enflamed human ☿ moaning in the world of matter ☿ wants to «*effect his redemption in fear and trembling*», as says Sacred Language (Phil.2:12), he begins the so-called *Imitation of Christ*. This is the path of *self-sacrifice*. – If a human bound in the *dichotomy* of this world of separation, pain and opposed Duals – **Y** – *really wants* to follow the path back to the Father, the Light of the CHRISTOS will come to meet him on the way. Traversing *the world of matter* in deep and serene humility without reserve, he will be given to unite himself with Him: This is the path of Alchemists through their *crucible* – earthen-vessel and *little cross* in one).

«*Without stinking black earth, no fragrant blossom can reveal itself*», said Jacob Bœhme along with all Alchemists.[62] By accepting the *Cross of Matter* + Man becomes a representative of Creation divided by the ‹Fall›, **Y**. By doing so in free will and full devotion, and in growing consciousness, he also fixes himself to the cross of the CHRIST: This produces the seal of VENUS-COLUMBA, ☩, and that is what the Cathars named their *Endurá*. – The symbol + now stands for both the *Four Elements* and *earthly Fire of the* CHRISTOS – and also for the *path through Matter*.

As soon as the Candidate is conscious of these facts, and if he fully yields to the Fire of the CHRISTOS, he will be completely consumed by the latter, until *merging with it*. – This *elevation* is symbolized by the Rune *Ýlhaz* –ᛘ, signifying *elevation* and *Transfiguration.* – *Ýlhaz* thus quite appropriately corresponds to the sign of the split world **Y** into which the *Fifth Ether* – ⚴ – has entered as the *power of elevation*: **ˈ**. –The ‹bipartite human› **Y** who thus *receives* the Fiery Ether and remains united with it, incorporates the Rune *Ýlhaz* ᛘ that now moreover says: *«Through Grace, Man is elevated beyond matter – and now in turn emanates* ⚴*, too!»*

A human thus standing in the *Christ Fire* and consciously clinging to the Cross **+**, hence forms the magic symbol of VENUS: ♀ and Her magic seal ⚹ analogous to the *Eagles or Sublimations* of Alchemists: In the sign of the Cross so-called Spirit-Soul Man will overcome Matter! – This Symbolism also implies: As in himself Spirit – O – dominates the material world of the Four Elements +, the Candidate ♀ makes *«of Two* **(Y)** *Three* (ᛘ)*», but of Three* (△) *and Four* (□) Seven ⌂ – and thence again ONE: ⊛.[62-A]

Oneness of the *Seven Spirits before the Throne of God*; – i.e. *macrocosmic* harmony of the *seven macrocosmic Elohim* ⊛ – is now re-established *microcosmically* in Man himself: Now the Candidate is an «Elect» – a Perfect One – sanctified and freed; and Transfiguration by himself, in himself, and for his World, has become a shining reality!

There is no contradiction in this if one understands the *joyful tidings* – *euangelion* – saying that since the first appearance of the CHRISTOS in this World – hence already *«in the Beginning»*! – The Christ Fire indeed dwells in the innermost core or focal center *of every creature*, just as says the *Gospel of Thomas*:

«I am the All. The All came forth from me; and the All entered into me. Go and split a piece of wood, and there I am; – lift a stone, and you will find me there ... ».
– Hence also in every human!

So, thanks to FIERY ETHER, and thanks to the descent of SPIRIT into the world of earthly scission **Y**, *«a new scion»* (Jes.53:2) shoots out of the latter. – **Y** thus again becomes ᛘ, then ⚹ – the *Venus Seal* – the sign of the *Morning Star* (2.Pet. 1:19; Apoc.22:16) – and of the NINE. – At last the new-born divine Son of Man **(IX)** rises from his grave in matter – joyfully: a young god!

The *Fraternitas RC* affirms that in the labOratory of the ancient Alchemists the Philosophers Stone obtained by Grace is *«the most noble and highest thing – a very high tincture, able to tinge the whole World and to transmute it into the purest gold (if this was possible, and agreeable to God – and if it {the World} be worthy of it)».*[63] – Evenly, *one sole human* transfigured while living in this world, would have the ‹potency› to transfer his proper Christ

Impulse onto a great number of other humans and make it effective for the whole world. – *This* is the concrete reality of the Mystery of Golgotha. – *This* is the shining and at the same time deeply moving ideal that needs to be grasped and held fast by every ‹pilgrim›, every Disciple, every Initiate on the transfiguristic Path. – *This ideal they should follow with all their heart, with all their soul, and with all their energy.* – «Should», so we say, for: this needs super-human devotion, super-human effort, and, from the first step to the final ‹Good End›, the inconceivable Grace of God – « ... *if (the Candidate) be worthy of it* ... »

So, on one hand «*has been realized the curse* {in fact: the ‹Geis›} *uttered by* YALDABAOTH *in Paradise:* « ... *you shall die by Death*»*!* – But on the other hand, when became a reality the threat: «... *you shall die!*», there were already set in motion the rescuing inverse dynamics to turn involution into evolution, and to bring about re-union with the One! – ‹Fallen› Man had to experience, and learn to overcome, illusion, delusion, illness and Death: This is the price to be paid for discrimination between ‹Good› and ‹Evil›. – It is also the price for said consciousness of the «*I am who I am*».

And it is what Man has to understand as his role and responsibility within the Universe of Creation: Learn to choose in free will the PATH that leads him to GOD, and to follow it *faithfully,* day by day, as a clear example to others: this path that eventually will turn him into a god – and the Universe into a new Paradise!

This precisely is another aspect of the *Double-helix* ⑨: The law of cause and effects leads from Separation to the Fall, from the Fall to the experience of Darkness, sufferings and Death – but then also brings about the opportunity for every human to attain to immortality – if on the grounds of experience, insight and conversion he will chose in devotion and free will the path of return to the ‹First Paradise›, and follow it, imperturbably, *faithfully and in Love!*

Indeed: Fall, perdition and Death were unavoidably contained already in the *First and Second Separations* (separation of the Four Elements in ‹CHAOS› ⊕, schism of the Elohim, and split-up of genders). It therefore is incorrect to impute the first cause of the ‹Fall› of Creation to the human ego-will that at that point was yet inexistent: Without an Ego, no ego-will can be. *Today's humans instead* – hardly in possession of a first ego-consciousness as they are – really serve the Great Adversary and a progressive ‹Fall› if they don't limit their ego-will to the minimum required for a normal existence in modern society (pic. 25). – The ‹curse› or ‹Geis› of ego-will, was indeed thrust upon ADAM in the form of an *unconscious ego* he yet *needed to develop* — and that was, and is, *indispensable* in order to recognize, choose and achieve the pilgrimage through Matter. Said *Geis* therefore is to be understood in a wider and more constructive way than is the custom in the judeo-christiano-muslimic interpretation of the *Ancient Law*[64]: – It is valid only «*... until you [knowingly and willingly] – will return to the humus whence you were taken*» *(Gen. 3:19)*. Here we need to remember linguistics: *humus is earth*; *humanus* is *the earthling* – that is: *Man of Earth.*

All this leaves out questions regarding (partially redundant) significations in dignity and power of ‹Ahura's›, Elohim, JHVH, ‹Anunnaki› or ‹Nephilim›, and whatever may be their names – and therefore also the myth stating that the gods created Man as *servants for themselves* – as hold Babylonian mythology, the *Popol Vuh* and other traditions in East and West, including the myth about the *Golem*. – Our present time demands to look forward: This is the Uranus Period of the Era of Aquarius; and it requires that *insight, longing* and *renewal* should hallmark the Universe. Today's call is: «NOW IS THE TIME! – HORA EST!»

May whoever can understand this call, understand it well! – The sacrifice of the few who undertake to follow THE PATH in order to open it also for many others, shall and will – notwithstanding so many (in)human efforts to the contrary in the world – *animate All anew*, in the light of the daily witnessed CHRIST-IMPULSE!

Light, Truth and Life are the flags to be followed now: *This future* we need to look forward to! – *This* ‹New World Order› must be realized! – *This* is what true humans got to witness actively – NOW!

‹Then› ... – in a very far ‹future›; – ‹then›, after times and times of cosmic, macrocosmic and supra-cosmic dimensions «*no human eye can see, and no human heart can grasp*»; – ‹then›, thus, we «*shall be with Him in Paradise*»? – No: TODAY! – For: ‹then› there will be no more Time; – ‹there›, there will be no more space; – ‹so›, there will be no more qualities, because again All will be in All. – Then, viewer, view and viewed object shall be all one again «*as it was in the Beginning*» – and as for timeless consciousness it really already is: NOW (Lk 23:43)! – *This* is what Jesus on his cross promised to the ‹malefactor› who – behold this proof of firm faith! – beseeched Him for His gracious remembrance in «His Kingdom» that He had announced!

This being so; – this eternally inseparable universal union existing NOW AND IN ALL FUTURES TO COME – TODAY! –, every human can already «*be in Paradise*» – NOW – for, even on the sole grounds of this deeply knowing faith «*every human of good will*» is elevated to this sublime bliss, NOW! – The famous *Path back* therefore is no sweet dream of some Future, but plain Presence. – It neither is a terribly far voyage, for: «the Kingdom of God is within ourselves – nearer than hands and feet»! –

The *Path back* is the fruit neither of efforts of a forced personal will, nor of a long pilgrimage on sore feet along wearing trails, over mountains and through cleft valleys; – nor either in bloody sacrifices full of pain and renouncement: The *Path back* consists uniquely in that Man wake up from his ‹Sleeping Death› of unconsciousness, that he stand up – and that, «undoing one veil after the other» he step forward, imperturbably, to meet descending divine Spirit – *the Rising Sun – «with an open heart and bareheaded, barefoot and rejoicing»*! [64-A] – This really means to encounter oneself as a god, *thanks to daily personal efforts* – and *thanks to divine Grace*!

Not the Ego as such is ‹bad›, but just its unchecked impulses. And it is not the human Ego who has to follow this long trail and to undertake all efforts to overcome towering inner obstacles: That would be quite impossible! – Highest *Grace* does all this for those who in *humble devotion and self-forgetfulness* open themselves to the inner process, sincerely repeating the well-known sentence of Mary (i.e. the new-born soul): *«That it be done unto me according to your* WORD!*»* (Lk.1:38).

Raised out of separation and pain, the Great Distractor, ‹Yaldabaoth, Master-Builder and Prince of Darkness›, once created a Kingdom wherein he sought to become as potent as the ONE FATHER. [65] But this was, from the beginning, a fake kingdom erected on the sands of double illusion; and it will have to wane into nothingness and disappear under the *waves* of the Stream of Living Water. –‹Lucifer› himself with his authorization to use all possible means at his disposal in order to seduce humanity as best he can – *«during seven days»* – will after all, at the end of those ‹seven days›, join the Light. *Out of free will*, he too, will merge with the one eternal stream of Living Water: This stream is nourished from the clear, sober acknowledgement of unhampered Love of All for each other, and for their FATHER-MOTHER – and through the positive realization of uninterrupted communion with the Spirit, as well as in the Love of Him and for Him who eternally IS LOVE.

Whoever understands well all these facts will clearly recognize the significance and the situation of ‹EVIL› – under whatever name it may appear: *«He who is all Death»* – the GREAT DISTRACTOR, the ADVERSARY of the Kingdom of Light, the PRINCE OF THIS WORLD of Ignorance and Darkness; – he who in full accordance with his dazzling mystifications and perversions is named «*Lucifer*»; – he is chained to the kingdom he himself built, fastened and nurtured with all the perfidies available to him: In fact, His game is *lost since the Beginning*!

For: the prison where he held all creatures, with the intention to attain control over the whole Creation and even over the One God, has become his own jail: Evenly as every creator remains bonded to his creation, and as every adversary is chained to his antagonist, the Great Distractor remains tied to his Kingdom of Darkness: As long as his reign remains intact; as long as the creatures erring around in it cannot find – *and consciously choose!* – their way out of Darkness and into the Light, the Prince of this world will have to stay in it himself – ‹separated› from the ONE – and impotent despite all his potency!

This is the tragic nature of the Great Adversary: Never can ‹Evil› become perfect as such: The Kingdom of Shadows is part of this twin Creation **Y** ‹outside› of the Kingdom of Light ⊗ – albeit (even this, against all odds!) being held in the loving ‹hand› of the FATHER. Thus, the cosmic law is valid even for Evil: Always it must bear in itself the seeds for the Good – same as whatever is ‹good› bears in itself the seeds for ‹Evil›. And like whatever is alienated from the Kingdom of Love «stands outside of it», even the Great Distractor must, and will ‹someday›, reunite with IT. –

And so the whole play of the Adversary – in spite of all his subtleties, and for all the time he may resist – will finally also curb itself back to its own source: BACK INTO THE LIGHT!

Every separation and every pain will then be neutralized; – all creatures, all beings, will then be reunited in the One Light – or completely ‹dissolved›. And so the jailer will be his own last captive, left at the mercy of his prisoners who finally, by way of their own salvation, *will free him, too*! – (see note 66).

And behold and understand! *Only humans* – only conscious physical humans entirely oriented towards the Kingdom of Light and Love can work the final redemption and liberation of the Universe. The *«End of all Days»* can appear only when all creatures – one way or the other – have returned to their origin, and when, therefore, even Lucifer has regained ‹his crown›, and has come to repose *in Oneness with God.*

That is exactly why the Adversary has ‹permission› – and even the *mission, «for seven days»* – to seduce humans, to probe them and test them: Because only such humans can reach the sublime Good End, as will – in unshakable Faith, in serene Hope, and growing in growing Love capacity – bravely and loyally keep their orientation towards the one Light, the one Path, the one Truth, and the one LIFE: *Elevated through the Grace of the Eternal One, but thanks to daily personal endeavour.* – Or, expressed more in the language of the *Aquarius Genesis*:

If the «crown on the head of God» is to re-acquire its crown jewel, fallen Man has to become conscious of God, of the World, and of his Self. Awakened by the fire of remembrance he got to learn and feel, i.e. to recognize and understand, his separation, his repentance and longing for Oneness, and at the same time his inseparable union with God. In faith and hope he then can make a firm decision to remain faithful to *The Path*. – Following this scheme, he also will learn to leave behind whatever could impede him on the way, and to hold fast whatever could be helpful or even necessary to attain his goal.

So ignorance turned into knowledge, separation into oneness, pain into salvation, and sadness and sorrow turned into joy. The dissonant jumble of a thousand vibrations of earthly personalities and æons – this is: the *«ten-thousand things»* of Daoism – flowed back into the harmony of the Seven pure Sounds (or vowels) – the Seven Spirits before the Throne of God – *«as it was in the Beginning»*.

Now the text of *Aquarius Genesis* moreover says that whoever will thus have succeeded can be named a child and brother of God, and even *«a god himself»*. – For this is what makes the difference between Man returned to the Father, and original divine Man in Paradise; and it is essential to deeply understand it:

Original divine Man was all one with God, and shining in perfect purity as the *«crown on the head of the Creator»*. – But this crown – to use this image – lacked the divinely human crown-jewels: the shining jewels of the seven virtues, including *Knowledge, free Will and Love.* – For: Quite easy is it not to succumb to any temptation never known; easier even to renounce what one never possessed; and easiest to let go of whatever one never was attached to:

Original Man in Paradise was indeed perfect without a flaw – but also lacked consciousness of his oneness with God, and self-consciousness in the first place. In order to acquire this knowledge, Man *had to* descend down to the world of Matter, and – overcoming Matter in free will and self-forgetfulness – ascend again. Separation of the original World of Light ⊗ into Spirit O and Matter +, Man had to reverse – Domination by

Matter + over Spirit O as symbolized by the seal of this World ♁, Man had to invert – to convert – in favor of LOVE: ♀.

To this end, Man had to develop a new kind of intelligence: the pure virtue of Mercury – ☿ – which represents the second force in the bipartite ‹Earth Epoch› (albeit interchanged for Venus ♀ by esoteric Tradition): This is the intelligent way of overcoming the unoriented impulsions by Mars ♂. – Subsequently, there had to be overcome the green-golden power of Mercury by birthing the living *Soul-Consciousness* – so-called Jupiter-consciousness ♃, where the SOUL ☽ arises from (or incarnates in) MATTER +. Finally – in the name of Venus ♀ – SPIRIT O will be elevated over Matter + again – by LOVE. And so indeed ♁ was inverted – *converted* – to give ♀. – And this now is not *vulgar Venus* but the *eightfold Sun-power* ✳ – i.e. the highest solar vibration in the whole Macrocosmos ⊕ – also named SOTHIS, as it were.

The ‹coronation› however consists in the third and highest level of the power of Mercury ☿: This is *purple Mercury* – physically speaking: the Philosopher's Stone ✡. – Microcosmically this corresponds to re-union of the *lunar force* ☽, cosmically named JHVH, with the *six-fold solar power* ⊛ named VENUS: Here Man will become a CHRIST : ☽ and ✳ are re-united in ⊛. – Cosmic THREE △ and FOUR □ become (cosmic) ONE again in ◎. –

From here, Man will finally achieve his ascent to the *Ninth Sphere* [65] , and thereby become able to *pronounce*, in full consciousness, *the name of God*! This is the real difference between the *«Children of the Sun»* returned home, from those who never left the Sanctuary. And thus we read in Lk.15:7:

«In Truth I tell you: Therefore there will be more joy in heaven for a trespasser who repents than for ninety-nine Just's who don't need to repent». –

The same promise is contained in the allegory of the *Prodigal Son*. And the *exultations by Pistis Sophia* as well are a glorification of this Path which, in its last consequence, exceeds by far human understanding [66] (pic. 26).

After lengthy *preparations* – named *The Path* – new divine Man – and in his succession *every creature* – can ascend and reunite with the One: as a tri-unity ᛘ with cosmic Trinity ♖, and also with macrocosmic △ – and finally fuse into supra-cosmic 👁 – the One-and All-and Nothing: This is the center of the vortex – the DOT: Source, eye and navel of the Double-helix ꩜ standing before, behind, and in the center of all Creation (pic.28). So Man finally became *«himself a god»* – just as it was the FATHER'S aim *«in the Beginning»*: emanating HIMSELF as a first new creation – as eternal FIRST NUMBER! Therefore one can say in truth that all those who achieved to return *«into the pure Light – into radiating Oneness with ‹the FATHER's Kingdom of Love»*, as the *Aquarius Genesis* puts it – have been elevated : *«to higher virtue, power and glory than ever before»*.

Thus, then, the often mentioned *‹Path back to the Father›* finally was but the path back to oneself – individual return of everything and everyone back to GOOD PROPORTION, good, i.e. eternally divine MEASURE, and to THE ONE NUMBER, the unique Principle, the sole essence of which is to radiate and give itself away IN LOVE.

This is the return of the whole Universe – back to perfect divine rest in DÃO. – It is the eternal moment of *«God resting»* between *retracting* or *inhaling* a Universe with its worlds – and *emanating* or *exhaling* a new *‹Day of Creation›*. – It is the *Great Silence* out of which, *‹someday›*, a new ONE, a new ZERO, and all other NUMBERS shall make their new appearance. Thus, a new circuit of Creation will become possible – but then on a higher level of the time-space spiral of NUMBER, RHYTHM and CONSCIOUSNESS: always a step closer towards the Prime Source of whatever is divine ... – until this inhaling and exhaling rhythm will at one point suspend itself completely.

Unconceivable, absolutely unimaginable is the perfection of the UNLIMITED STILLNESS that will then reign!

«Come to that, you shall meditate about what is God – and what is a world; – what makes an immortal living being – and what makes a dissolvable living being. You also must know that the world is both of God and in God, but that Man is of this world and in this world. The prime foundation however – as well as what embraces all and preserves all – is God».

From: *Corpus Hermeticum* (loc. cit.):
Hermes for Tatios, about mutability, transformation and Death.

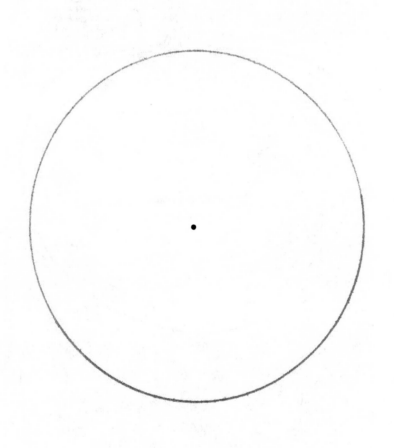

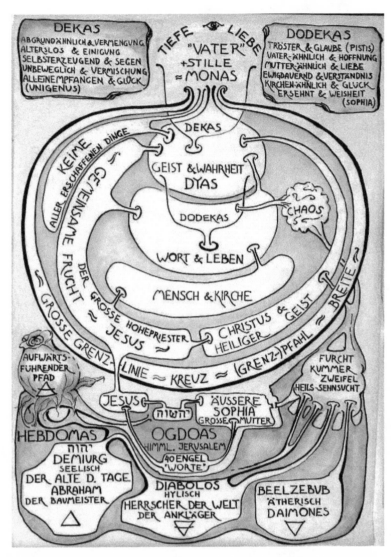

‹Aeonology› of Valentinian Gnostics describes the generation of supra-cosmic Pleroma, of the Macrocosmos, and of the macrocosmic realms – especially those of the Seventh (Hebdomas) and Eigth Sphere (Ogdoas). These may be equalled – *cum grano salis* – to MALKUT and JESOD in the Tree of the Sephiroth, resp. the quoted passages in the *Secret Book of John*, contained in *Nag-Hamadi-Codex* 2, 5 – as mentioned in the text.

APPENDICES

Appendix 1: Index of Symbols

○   SPIRIT – therefore also: The wholly spiritual, all-one, divine *universal* WORLD OF GOD: space-less, time-less, shape-less … : ‹Potentia Dei›.

●   *Supracosmic* PRIMARY CHAOS, unconceivable in every respect.

●   *Macrocosmic Chaos;* ZERO-POINT OF ENERGY, ‹moist Root-Substance›, still entirely spiritual); PLEROMA; the MOTHER of all potentialities (‹germs›) of all (eventually, or never) created things.

◇   RHOMBUS: supra-cosmic, divine ONENESS OF ALL CONTRARIES (‹DUALS›).

◆   CHAOS: unorganized MOTHER of the four cosmic Elements.

◈   Spiritual conception of the 4+1 Elements in the Universe of PLEROMA.

+   The ELEMENTAL CROSS OF MATTER. – Also: CHRIST-LIGHT in Rhombus.

×   The omnipresent LIGHT-CROSS: CHRISTOS, SON, LOGOS, ‹DATH›.

⊠   Supra-cosmic MOTHER-SQUARE OF MATTER; in it, the LIGHT-CROSS.

⊗   FIRST PARADISE: the original, entirely spiritual, divine Light World

⊕   SECOND PARADISE: etheric paradisiac World, constituted following ⊕.

ð   Material World ‹outside› Paradise: Matter dominates Spirit. – Earthly Man.

◉⟶   AIYN-SOPH-AUR: *Supracosmic* source and guardian of each ‹Day of Creation›: space-less, timeless, nameless, indescribable; the ‹Eye›, ‹Navel›, ‹Depth› or ‹Silence›, the sublime, unspeakable FATHER – HE who «visions», or «contrives» all Universes, worlds and Himself – and wherein, *«at the end of Days»*, He returns again – exhaling, sustaining and inhaling Himself and All, as the cause of all causes. The Presence of all inner-most Life in all inner-most and outer-most existence.

△   AIYN-SOPH: The *macrocosmic* Fiery Triangle (‹Trigonum Igneum›); *macrocosmic Trinity* consisting of **I** (FATHER), **O** (MOTHER) and **X** (SON), with **IO** (the Arabian NUMBER 10) as the ‹FATHER-MOTHER›.

♈   SOLAR (i.e. cosmic) TRI-UNITY of FATHER-MOTHER-SON.

☉   COSMIC TRIAD (‹TRI-UNITY›) *«in the Beginning»*: ⌒ («Osiris»), ⌣ (‹Isis›) and × (identical with the • – i.e. the *cosmic* CHRIST, through Whom radiates the macrocosmic Fire-Ether: *Jèsoūs* — the *Fiery*).

✳   The SIX SOLAR ELOHIM.

⊛   The CELTIC SUN-WHEEL: The six solar Elohim as a *Unity*.

⚹   Commonly so-called CHRIST-MONOGRAM («CHRISMA»)

⊛   Full CHRISMA: Six solar, one lunar Elohim, united before God's Throne.

△   Spiritual and elemental cosmic FIERY TRIANGLE; – ‹male› aspects

⊿   Elemental AIR-Triangle; *«in the Beginning»*: LIFE-ETHER.

▽   Spiritual and elemental WATER TRIANGLE – ‹female› aspects

▽̵   Elemental EARTH TRIANGLE (Spirit condensed into shapes and matter).

♀   FIERY-ETHER OF -SPIRIT; – Force of Elevation. In Alchemy: ‹SULPHUR›.

⊙   The SUN; – whatever is solar in elemental or spiritual Worlds.

☽   The MOON; – whatever is Lunar/Lunic in elemental Worlds.

☿   Planet and God MERCURIUS: Soul ☽ controls Spirit ⊙ controls Matter +

♀   Planet and Mother-goddess VENUS (Spirit dominates / projects matter)

♂   Planet and God MARS: Low astral impulsions – and new astral will.

♃   JUPITER: Soul ☽ arises from matter + (= concrete thought-streams).

♄   SATURN: Matter + (elemental structures) dominate the soul ☽.

♆   NEPTUNE: Soul ☽ dominates + and ascends as a new mystic Trinity.

♅   URANUS: Solar spirituality; renewing soul-impulsions; absolute LOVE.

♇   PLUTO: ⟨THE LAW⟩, KARMA (Persian ASHA; Daoist DE).

◉   DOUBLE-HELIX of ⟨Sleeping Death⟩ unconscious of Light (Hyperborea).

S   SOLAR S – unconscious hunch of The Light (Lemuria).

𝔞   TRISKELL – Dream-consciousness of ascent to the Light (= axis!)

卐   SWASTIKA – first consciousness of the Christ-Impulse.

✪   PENTAGRAM – New Soul-Man (→ Druids, Holy Grail).

✡   WISDOM-SEAL OF SALOMON: △ and ▽ consciously united.

✡   Seal of perfection in the PHILOSOPHER'S STONE – ⟨a Christos⟩.

◎   Arch-divine FIRE OF SPIRIT.

⬚   SEVEN ELOHIM united (three fiery spiritual, four earthy spiritual).

◎   Union of the 7 Spirits before Gods Throne reset. – Transformation.

◎   Fully conscious oneness in the Universal Brotherhood; a Transfigured.

Y   Cleaved / twofold Man. – World in Dichotomy.

Ψ   Rune ÝLHAZ: Elevation, Transfiguration; Spirit enters ↓ into Y

⧻   MAGIC VENUS-SEAL (VENUS COLUMBA): ÝLHAZ and CROSS united.

⚹   ⟨WITCHES FOOT⟩ (a goose foot) – a LUNAR CROSS, really : ⊤

♀   The ⟨ANCH⟩ – Cross of Life – a SOLAR CROSS, really. – Or: ANCH-OR SIGN (!) ⚓ combines SOLAR CROSS and MOON into one.

NOTICE:

Most symbols are polyvalent: They often have multiple – and according to view-points even contradictory – significations. Most important for present book: to clearly differentiate the four main ⟨planes⟩, or ⟨levels⟩ of *supra-cosmic, macrocosmic, cosmic and microcosmic consciousness*, awareness and simultaneous existence. Main basis for this book: There is only one Universe, comprising all galaxies, all milky ways, their worlds, their humanities, etc.

Appendix 2: External Sources of pictures

Fulcanelli: *Mystery of Cathedrals,* loc. cit., plate. XLIV; – In the present book: detail of this plate as a vignette p. 22 .

C.A. Agrippa a Nettesheim, *Occulta Philosophia.* Colonia, Sotèr, 1531 (pic. 6, 7)

E. Canseliet, *Trois Anciens Traités d'Alchimie* ... – Paris, J.-J. Pauvert, 1972 (Pic.19).

Rev. E. Cobham Brewer, LL.D.: *Dictionary of Phrase and Fable* .... – Cassell Peter and Galpin, London, Paris & New York, 1877 (pic.1).

Photo book *Gallia Romanica.* – Schroll, Wien & München, 1955 (pic.12).

Die Geheimen Figuren der Rosenkreuzer aus dem 16ten und 17ten Jahrhundert (Secret Emblems of Rosicrucians of the 16th and 17th century) ... – Altona, 1785; Reprint: Berlin, 1919 (pic.23).

H. Hartmann & H, Mislin: *Die Spirale.* – Basel, MG-Verlag, 1985 (Frontispiece II, pic's. 2, 4, 5, 8, 9, 10, 11, 12, 14, 15, 16, 22).

Pierre Martin, *Esoterische Symbolik heute* ... – Basel, Edition Oriflamme, 2010. — In French: *Symbolisme Esotérique actuel* ... – Ibidem, 2011

R. Schubart: *Der Babylonische Turm* – In: *ANTAIOS III* – Hrsg. *Mircea Eliade und Ernst Jünger.* – Stuttgart, E. Klett Verlag, 1961 (pic. 33).

Alfred Schütze: *Mithras.* – Verlag Urachhaus, Stuttgart, 1972 (Pic.13, 18, 20, 24, 25, 26).

Theodor Schwenk: *Das sensible Chaos.* – Stuttgart, Verl. Freies Geistesleben, 1962 (Pic.3, 11, 21).

Lewis Spence: *The Encyclopedia of the Occult.* – London s.a. (ca. 1920); Reprint: London, Bracken Books, 1988 (pic. 28).

M.P. Steiner (Transl. & Ed.), *Corpus Hermeticum Lateinisch und Deutsch, nach dem Druck von 1503 der Übersetzung von Marsilio Ficino (1468).* – Basel. Edition Oriflamme, 2015.

M.P. Steiner (Transl. & Ed.): *Dao-De-Ging – Die Gnosis im Alten China.* – New translation and commentaries. – Basel, Edition Oriflamme, 2013.

M.P. Steiner (Transl. & Ed.), *Jubiläums-Gesamtausgabe: 400 Jahre RC-Manifeste (1614-1618),* neu-deutsch. – *Die drei Manifeste in einem Band, mit drei Zusatzkapiteln sowie 10 Sendschreiben an die und aus der RC-Bruderschaft (1612-1618).* – Basel, Edition Oriflamme, 2015.

W. Eilers (Hrsg.): *Codex Hammurabi.* – Wiesbaden, Marix-Verlag, 2009.

Appendix 3
Three Mythic Texts from Paradise

The End of Wrath – or why Eve was created

This free myth is not based on the contents of the Aquarius Genesis, but rather on famous Babylonian Genesis as transmitted by the AT since ca. 300 b.C.

In the Beginning when everything was still fresh and new, God created, as is well-known, Man – ADAM – as the crown of Creation. And He saw that everything was very, very good. And this couldn't be otherwise; for the unique Perfect One who is All in All, by virtue of His perfection obviously creates perfection in everything – just as Man by virtue of his great imperfection is bound to create flawed things, everywhere. – And thus everything was very, very good indeed.

And also Man – ADAM – saw how wonderful and just everything was, and he ambled through the Garden of Eden, rejoicing with all the creatures who were his younger brethren, although created earlier than he; and he named them by their names and taught them things useful to himself ... –

But best of all Adam liked to rest under the big mighty Tree of Life in the center of Creation, dreaming in sweet dialogue with his soul. So, everything was peaceful, harmonious and very, very good. And God beheld his son Adam dreaming and was delighted with the latter's perfection and childish happiness; and thus things remained perfect during an almost endless moment. – Times and times did this last, until at once the Creator became aware that – yes – everything was very good; but everything was so good that never ever would there be any reason why anything should become better, still. – In other words: First Man, divine Adam, was so full of harmony, so perfectly content and in oneness with his soul and with the whole of Creation that he would have remained dreaming and slumbering under his tree forever; and never would he have had any cause to evolve further.

And God saw that in order to make perfection absolutely perfect, a little flaw was required – a grain of sand more on one side of the balance that otherwise could never have moved: Adam would eternally have remained a playful child. – Never would he have become equal to his Creator. – But this precisely was the innermost intent of the Lord: that His creatures should – step by step – grow up towards Him, and thus become equal to Him. –

So what could be done? –

There are several traditions regarding creation of the ‹Female›, and we add here just one little ‹point› more: When Adam had attributed their names and utilities to all beasts and plants, there was nothing left he could do really, and so he finally remained resting under the Tree of Life, and «fell asleep».

And precisely so that he should wake from his dreams, realize his destination and follow it, God created a division of Adam: The realizing part of his soul, equalizing his impulsive eagerness to reach new goals while spinning his harmonious dreams under the Tree – this shaping female part of his, God extracted from Adam, so to speak.

Adam «awoke» from his contentedness and «recognized» the part of his he so harmoniously had been one with, and he extended his hand in order to reunite with it and continue his heartfelt dialogue with himself under the Tree. And the ‹Female›, too, stretched out her hand in order to re-unite with the creative will of the ‹Male›. And the Creator beheld the two of them and was very satisfied, for He saw that it was good what He had done, and that He had instilled movement into the childlike contentedness of Man under his Tree.

And Adam spoke to the Female: «Come back into me where you belong, so that all may be good as it was before, for I am now lacking you, and without your being-in-myself I cannot be happy under the Tree of Life: Come back then!» – And the Female in turn spoke to Adam: «Eh – what? You come back into me; for you were in me, and the Creator took you from me and delivered me of you so that finally I can freely reveal myself, as it should be!»

Thus they argued for some time until Eve, the Female, began to resent the lack of goal-oriented will-fire required for successful manifestation. And so she approached Adam again, saying: «Adam, my dear, we'd rather combine again, for your will needs me to make your goals manifest; but I, in order to manifest the divine Plan, need your directed will – therefore: come into me, and let us be one again, as it was in the Beginning!»

But Adam had already returned to his Tree, spinning his dreams and thoughts; and so much had he remained the primitive child, that he sufficed to himself to activate his creative will: Whatever he visioned and thought out was as real to him as if it had physically stood there already. – His plans and imaginations were so clear in his mind that they needed no physical realization. And while Eve called for him again and again, Adam saw no need to chase after her, speaking onto her: «You go and manifest yourself as much as you like: To me, my thoughts and visions are quite satisfying manifestations!»

Then the Female went to see the Lord and bitterly complained:

«Lord!» – spoke she –«Help me; for your Adam refuses to unite with me. Was not this your will, when you separated us?» – For the Female had received from the Lord this gift that she could divine and speak out His will. – And God spoke onto her: «True is what you say, Eve, and I shall help you achieve your goal. Adam indeed needs you no more, yet you need him, in order that through your manifesting my will you will be able to follow your destination, so that, at the End of Days, everything can re-unite again as is my will!»

And God gave the female the stature we know today, and gave her the attractiveness she uses to seduce Man and to entice him to mating with her, so that he should, like before – and as if asleep – commune with her under the Tree of Life. Awesomely did the Lord endow her: with sweetness and softness, and with a fruit that, tasted once, can never be forgotten thereafter. All these attractions and this might of seduction gave the Lord to the Female, Eve, in order to help her fulfill her purpose. To the Man, Adam, he gave his generative parts instead (that is the power to visibly generate) so that the creatures of his will could become visible and that, out of the symbolic union of Male and Female, there should result some fruits to demonstrate the Plan of the Creator, and fulfill it at the End of Days.

And the Female went and enticed Man to act as she wished, and separated from him again whenever she wanted; but her Adam was saddened, for the Female he could not hold, and his Tree he had lost from sight. So he was full of grief, erring about in the Garden until he met the Lord; – and he complained to Him:

«Lord! – exclaimed he – You separated me, and You gave to my part the power to attract me even against my will; but I cannot hold this Female – and I cannot either return to my Tree where I was happy and content, having no need of her: Help me, I beg of you, for she whom you took from me is too much of a nuisance to me, with her fickleness!»

Then, the Lord had mercy of him and spoke to Man: «Adam, my son! I will help you. I shall give you the power to subdue this Female by your strength; but the pain you are suffering of her, I cannot take from you, for you yourself must learn to overcome it, until you will have found the way to unite with her permanently at the End of Days. And the Female as well needs to learn – someday – to unite with you without the ruse of seduction.

And this I give you as proof of my love: As long as the Female will treat you the way she does, male humans and female humans shall be multiplied. However: in every human that you will engender with her, the spark of your knowledge regarding the purpose of being a live creature, shall be increased at the moment of each birth – until there appears a Female completely free of temptation, and who will approach you in purity of the soul. Inasmuch as you then shall remain pure concerning your will, you shall unite with her, the pure one, without any pain – This will be the End of all Days – the end of all sufferings, the end of all quests, the end of all aberrations. – Then you shall be able to return to the Tree of Life; and again you shall dream there – not as a child anymore, but as one who creates; – and as such you shall enjoy the dialogue with your soul again, as at first it was, in the Beginning!»

And to the Female God then spoke thus:

«Female – Eve: badly do you serve the Plan of my Creation: The good I gave you to attract your Adam, you use to distract him.– Willingly you make him suffer by your inconsistency and your abuse of the powers I gave you, in spite of you needing him. – Also you must learn what all this is about, and what for. – The powers I gave you I will not take back: Go and learn to use them well! – Until then, however, you will be constrained to carry yourself the fruit of your seduction, until its maturation. Thus you shall resemble the Tree of Life. But while the latter carries its fruits without toil nor pain, toil and pain shall accompany your carrying your fruit to term, so that the suffering of Males and sufferings of Females be equaled and balanced until the End of Days when everything will be One again. – Thus, go now and be fertile so that your enticements may bring the world advantage – evenly as does the impetuous will of the Male!»

And Eve went hence, playing with her hair and with her might, and learning a thousand and one artifices to bend the Man's will as ever she wished: with charms and admiring words, with tears and railing, with clever acting, with weakness and a mellow voice; by monopolizing her fruit because she had carried it; and by asking for counsel where her mind was long set ... –

And Adam erred about, searching for peace and never finding it: Thousand and thousand times he let Her ensnare him, then took his revenge through his physical strength, but got all the weaker in turn; – uniting with Her, yet feeling still more lost and lonely; seeking for the Tree of Life, yet finding only the one of discernment of ‹Good› and ‹Evil› ... –

Original divine Man had been the crown of Creation in the Beginning, reflecting the whole Universe and its perfection. – Now the schism in Man was reflected throughout all Creation. – Nothing was as it had been in the Beginning; and as often as Adam strolled by the Tree of Life: he did not recognize it and stumbled on ... —

The end of the tale has not been handed down to our days. No-one can tell it: Those who – following the will of the Father – united with Him at the End of *their* days – they speak to us, but our ears won't hear them. We, too, humanity after Adam and Eve, continue to err through the Garden of Eden until we shall recognize the Tree of Life again – free at last of all contraries and contradictions; – free of Ego-will and genders' play; - free to manifest the Good without its contrary.

Those others instead who before us walked the Path to Eternity: they keep calling us until we can hear them at the End of *our* days – at the End of all Wrath; at the End of all pain; – at the End of all ruse:

Smiling will then radiate from the summit of the Tree of Life – in purity of the soul – the New Adam-Eve — new divine Man!

Cain and Abel Today

Cain-humans and Abel-humans carry on the conflict of the first sons of Man since the beginning of the world until today. The hostility between the two contrasting brothers is akin to the continuous conflict within every human individual – conscious or not.

From a standpoint of human psychology, this situation could be named the *Cain-and-Abel-Syndrome* – or: the *syndrome of the two hostile brethren*. Indeed this complex behaviour is at the origin of so many wars – of so much perfidy and painful love … —

The *Cain-type*: This is the first artful human, the artist (lat. *ard-/ars-, be on fire*); – man who turns up the earth, with the help of celestial fire – the fifth Element, or Ether – the ‹*Quinta Essentia*›: He is the creative craftsman, the human who shapes whatever he touches; – man who is movement and sets things in motion, holding up in his elevated dexterous hand the torch of Sacred Fire.

In the Beginning, the sons of Cain – and especially those of *Tubal-Cain* – worked with the fire of Spirit: with the divine force of creativity and formation. – Today, they tower up dead matter, running after a thousand idle thoughts and objects, yet often producing but empty shells. Rare have become oeuvres reflecting a divine creative spark, be it in literature, architecture, fine arts, or music. – Indeed: To be an artist needs more than to produce, as an exclusive personality, exclusive original ‹arti-facts›!

The *Abel-type*: This is the first priestly human (lat. *sacerdos* – i.e. *gifted with knowledge of sacred things*). – *In the Beginning,* he was in direct communion with God (lat. *religio – communion*). He is man flowing with the water; the mystical Disciple and faithful guardian of laws; the herdsman or Good Shepherd (lat. *pastor*); the reproducing preserver, the guardian over the *status quo*.

In the Beginning, the sons of Abel worked chiefly out of pure sacred soul-force: out of the Waters of Life (see *Priest Oannes*). – Today (since ca. 3'500 years) they are rather motivated by the etheric forces of the blood. Faithful Abel has largely degenerated to become a tepid caretaker of traditional forms that often have become obsolete, and lacking life. Forms the substantial content of which over time and social changes has waned more and more – as is often the case in economic, political, social, and ecclesiastical forms and norms. – Indeed: To be a priest means more than to faithfully (or not) watch over sanctuaries, to read the Scriptures, and to solemnly recite their contents.

It would be no use, however, to insist on the differences between Cain, Eve's ‹Son of the Elohim›, and Abel, her ‹Son of Jhwh› by

Adam: Dr. Rudolf Steiner, precisely a century ago, has comprehensively explained the same in his lectures and books. It will prove much more useful instead to study the role of the two hostile brothers *today* – and to shed some light onto their *future spiritual evolution*, along with the fact that their (ever unpronounced) conflict represents a task to be fulfilled by each and every human individual, deep inside their personality.

In every human west of Babylon, the names of Cain and Abel promptly evoke the association of the famous fratricide – and with it: a mixture of indifference and a hardly conscious partisanship. Where and how should this biblical anecdote be classified? – What might be learnt from it? – The above mentioned characteristics of the two brothers allow for an approximate answer.

In order to make evolution of Humankind possible, and in order to achieve that the ‹family chased from Paradise› and still living in every human individual of today, should find the path back into the shadow under the Tree of Life, it had to occur that autonomous laborer Cain should get the upper hand of Abel, the devout pastor. – Expressed in the language of fables: he had to ‹slay› him.

Later on, Cainite Man developed into an artist, a craftsman, and lastly into the triple figure of blacksmith, magician and warrior. Original warriors fought «with Fire and sword» – two expressions for one and the same: They fought in the Spirit, with respect and compassion. They fought for the highest invisible spiritual aim – holding their adversary in high esteem!

Warriors continued to be respected as a priestly caste (Indian Kshatriyas) even when their fight had long degenerated from the sacred solar plane (Jupiter; the pure magical power as a balance to spiritual forces) down to a purely Martial plane, destroying life of all kind in every way. – The world of once sacred art underwent the same degeneration as the rite of warfare: On one side, human spirit soared up to become an *incarnate spirit-soul*, achieving original divine purity and magnificence again – passing beyond Jupiter-consciousness and pure Venus-Love – until meeting, and uniting with, the radiant divine blacksmith VULCANUS. – On the other hand, arts degenerated until sinking into the swamp of dense matter. The Cainite «Work *of the Sun*» with spiritual gold as its highest goal decayed to become the Saturnial work with ‹electrum›, quicksilver and lead; passing through working with bronze, and lastly raging in war for its own sake: using iron and spiritually dead (and death-bringing) matter. – So much about degeneration of ‹Cain's Sons ›.

The old Conservative instead, Abel, remained seated in the Temple – guardian of the fire that Cain carries to the battle-field: A preserver of sacred rites and traditions is what Abel became: he who was meant to help shape peace and keep prosperous dynamics alive through sacred rites.

But Abel with his soul of Nature – the BA of Ancient Egyptians, Hebrew NEPHESH – invents and stimulates war by ruse and intrigue. – Cain, the ‹First-Born›, predestined to be the first Re-born in a living spirit-soul – Egyptian KA, Hebrew NESHAMAH – Cain carries it out.

This should still be the task of Abel today: to keep alive good forms in morals, ethics, usages and society, so that the deeds Cain achieves as first servant of the Fire in steadfast faith and deep humility, may be *justified* — and thereby *purified* while taking upon himself the guilt inevitably linked to his deeds. – Abel instead repudiates his brother Cain: He mistrusts Fire; he expelled it from the Temple! – And so much about degeneration of ‹Abel's Sons ›. —

So far, so good – or as good as these things can be understood in our days where Man, as a consequence of exaggerated individualism, values particular egocentric interests higher than original rules and values defining the meaningful task of the Kingdom of Man within the Universe, from Eternity to Eternity: The original Law of *Universal Brotherhood of Love* among humans was bent and flattened down to become vain pious behaviour: Its practical realization fell into oblivion —.

So Cain ‹slayed› his opposite brother, Abel; – in other words: he suppressed him. It would seem that this occurred as a result of a simple sacrifice; and one might be inclined to say: out of jealousy, because Jahveh *«unto Cain and to his offering had no respect»*.

«Cain was very wroth, and his countenance fell», as official Bibles have it (but συνεπεσι, rather than *fell*, means *did accordingly*). – «He lost his face» one could also understand, following Asian Tradition. – And Cain took revenge for this loss of the face, by hurling his fire against his brother when they *«were on the field»*: Just as if it had been the most natural consequence of his talks with JHVH, Cain ‹slayed› Abel. With his ploughshare he ‹slayed› him; and his brother who must have known all in advance at a time when Man was still conscious of his seven senses – Abel just let it happen!

He, too, let it happen – He who had spoken to Cain just shortly before: Having warned Cain beforehand, after the latter's deed He sentenced him to henceforth live as an Earthling – But He also gave Cain a signature as a sign of His love, granting that whoever would slay him, should undergo *«sevenfold vengeance»*. What this sevenfold vengeance should be was probably known at the time, but today we have forgotten it. – Cain instead went off to his exile, punishing himself harder than God had meant to do it, for: «*nothing of all this shall happen [to you]*», said the Lord when Cain named other reprisals he expected for his act.

It is quite hard to understand without a judgment, this tale about Cain slaying his brother – deliberately, and with the Lord foreseeing it and silently letting it happen: – Cain then suffers terrible remorse, and lives on ‹cursed› by the Lord, though remaining under His ‹personal› protection forever. – Difficult as well to appreciate the position of Abel who, foreknowing that his brother was going to slay him, followed the latter onto the fields and – as cool as could be, so it seems – let himself be slain.

Was Abel really so placid, mellow and stolid? It is possible. – Evenly possible it appears to us today – knowing today's reality of the myth – that he intended to put Cain in the wrong, in order to take his revenge – sooner or later. For: That the stroke by Cain could only slay his appearance but not his essence: this Abel knew very well. The ‹Sons of Abel› and of Seth not only excel by their ‹conservative› behaviour, but also by a very typical and exclusively human feature: *smartness*. – This is the capability to use subtle speculation and dazzling syllogisms so as to let untruth appear as truth, and by artfully faked causes bring forth real effects.

In early times, Cainites – as the strongest warriors, best endowed orators, most illuminated prophets – led their people in war and peace: as strategists, ship-owners and patriarchs. Today instead, it is Abel-Man who is ‹at the helm›: as managing and also mismanaging directors, or ministers over funds and laws; – as preservers and pervertors of rules, eternal lore, and Truth. This is part of the revenge of Abel against Cain: that over thousands of years, and thanks to subtle manipulation, he achieved to take the lead, while he let his brother Cain only just live, lest one should accuse him of having killed him. This is the primacy of Abel over Cain as promised by Jahveh. Who ‹only› injures, or incarcerates, or tortures his brother (or all three of that), evidently has not killed him – even if the other should die as a final consequence: this is the proverbial *Atlantean Guile* preserved in Abel's blood until today – over thousands of years, over worldwide migrations of humanity, and despite all kinds of cross-breeding of ‹races›. – Cain however did neither kill Abel as a living being, but ‹only› ‹inflicted a crushing defeat› on his physical appearance. Nonetheless, Abel never forgave him, and since thousands of years seeks revenge – on and on.

Following what relates the Gospel of Matthew, Jesus comments on this: «*The chair of Mose* (i.e. of a *Cainite* who like Himself had

brought a new Law) *has been usurped by the Pharisees and Scribes*».
– These were Abel-Sons who, notwithstanding all changes, preserved unchanged a once given law – while not actually keeping it
themselves ...

Evenly, the author of the ‹Letters of John› – an Apostle brought
forward by the church in the first days of Christianism, but who's
existence never could be proven beyond any doubt – evenly this
‹John› affirms (see I.Joh. 3:10):

«*In this the children of God are manifest, and so are the children
of the Devil: whoever does not live justly is not of God, neither he
that loves not his brother ... as Cain who ... slew his brother*».

This sentence today – if it is applicable at all – is valid for Abel's
Sons and Cain's Sons alike, so that the «*children of the Devil*» have
become very numerous indeed, while the *children of God* instead
must be regarded as very few, alas ...

Above quotation already points at the Abel-like tenant of a dogmatic Church that, more than 16-hundred years ago canonized a
Christianistic (but hardly Christian!) «correct teaching» – an ‹orthodoxy› crystallizing more and more since then, unable to gain new
life, despite progress of time and spiritual awareness in Man.

Now who indeed is allowed to argue that Cain did not love his brother Abel because he «slew him»? – Jesus himself who preached the
Gospel of Love, said: «*Love your enemies!*» – He did not say: «You shall
have no adversaries!» This is an important difference; but Abel still
does not notice it: Even today and at every given occasion, Abel
cries for revenge, whenever he believes (or pretends to believe) that he
has been beaten. Yet «beating» – especially with a rod, or whip, or
sword – is a classic image for Initiation with the Fire of Spirit (see
Michael signaling the entrance to Paradise with the *fiery sword of
esoteric Initiation*) – and for direct confrontation with often hardly
understandable truths of The Light.

So until today Abel's heart remains filled with insatiable thirst of
revenge, hoping to «slay Cain as well», wherever he might find him –
i.e. whenever he is confronted with naked truth as Cain transmits it:
he who does not speak in ambiguities and sophisms, nor designs
machinations but overtly appears with the flashing blade of flashing
words, fighting with tools ripened in himself, daily renewed and
sharpened by himself so that he is not calculable the usual way ...

This is what most scandalizes and nettles Abel: Cain is so autonomous, so polyvalent, so flexible! This fills Abel with wrath and
even hate against his brother Cain: Abel *cannot* believe that Cain
loves him despite his, Abel's revengeful beatings; for he, Abel,
cannot love his brother whose love he so desperately yearns for, while

so *intensely wishing to love him in turn.* – Instead he fears him for his untamed strength, and for the fire that Cain is capable of briskly hurling about, ere one could think of it. – Thus, Abel follows the ways of his wounded heart since thousands and thousands of years, hoping for a great moment of revenge at the first sign of weakness of his belove-hated brother Cain:

Then he, Abel, will deliver to his brother Cain the evil but not deadly blow: the blow dealt to ANFORTAS, guardian of the Holy Grail; – the blow delivered to their brothers and sisters by so many men and women, through so many ages, rejoicing over the evil wound they are able to inflict to them – and yet in the next moment regretting it in grieved repentance as did Cain, erstwhile, when he had slain his brother. – But it is Cain, not Abel who bears the signature of God: Cain took guilt on himself and repented for it, and in turn was sealed by his Lord, forever! – And Abel's blows heighten Cain, not Abel!

– But Abel – how about him?

Abel's «*countenance fell*», and tortured by envy, he today smites his brother Cain in revenge, whenever he can:

«Haah!» – he cries out – «I shall show you! – Haah! I will smite you where it hurts you most! – Haah! I want to see you bleed, and turn pale, and squirm, as a punishment for the smart you inflicted to me!» – And Cain in turn: «Not to cause you pain was my intention, nor did I cause you pain when I hurled my fire at you. Not for your smart namely do I use my strength, but uniquely moved by my love for Truth, the Light, and the Fire. Without anger I smite, and my aim is not the wound but indeed the healing of the wound! – That wound, really, that still causes you pain! The smart you believe you are suffering, issues from you alone, out of yourself. It is the pain that falls back on you because neither with subtle schemes nor with gross blows you are able to hurt me. – Think, I pray, Abel, my brother! Do understand that I love you – love you forever and always! – Nevertheless, I have to indulge neither your machinations nor your blows, lest I should burden with guilt both you and me. Receive my love, then, and be free of all resentment and all pain!»

And Abel in return: «Hahaaah! – The hypocrite! The bigoted devotee! The pompous arrogant good-doer! Can you hear him? Listen how he reviles and derides me with his false generosity and trumped-up love! – Do you hear him?! – Smite you is all I want, Cain! – Yes, smite and beat you, until whimpering you shall implore me for mercy!

«To rejoice of your pain is what I want, and of the blood that trickles from your nose and ears: Why don't you smite me, too?– How I hate you – hate you – hate you! The humble did I play. the mellow, the dopey preserver: From now on I want to be the strong one, the great one – the relentless fighter and triumphant destroyer; – the stringent judge, the merciless!»

Unconceivable pain is what Abel suffers from the love of Cain: He cannot understand it, cannot see it, wishes not to have to believe it: He wants to smite, smite, smite and be the strong one ... – and as his blows leave Cain unmoved, Abel suffers the pain he sought to inflict on him: on his brother who is no martyr of Evil anymore, but rebuffs feeling injured or belittled, and turns his back to the hatred of Abel in silent astonishment, and in compassion for Abel's pain in which he has no part anymore.

✳

Thus far the tale. – But Reality? How about it? Since long Cain's sons have mingled with Abel's daughters, and *Abel-Seth's* sons with Cain's daughters; and *Tubal-Cain* as well, the greatest artist of them all, has dispersed his seed among many; – but few are those who received it. – Cain's sons have also Abel's blood; and Abel's sons also feel the fire of Cain in their veins. Cain's flaming torch and Abel's ruse – they are present in every human, despite that in each of them one of the two prevails.

Cain's task is today the task of all humans: Learning to control his divine fire and to calm down his sacred temper in the service of All! – And likewise, Abel's plight: To let fairness, fidelity and justice neither depend of his own profit, nor of ‹good behaviour› of others! – Cain needs learning to respect normality and mediocrity, same as Abel needs learning to acknowledge without resentment excellency and genius: the Light-Fire of Truth in which no Darkness can exist!

The task of all humans together on their common path towards immovable peace however is to unite Fire and Water in the right proportions, so to cast the Sea of Glass in pure, brazen, brotherly love, «in wisdom and great diligence», as says the *Tabula Smaragdina*: Free of the sluggishness of Matter; – free of that old, pathetic Ego, which in its resentful ignorance always is busy to abuse Truth and whatever is pure Spirit, abasing them into the shadows akin to itself, down there where Life molders in lack of light ...

Achieving this *common sacrifice*, the two brothers, Cain and Abel, will finally be reconciled – for the benefit and prosperity of mankind and of the Universe. – Shining glass will be the surface of the Brazen Sea, and show one amalgamated reflection of unified adamant Love!

United then the two brothers will return to where they came from as two foes. Smiling in the Garden of Eden they will stretch out their hands one to another, in pure love now that they have united *in consciousness*, uniting their Fire and Water. Not separated are they anymore as are Earth and Air. – The *Great Rebis* they have solved; – through a *new will* and in subtlety and *wisdom* they have *realized* the powerful *Salt*! – Then will shine the purple glistening Star; – the Seal of the Priest-King Solomon; – the magnificent star shining beyond the eternal temple, in the glory of the sole solar Light:

Solo Deo Gloria!

Eve and Lilith – The Second Woman
A mythical scenic Dialogue

*«Since the day Eve met Lilith in Paradise it has always been
the Female that made the World spin!»*

This little one-act play from an early hand fits in harmoniously as a
third Appendix, while remembering the situation after Thesis 6 of
Aquarius Genesis. – It should be noted that, following its text, Eve is
not the Last-born, but the First-born – *«after the World»* (Hermes).

*Mid-summer morning-light. – Birds are chirping. Under a mighty tree, rises
– lightly and girlishly – EVE, braiding a freshly made wreath into her hair.
Humming a tune she sways her figure in innocent seduction ... –
In the distance, repeatedly a crow croaks both imperiously and warning.
Then, unnoticed at first, appears from the background LILITH, enveloped in
the wide, night-blue cape of ASHERA-ISHTAR: Mysteriously – solemnly; –
but at the same time menacingly like the Thirteenth Fay in the fairy-tale. –
Unseen herself, she observes Eve for a while but soon advances from behind
the tree, placing herself in front of the trunk: a sudden, priestly-royal
appearance: imperiously but discrete ... —*

*During the following first scene, the warm morning-light gets cooler and
cooler, bluish pale, and hardly more than silhouettes remain visible ...*

Eve: *(sees Lilith. starts)*
Who are you, sinister woman?

L: *(imitates her, mockingly)* – Who are you, sinister woman ...!? –
Who might I be, you pretty pure one? – I am your shadow!

E: My shadow? – How that? – What is a shadow? – And how can
you be mine? I know you not!

L: Indeed, you know not yet what Shadow is, you light, lightful,
lovely EVE! – You know me not yet, and yet know me: You fear
me ... – and yet you are but my other face, same as I am your
other face; – better – viler – that be undecided; for, in front of the
Great Tree we are all alike: Adam, you, der Great Jealous One,
and I. Each of us is but one of HIS members – but without us,
without HIS members, HE is not whole either: If HE did not em-
brace us as well, HE would not be the All-embracing. Had he no
place for us in HIS Plan, we were not here, nor elsewhere either –
and HE? – No-one able to speak of HIM could see HIM.

True: Stars see HIM, and suns and moons – but they are only
eyes, are just glance empty of consciousness, empty of Life:
Unless they were allowed to reflect HIS Light all the time, they
were ... — NOT!

171

When speaking of HIM, *the Lord, she makes a gesture with her right hand upwards, in half-sincere and half-mocking reverence. Her left hand pointing downwards alludes to* HIM, *the Great Jealous One: Yaldabaoth, Lord of Darkness. – Distinction of the two is left to the consciousness of the spectator.*

Look at all the plants – flowers, herbs, trees and their fruits! – What were they without HIM – and what without us? Just eyes and senses swinging in HIS breath that nobody understands who cannot himself or herself breath HIM; – who is unable to become and remain part of HIS breath, as do we, little Eve, you and me – and your Adam of course whom you run after so obsessively that already he hides from you in order to finally be able to quietly indulge in his day-dreams, in his brooding and in his ‹thoughts› he is so proud of!

E: *(dreamy, ravingly)* – Adam? Beautiful is he, and noble and strong! In his thoughts I see reflections of the LORD! – Is he not akin to HIM in his loftiness, as he ambles through the Garden? – Is he not like HIM in his glorious attitude, – in his knowing and calling and making obey?

L: Oh-yes, yes, little Eve – oh yes, indeed! Strong is he in treading down the grass, in his claiming and calling – in his naming and ordering ... – but in his understanding? – But in his feelings? Can he compare with us in vision and senses, in shaping and realization? – In loveliness and warmth?
Does he not surround himself with animals of the fields and forests – the wild, wooly wood-beasts he calls his Brethren?
Does he not exploit their senses – their view, their scent, and the swiftness of their hooves or wings? –
Their defences even he looks upon with envy because they are so strong and matchless in the diversity of their physical attributes and virtues! – This Adam indeed do you revere, little Eve: to him you are subservient – him do you follow, everywhere! Is this the freedom HE promised you? Is this your resemblance to the Creator whose crown-jewel you are?

E: A crown-jewel – I? – Odd ... Thing: It is not I who ornate HIS crown; not I who am the crown, nor its adornment: – It is he – Adam, of who's flesh I have come forth; he who was ere I came forth, shaped by the hands of HIM who's Plan is perfect: HIS doing is non-doing, HIS thought needs no thinking, HIS feeling needs no senses, HIS view needs no eye, and HIS will needs no audible word! –
And Adam is like HIM: – Like HIM he ambles through the Garden in well-considered paces, in well-aimed actions. – Clear are

his thoughts and feelings, and wherever he directs his will to, there it happens, faithful to the word of HIM who gave him the task to be a Lord over all creatures .....

L: Oh really, a Lord! – And what a Lord! The only one is he – yet – So it is easy for him to be the greatest as well ... ... as long as no-one can be compared to him. – But soon this will change:

(Vague gesture of both hands: Right hand up – the left one down ...)

Others will come – other «Lords», who will do as he does – wanting to compare with him in will and knowledge, in speaking the WORD to which all Nature must obey, because HE wants it so ... – Ha! – No! – The crown, that's you – the FEMALE! – The Last-born!

— But woe! — Woe to all ... ! —

E: Oh – don't you speak that way, you wildish woman!

L: *(Jealously, fiercely)*

Wild do you call me? – Just let me talk, for what I say is true — *(in motherly possessiveness)* — and you do feel that, don't you, little Eve?

E: *(abashed)* True? – True say you? – What then is TRUE? – What is the meaning of this word?

L: TRUE is, what IS – but as it is, it already was, if true it was not or does not remain: True it can have been and yet is true no more – and yet remains so: For, while something is true it cannot change, ceasing to flow it steps out of the Whole, out of the flowing existence HE made for us all. And because this is so it will also vanish, this ‹TRUTH›, in its whole and magnificent glory!

E: And why should it not? – Would it be good if it never should wane, your TRUTH? – Is not all that steps out of flowing Existence annihilated? – Is not *vanishing* the source of *appearing*? –

Withering of the flour only brings us the fruit; fouling of fruits only brings us new trees; and the fall of trees only allows for new life of beasts of all kind, for new earth, for seeds and beings and new existence?! – Is it not so? – So what is then the strength of your TRUTH? – Explain!?

L: My dear little Eve: so clever have you become so fast in your garden! – Did you learn all this from your strong Adam, the beautiful, the excellent one? – Did he prompt you such humbug? – And you, you believed him?! – Oh phew, little Eve, how very ashamed am I of my little sister! — Listen to me ... !

(To offer the seeds for lies and perversion amidst pure fruits of Truth: this special talent Lilith – sister of Enlil-Yaldabaoth, the Great Jealous One – shares with Mephistopheles-Lucifer.)

With a wide generous gesture Lilith is bracing herself up for a long speech; but her gesture freezes underway and crumbles away as Eve interferes:

E: Your little sister? – How can that be? Never has Adam spoken of me having a sister; and neither did HE, who loves us! – Who are YOU, really? How are YOU named? *And who* named YOU? Whence do you come? What is your task here? – And why do you speak badly about *him*, to whom I belong as one leg to the other leg, as one eye to the other eye, as one star to the other star – as the Moon to the Sun?

L: Eve – Eve – Eve ! – So new on this world and so many questions! So young and so little, and yet she doubts of what her eldest sister tells her! – So slim, neat and bright, and yet has not learnt who I am, – indeed, not even *that I am* at all! –

During what follows, Lilith step by step approaches E., almost absorbing her into her night-blue cloak.

Eve! – Eve! – ... – Eee-v-e! – – Wake up! Look deep into my eyes and know me!

Your dark reflection am I: your shadow – the night-face belonging to your sun-face!

I am who you were; – I am who you will be; I am who you are, when you wake from your day-dream of light-brilliant being. – Bright am I, too, albeit of a different brightness and of a different light; – of that brightness namely do I come, little Eve, which is *(menacingly)* the SHADOW of HIS Light, who's eye we avoid, who's breath we fear, who's WORD we flee!

(Translators remark: German alliteration of Helle/Hölle for brightness as light, smartness and Hell, light and fake light, must be well understood by actors!)

HE who loves us, do you say? – Little Eve: wake up! – Wake up to your strength – to *our* strength – to the strength of night and stillness! – To the strength of secret revelations, and of appearances that need no light and even avoid it, lest they might be spoiled in their pure, whet and warm blackness *(with as gesture down her womb)* that is our secret – yours too, little Eve – yours too: don't you feel it?

Feel how it lustfully makes you shiver, through and through, now that I remember you of this darkness! Feel the warmth and pleasant sensations that run through your whole being at these my words! Feel how you wake up to true life – how you become part of me – of us – of all other sisters who dwell in the deepest brightness, triumphant in strength – in the TRUE Light that belongs to US, the daughters of *Him* (meaning *Yaldabaoth*) – we who deride that Adam – him who cannot live without us; him who names us but never will understand us!?

Eve!... – ... Eve!! ... – – ... Eee-v-e ... ! ! !

Thrice I have called you, and thrice again, and for a third time thrice! – To *me* you belong – TO MY LIKENESS you are: more divine than Adam! For he, «the strong one, the beautiful and lofty one» – the «reflection of the LORD» as you name him: what is he good for? Has he a purpose left, now that he has fulfilled the task of bringing forth you – of setting free you – for you to be created? – To be useful is his only purpose: now that he has been useful to produce you, he is past use; for all the rest has no need of him: all the rest you can – WE can – well do without him!

Lilith seems now to speak just of Adam, but in casually raising her right hand also indicates HIM, the LORD:

Did you think there was only HIS name? – Did you believe there is only HIS Law and Order?– Did you believe there was only HIS call? – How wrong you were, little Eve! – How verily you were deceived!

(Now about Adam again, pointing behind her) :

I shall teach you to call him so that he must obey; I will tell you names that you shall give to your god-like Adam, so that he must crawl under your will! – I will teach you images and thoughts he shall beg of you, wringing his hands! – Mild will remain your speech, as he is used it; but the power of your words will exceed his by far! – Mellow will be your will, as he wants it; but the power of your will shall be like the trunk of that tree of which he is but a leaf, your «strong Adam»! –

Sweetness I will give you – some sweetness of the fruit HE forbade to both of you ... – *(foxy, half-aside, vaguely)* – that He forbade to you both ... – why ... ? – yes, why indeed ...???

E: «Why indeed» – WHAT, my sister?

L: *(starting eagerly, triumphantly, at Eve's expression: «my sister»):*
Why indeed – WHAAT – ... – *(hypocritically)* – deeear sister ? ? ?

E: I heard you say *«why indeed ...?»* – Was it because of the fruit? – The fruit HE forbade us – what do you know of it? What is its secret? – What harm can it do us? – Do you know that as well?

L: Oh no, little Eve, ask me not that, ask me something different! For, if HE wants it to be a secret to you, surely it would be no good to blab it out here, and now, and in front of you – don't you think so, too?
Also I know nothing precise about it ... – no, nothing precise ...–
no, not really, indeed!

E: But just roughly? — What do you know just so roughly about it? – *(begging)* – Oh, do tell me about it, my dear sister, oh tell me, – pleeease!

L: *visibly proud of her successful seduction:*
No-no, let it be, don't bother about it; for, is it not so: «the half-known impedes true knowledge» – only an Initiate may understand these words, but believe me, they are true; and because – as compared to HIM – all our knowledge is but half-knowledge, we really know nothing at all – even if we think we know something!

Just one thing I know for sure, namely: that this forbidden fruit is sweet – OH SO SWEEET, and sweeter than everything else here in this garden – albeit outside of it there may be other things, sweeter still, but whereof we here inside should not know. – That is at least what I could understand from our LORD. But I would not want to seduce you. I should hate indeed to awake in you the curiosity for forbidden things – even if besides all the rest I know, I can't see what there is so secret about it, nor what needs so much secretiveness ... —

But let us speak about other things: It was just a comparison anyway, this sweetness that slipped off my tongue, and that I might donate you. So sweet shall you be for Adam that despite the soaring heights of his dreams and meditations he never shall be able to forget it, and thus he shall become your slave, obeying your lightest bidding; – following your faintest call; – living at the mercy of your grace, while surrendering to your sweetness – the sweetness of the fruit ... – YOUR fruit ..... !

E: Sister, I beg of you: tell me after all, how are you called? – Your name in your reign, how is it? – And how in ours? – And what is your calling within the Great Plan?

L: *(pompously)* My names are as numerous as the stars of which MANY have my name – and almost NO-ONE knows it!

L. slowly and with outstretched arms opens her cape, thus revealing herself like a night-blue equilateral triangle, so that slowly the LITTLE CHILD becomes visible on the height of her navel, softly glowing)

... and hardly one knows, who they are looking at, for my names are many ... – oh, many ! ! !

Menacingly, mysteriously chanting :

Names of stars bear I, and names of gods; – names of gods that not yet are; – names of mountains, of rivers and lakes; – names of temples and fields and grooves; – names of tears, and names of dance! –

Chanting, passing into dancing movements:

Names of mothers and names of children; – names of beasts and spirits and plants; – names of air, and names of stones; – names of heavens and times and obscurity; – of grievance and joy and of brightness and light!

My figure as well is ever changing: black as the womb of the mountains – and silvery bright as the crescent Moon! Dark velvet green as the pinnate pine-trees; luminous green as the morning light, ere the rosy dawn appears on the hills!

Pauses – priestly, then fiercer and fiercer:

Azure of the Sea, and the redness of burnt earth, and then the whiteness of purest ashes, and silvery then as the snowy salt; then golden green as is true life, and the ash-grey after, that comes behind ...

The light is dimmed completely now; against a cold bleak background just outlines of the silhouettes of Eve, Lilith and the Tree remain distinguishable; Eve shrinks back from Lilith, until her silhouette almost melts into the trunk of the Tree)

LILITH am I, the One Great Mother: LILITH, she who always was – ere there was Creation! – LILITH am I, the Mother of mothers, the Woman of women, the Shadow of Light!

The head of the little child glows up, golden; Eve beholds it, rises her arm to points at it; opens her mouth for the question ... – but swiftly the glow dies out; Lilith quickly has closed her cloak – only to reopen it, wide and shady; and in demoniac paces of her dance she turns around Eve, her chanting swelling up to become a magical incantation :

Strength am I that comes out of darkness; life that swells, completely unseen; – Power that thrives in secrecy only:

Honor I merit, and fear and obedience; – joy am I, and awe and trance. – Sweet seduction; – mild submission and cruel coercion; the vigor of being, the power of Time! —

My dance is the dance of all days and nights – the dance of all women in all the worlds, in all the heavens, and on all stars! —

My dance is the dance of all-revelations – the dance of you humans, the dance of decay ... – the dance out of deepness ... ... – – the dance out of night .... — !

Lilith, dancing and chanting disappears in the distance. The light, timidly, grows somewhat warmer and more golden ...

E: *with her arm still raised, advances a few paces, hesitating ...*
Lilith? – **Lilith!** – – **LıLiiiiTH** ..... ! ! ! —— .... —— ......
There she is gone! I'm all confounded! – Where might she have gone? – Whence might she have come? – What might be her signification for me – for us all, and for everything? —
So many words – and so much power!

— — —

Is it then true that she is my sister? – MY sister? – And what kind of a sister? – And Mother?? – And Shadow??? – – I'm so confused!

And yet, I feel: light of a new brightness dawning inside me: a brightness I never knew before!
New sounds, new movements, new thoughts and a new way of being alive runs through all my being, simmering, in a mixture of trembling and lustful shivers — of a strange coolness – and warm familiarity ...: –

Am I still Eve? Am I still Adam's wife? Am I a human woman still? – Or am I a Goddess? ——
Both boil within me since SHE spoke to me!
Lilith? - Lilith! – Queen of the night! – What has done to me your might??? -

Departs in thoughts.

Appears Lilith in the outfit of a modern business woman in a night-blue, strict deux-pièce costume, a silvery shining brief-case in her left hand, a silver-gray travellers cloak over her right arm. At first just a dark silhoutte, she then is illuminated more and more by a faint silver-blue light.

L: Where has she gone? – Eve! — EVE ... ! – – EEE-V-E ... ! – –

There she is gone! – Gone from her is the sleeping innocence of the pure girlish female; gone also her humbleness, and her blind obedience: To questions and doubts will she give birth; and she, the lightful one who never yet saw any darkness nor shade, she has a shadow now that never will abandon her!

In an unconvincing tone of compassion giving way to a growing under-tone of true repentance that seems to shed a softer light on her character:

I almost regret now what I told her – what I did to her ... – evil, black, nightly Female that I am!

During what follows she advances to the front and center of the stage. Here she stops as a slim figure, puts down her little suitcase, draping her cape across it ... – pausing – thinking.

Then she slowly raises both hands to cover her face with them, yet peeping through between her fingers, in a mixed expressive countenance ...

What might HE have to say when HE sees her? – And what will Adam, the faithful one, ask her when she will call him and he comes, while *she* only rarely will come henceforth when *he* calls *her*? – She herself does not understand it – what can she say? – And I? What can I tell HIM?

I don't know all answers to all her questions myself: Whence I came forth, who I really am, why I am how I am, and through who's will?

Who named ME? – Who calls ME? – And ... – what for? ? ? —

How I envy her, this little Eve ... – How much I did envy her! –

(In a soft, longing echo to the previous:)

«As one leg to the other leg ... – as the Moon to the Sun!» –

(Bitterly:)

Las ! – Thus she once spoke, the little pure one – and I did awaken her from her dream ... — from *one* dream ... – into this *different* dream ... – out of smart ... — — OUT OF SMART ! ! !

How great was my longing to be great like HE; to be sweet like HER – to appertain to someone, like she does to her Adam! – – Now we are separated, *all of us* ... ! ! —— And soon Adam as well will be infected by the fever I gave her as a dark, shadowy legacy ... – according to whose plan? — Following who's spell? — whose pain did I heal? — What destiny did I fulfill? — Who's aim has been achieved through me?

Darkness was what I wanted to sow – and I sowed motion ... — Motion is LIFE! — Motion is LIGHT!

Inertness I wanted to sow by using so-called ‹Truth› – and what I planted really is nothing but vanity – and pain – and corruptibility!

For ‹Truth› as well will be discarded — by our sisters —— or by our sons!

Doubts I wanted to sow – and I sowed discernment; – Eve's light I wanted to take – but I just gave her my shadow!

Never will she completely forget whence once she came from:

Never will she loose completely her innocence, however deeply she may be engulfed by Shadow. –

And always she will also remain little Eve, the tender one, the light one ... – even when one of them will be entirely enslaved by me, she never will completely *belong* to me! –

179

Each of those whom I will seem to have won, I shall also loose thereafter!

If she eats the forbidden fruit – and she will! – and if she has Adam taste the same – and that she will, too! – then there will happen what *can* and *must* happen. But *all mine* they will never be; neither of them: Neither mine, nor YALDABAOTH's, nor of one of my brethren who revere me so deeply as the eternally ruling Lady, as the Eternal Mother – as the ETERNAL FEMALE!

— — —

Thus she goes hence, the imperiously tender one, the shadowy light one, the *spotted woman* that lost her innocence in order to taste guilt and remorse – to sow shame and harvest blame, in whatever she does!

Thus she goes hence, whose light I wanted to put out – leaving me behind in my own darkness. - In a new appearance she follows the old destination – only that soon *she will know* what she didn't know: who she is herself: A shadow, destined to find its light ...
...: ——

(her arms desperately reaching forward)

EVA–LILITH — THE OTHER WOMAN !!

Her face drops, freezing in this position. After a little while, she drops her arms as well. — Front-lights off.

At once however, in the background very dim the white light goes on, becoming bluish like a moon-night, then more vivid, greenish golden like dawn before the aurora. – Lilith, as the dark silhouette of a modern woman remains quietly upright in the center of the front-stage, then wanes into darkness ...—

Golden-rosy glow from the edges; – in one corner a nightingale or blackbird sings; – a warbler calls: zizi-zit! – zizi-zit! – zizi-zit –Then the voices of trilling birds like in the beginning, but slowly fading out ... — Silence for a while ... –

All lights out completely ... ——

Appendix 4:
About the Essence of Being
(following an ancient manuscript)

‹NOTHINGNESS› ...

... is both the integral plenitude of all possible manifestations in thoughts, acts, or any other perceptible form NEVER manifested in any Past, nor in any Present, nor in our or any other Future — AND the plenitude of all possible manifestations in thoughts, acts, or any other perceptible form EVER manifested in some past, or in some Present, or in our or any other Future, when, where and how so ever — BUT which are not accessible to common human awareness. – Therefore, for higher human awareness, Nothingness does not exist: «THERE IS NO EMPTY SPACE»!

(P.M.)

182

Introducing remark by the Editor*: Friends of old books and manuscripts experience many a surprise, as knows whoever shares with us this same predilection. That's how a booklet in black wax cloth came into our hands, containing the following tract among others – hurriedly written in a hardly legible hand, as if the author had feared his pencil not to be able to follow his thoughts. – Interestingly, what at that time would have been classified as weird phantasms of an overheated brain (in one instance the author speaks of ‹heresy›), today marks exactly the crossover of Natural Science and a strain of Philosophy that today is ‹bon-ton› under the swell denomination of ‹Quantum Philosophy›. – We here reproduce said manuscript including the original sketches accompanying the text. It reads as follows:*

ABOUT THE ESSENCE OF BEING

Wherever we may move about, at home or on the street: we always are surrounded by an infinite number of things and animated beings. Wherever we may stop, never will we stand completely alone, nor walk all alone anywhere: Always we are surrounded by *something* existing outside our own individuality. – We are used to see furniture and dishes inside our house, or the street running in front of it, while up and down this street almost continually circulate cars, bicycles, horses, humans, and so forth – and houses of gigantic dimensions grow out of the soil around us, like giant mushrooms. We also mostly give no single thought to the fact that all this surrounds us. In the contrary: Immensely astonished should we be if one day all these multifarious surroundings had disappeared; ~ if we should find ourselves floating there all alone, ~ yes, floating in some space, unable to behold any object outside ourselves – or maybe even unable to see, smell or palpate our own personality.

And yet, we not only *can* – we even *must* admit the possibility that some vast time ago, there existed nothing of all these things which during our earthly existence we have taken the habit to take for granted; – nothing but some ‹emptiness›, some space without the slightest content perceivable to our five or six senses: – There was just some extended space without any limit.

Whatever we *can* see, hear, sense, smell or taste is built from constructive elements that in turn consist of small and smallest parts and particles, so that in the continuous dissection of, let us say, a horse, there can be seen no end, while we are incapable already to clearly imagine anything thinner than a hair. And yet, – compared to entirely unimaginable small sizes like e.g. a virus of one $10'000^{-th}$ of a millimeter, which nevertheless is infinitely far from being ‹nothing› – even this hair is already a giant among the smallest objects. – Despite that, we are hardly able to correctly investigate such a

183

relatively ‹big› object like a hair, unless we are permitted to study it by means of a microscope or a similar contraption.

Science in fact since long undertakes all possible efforts seeking to define the First Origin of «everything». Once the *atomos* was presumed to be the smallest particle of matter, and any further dissection was long affirmed to be impossible. But Man has penetrated to the components and, so to speak, into the bowels of atoms – yet without being able to find their HEART – the true inner-most core of live manifestation in Matter. For: given that every single atom manifests luminous motion and warmth, it has to be some form of LIFE – and hence: contain live Spirit! All mathematical formulæ and intellectual super-efforts are impotent to change these facts. And all swiftly stamped special terms and forcibly introduced ‹natural constants› fail to prove total submission even of smallest thinkable elementary particles to the vanity of human intellect: GLORIA DEI INTACTA! – Man names, classifies, formulates, numbers ... – and many should like to think that as soon as they should have succeeded as much as to describe and even imitate every possible physical motion, they would hold the secret of Creation in their hands! – Natural Science – and as is well known, Medicine as well – mistake phenomena, effects of natural processes and the measurable remnants thereof for the process itself – and even for its essence: Poor Science!

The servants (or slaves) of academic Science should certainly like to oppose such statements in many ways: They might want to state the motive for everything to be very well known – advancing acceleration, magnetism and so forth to be «fundamental» measurable and reproducible forces – «natural quantitative properties» - and more such things. But as soon as we begin to ask: WHAT really IS this acceleration? – WHAT really ARE these forces, vectors, masses? – soon we will be set back to new tautologies – and finally to another inexplicable term: ENERGY!

Energy as warmth; energy as motion, as sound, light, smell and taste; - energy as ‹feelings›, as ‹emotions›, as the ‹voice of blood›. – Energy is Life, is Spirit! – WHOSE life? – WHOSE spirit?

All the manifold forms of energy are indeed only expressions – WHOSE expressions? – and so we are not allowed either to assume ‹energy› to be a prime particle, some prime ‹thing› - prime existence of whatever IS. For, even if we pretend the basis for every body *in the Beginning* to be a prime form of energy or shape – relative only to this body, or common to all – there would still remain the even more multifarious world of thoughts, feelings and ideas untouchable for such approximations – unless all these fundamental forms could be reduced to one sole and basic prime «energy particle» ... —

Now it is certain that whatever exists – be it of a physical or non-physical nature – must, and therefore duly does, come forth from some common prime foundation – a inner most primary cause – a «*prima*» or «*ultima causa*». – Only: Where is this primary cause or source to be found?

Let us imagine for once that we let a given body, assumed as being neutrally homogeneous – like some water drop for example – shrink down until its mass becomes infinitely small (in what follows, small indices are put for reductions [v], large ones for enlargements [V]). There, in infinite smallness, we must stop speaking of masses however: This ‹limiting point›, we will name *Limes m: Lim m (v → ∞)*. – And this point or limit, using *Figure 1*, be located in L, notwithstanding that it is impossible for us to locate it in reality.

Nevertheless we assume that here we have found the true origin, the ‹Navel› of formation of matter – namely the «universal prime particle» we have endeavoured to find (compare *Aquarius Genesis*, commentary to Thesis 1, p. 40 of the present book).

$$\infty \;\leftarrow\; M/m \;\rightarrow\; \odot \;\leftarrow\; i/I \;\rightarrow\; \infty$$

$$\textbf{M} \quad \text{(mass-world)} \qquad\qquad \textbf{L} \qquad\quad \text{(world of ideas)} \qquad \textbf{I}$$

FIGURE 1: Seemingly one axis leads from limes M – ONE infinite mass (Universe), over Limes L (infinite shrinking of masses m; and an infinite quantity I of infinitely small ideas – ‹prime ideas›) to the ONE infinitely big idea I (the all-embracing ONE idea of the Creator for the whole Universe).

If now, as said before, we again and again ‹split› our drop of water or whatever it may be, until its mass will finally become infinitely small, then, at a certain moment, we will reach a point where this particle of matter will stop *to possess* any kind of a mass, and consequently also *to be* any kind of a mass. Particularly significant for Natural Science is the fact that we find *no definition* for the existence of ‹mass› as such, but only definitions for its measurable phenomena; namely the presence of *relative quantities, qualities, properties, effects*, a.s.f., described only by so-called measurements, i.e. comparison with *arbitrarily defined and established parameters*. –

Progressing between *L* and *M* on the *axis M/m*, we penetrate deeper and deeper into the zone of smallest and largest bodies *in all their forms of existence*. These will necessarily create not only a straight line, but sort of *a conical space R* (Fig. 2), the mantle-lines of which have to be imagined as hyperbolic. Its largest, infinitely wide diameter *S* with its infinitely big radius *r* is described by an infinite number of *undistinguishable and hence uniform* prime particles without any volumetric expansion at all. – The ‹tip› M of the cone, situated in an infinite distance as it were, however ‹defines› one single infinitely large space embracing All, even the infinite number of all other spaces.

But what lies behind this?

If now we let shrink our supposed ‹body› – whatever its nature – until it gets lost in infinite smallness, it will finally be impossible to call it a mass. Nevertheless, nobody will dare to contest that *in its essence* it still exists. True, it neither is of any dimension anymore, nor has it kept any property as defined by the measuring and measurable world – and therefore we are unable to describe it either in figurative or pronounceable terms. But given that we still are able to speak about it, it must still be there: Our thought already – our WORD – keeps it in existence. – But WHENCE is this thought reaching us? – In order to include both, yet existing and anon inexistent ‹things›, let us name it *‹the IDEA of the object* or *thing›.*

Admitting into the *world of ideas* the same thought-construction as for the *world of matter,* a second cone appears, the basis of which – situated for all three dimensions in the ‹Infinite›, as it were – is similarly ‹defined› by the already mentioned largest diameter *s* : This is precisely the geometrical ‹locus› of transition for the infinite quantity of infinitesimal prime particles to become an infinite quantity of infinitesimal and indistinguishable *idea-particles* (thought-elements).

Progressing on the *i-axis* towards *I,* we attain ever larger ideas that can be described in a more and more precise way. The *tip I* of our new cone then corresponds to one single idea that ‹contains› all other ideas, hence one sole idea, all-embracing and infinitely ‹big›.

Thereby is created a spindle, the largest ‹diameter› of which lies in the Infinite – and so do its two ‹tips›. It therefore twice reaches into the Infinite. In fact, come to think of it, in the whole Universe there not only exist already now more objects and beings than anybody could count; there also is created in every second another countless quantity of bodies and ideas. Thus, ‹Space› as defined by academic Science is now *filled twice* – but in reality more than twice!

Meanwhile, *figure 2* is but a gross simplification: Not only must *Lim M* (same as *Lim m*) be situated in the Infinite – but also the Prime Origin (Navel) *L* itself (*as Lim m*), and the same goes for two other ‹loci›: *Lim I* and (simultaneously!) *Lim i,* bot commented on later, as well as the ‹mantle› of the spindle as a whole, albeit it is impossible to delimit this mantle in whatever way!

What now must – and therefore will – remain extant in the infinite distance of our shrinking process – so we postulate – is its *primary idea.* And we insist on that any IDEA to us is no ‹abstract thing› in a general sense of the word: The way common people understand the term, nothing abstract does exist at all!

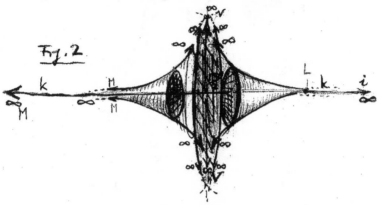

FIGURE 2: *Only one* infinitely big mass M, and *only one* infinitely big idea I are possible; – but an infinite number of infinitely small mass particles m, and of infinitely small ‹prime-ideas› i – or ‹elementary particles of God› – creative sparks. – Lim m and lim i both lie in the Infinite of the widest diameter of the spindle – and *they are identical.*

If we can understand the waves of electrons, and possibly of their ‹particles›, as a form of motion – a motion ‹rotating around› an assumed ‹nucleus› – then each idea in its emanation has to be formed by some waves of a very high frequency, rotating around some nucleus or CORE (i.e. HEART!) – the *nuclear idea* or *core idea*, or the creative spark corresponding to it and ‹held together› by it – as by a so-called gravitational force. Only after a relative ‹enlargement› would there indeed appear a «palpable idea», so to speak, corresponding to a seizable *idea-atom* (Fig. 3).

The spherical space symbolized by *e* in *figure 3*, serves to indicate an enlarged section of an *idea-orbit*, analogous to an electron orbit. This ‹orbit› itself be defined as W, its group assignment as w, and its individual character as *Bigamma* (ϝ).

In order to *somehow* yet define the idea and its physical effectiveness by which it affects the human mind, a physical mass shall be assigned to it, namely at the limes of reduction: *Lim m* ($v \to \infty$). [1]

---

[1] Note by the Editor of the original text: *At this point, let us emphasize that transition of spiritual energies to their physical expression in the human body can be physiologically defined by hormonal triggers (so called hormone-directing hormones) – This critical transition can be clearly localized. in the human pineal gland, the PINEALIS: This is a tiny organ to which spiritual traditions throughout the world and over all ages up to date have in fact ascribed exactly this same function. – However, this Pinealis today is – as compared to The Beginning – a totally curtailed organ, having*

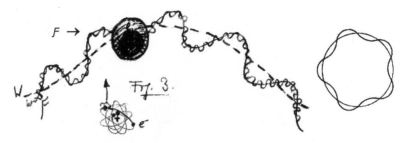

FIGURE 3: LEFT: Inside the *idea-atom*, waves of a super-high frequency orbit around the nucleus, or heart of an idea – i.e. of a divine creative spark in turn ‹moving› through universal space, rotating on its ‹idea-orbit› – *bigamma*, **F** – and the latter on its group-orbit **w** as part of a main orbit **W** (*‹consciousness›*?). – RIGHT: The track of an electron according to the model of *Niels Bohr*: a so-called *standing wave* with n = 5; «condition fulfilled».

But in its core or heart the idea becomes identical with said nucleus of a *prime atom*: Both are immaterial centers, and by their magnetism make possible materialization of the idea: They therefore are *elementary particles of GOD* – spirit-atoms – sparks of THE ETERNAL – *prime particles of prime Chaos*, ‹blown into› our world – «inflated to it» (like in Genesis). Obeying the Universal Law, they manifest as what now they are. – Thus, the atom as well has as its prime center the *idea of the atom* – the *creative primary atom-idea of God*. However, in order to satisfy modern scientists, this thesis shall be endorsed by a simplified formula (neologisms are inevitable here!):

The ‹end› of reduction of masses shall be *lim m* **(v → ∞)** with the *carrier-wave Bigamma* **(F)**. In the end of reduction of the idea – i.e. in its center, and thus in the center of the largest ‹disk› of the spindle **S** – there shall be the *prime idea* – i.e. *lim i* (v → ∞). To it (as to the inner-most center!) no **F** –wave can be assigned but, at the most, an infinitesimal *star*. – Now, we previously found that the *prime idea of the atom* must be identical to the prime nucleus of the *idea as a spark of Creation*. This means in fact: For the ‹prime atom›, the mentioned wave-length *F* appears, so to speak, at ‹half-Infinite› (where then begins further reduction until reaching the primal idea). – Or,

---

ceded its original space to the brain, which, in turn, in its prime state of evolution was nothing but a tiny gland. That is how Man, once visionary and wise by Nature, became an intellectually speculating animal with literally parched reasoning. – Nevertheless, it is possible to Man in his actual relative blindness to find the Path back to original wide knowledge, where intellectual thought – entirely put into the service of spiritual striving – can and will be of great benefit, similarly to the human Ego that built up during ages, but then has alienated humans from their union with Creator and Creation – and therefore of the original communion with all natural Kingdoms of the Universe. Thus earthly Man became the ‹Lost Son› of the biblical parable ... —

verbalized differently: We here have already reached the cross-over of concretization of the prime idea to become prime *matter* – and sublimation of the prime atom to become *Spirit.* – However that may be: To continue our reflections it is of no importance. For, as these crossings *must exist somewhere* within the ‹Non-Foundation›, the two *limites* will coincide at any rate, namely at the divine *Zero-Point,* or *Navel of the Universe*:

$$lim \ m \ (v \to \infty) \ \equiv \ lim \ i \ (v \to \infty) \ \ [\approx F]$$

Thereof follows that *figure 2* has to be completed in such a way that *two spindles* must appear (fig. 4):

Spindle S_i has hyperbolic mantel lines, – just as s*pindle S_m.* – This is to say: *their tips as well* reach into the Infinite; and *their mantle lines as well* are infinitely far from their axe. Two of the tips are identical as pointed out earlier, namely the tips $\Sigma \ [\ v \to \ \infty \ ]$. – This is the ‹point› where the two limites Σ_i and Σ_m *coincide in* F .

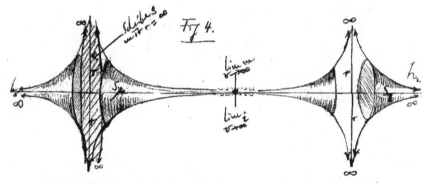

FIGURE 4: The *spindle of all masses* (M → m) is mirrored at the wave-length F (expression of limes m *and* limes i *at the same time*) and thereby transitions into the *spindle of ideas* ($i \to I$)

At this point, a very human question comes to our minds: *What is going on here?* – *Who or what was, or is for that matter, the origin or cause bringing forth said prime wave?* – We already found the answer earlier: It is the *divine prime idea*, the *creative prime spark* – the *spiritual prime atom* – and therefore *Divine Spirit* – also named *Holy Spirit*, or: *the LOGOS.* – And thus, even using a simple graphic model, the wave-term F has – although in a completely insufficient way as compared to all-embracing reality – been brought back to the arch-divine Prime Idea!

To whoever might find this arrangement shaky – or entirely impossible even, we like to reply that this thought concept, or ‹theory›, or model in which we reluctantly use the three-dimensional terminology or *imagination* of our numb mind and senses, in factual reality can in no way be of a three-dimensional order: Neither are the axes of the spindles geodetic lines, nor are they ordinary straight lines of an Euclidian geometry (see methods for geodesy!). Rather they should – as are their hyperbolic mantle-lines, and because every infinite straight line is a cycle with an infinitely large radius – be imagined as ‹hyperbolic curves› as well, approaching one common assymptote in (inconceivable) Divine Space; – an assymptote that – as far as we are bound to use our two-dimensional graphical representation and poor three-dimensional imagination – is to be visioned as standing perpendicularly on the plane of the drawing, same as in *figure 4* (see *figure 5*).

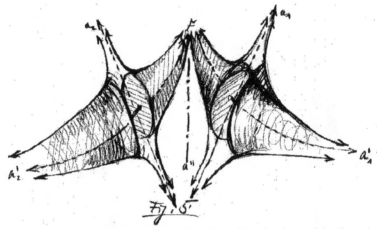

FIGURE 5: The spindles of mass- and time-dimensions plus those of the dimension of ideas are converging *by all their tips* in the ‹One Infinite›. – These nine dimensions form as an ‹intersecting space› a tenth and all-round infinite dimension – namely the tenth *dimension* – the dimension of God all-one – hardly thinkable, wholly unimaginable.

In reality, under these premises, ‹since long› no ‹vertical line› can exist there anymore: ‹Since long› our arguments go far beyond all possibilities of stereometric comprehension and common imagination. Already in the frame of scantily described relations as in figure 2, we have *trespassed* beyond a fourth *stereometric* dimension. – In *fig. 3,* an additional *dimension of time* comes into play, which cannot possibly be ‹steric› in any way: Here again we fundamentally and in a self-proving way contradict today's state of awareness of academic Sciences. – In *figure 4* there would appear an additional fifth dimension; and in the ‹complete overview› according to figure 5, *a sixth dimension* is reached – hardly thinkable, and absolutely unimaginable.

190

The SEVENTH DIMENSION is one more step further, however: Here all expansions of the sixth dimension push towards the Infinite, and simultaneously, incessantly, return to their origin. This is the DIMENSION OF OMNIPRESENCE: being «*"present"* at the same *"time"*» in the starting point, in numberless end-points, and in *every point in-between*. – Therefore, in the seventh dimension not only every think-able space is omnipresent (and concurrently suspended!), but so is every conceivable element of time. All dimensions – space- and time-wise – have here become One – coinciding and collapsing – and so «*all fall together*» (!!). – This is omnipresence in time and omnipresence in space, of whatever is imaginable, or thinkable, or unthinkable, and so of whatever is physical or metaphysical, and of whatever is imaginary or spiritual, or otherwise *sensible – or not.*

The SEVENTH DIMENSION thus is (to us) the OMNIPRESENCE OF GOD: space-wise and time-wise, spiritually and physically – and even (somehow) materially. – All has become one – $^c εν \ το \ π άν$ – *hen to pan* – *each particle is the whole Universe.* – This fact, on one hand, yields an interpretation of the beginning of biblical Genesis; – but on the other also the beginning of the gospel of John: «Eν αρχη ην ^{c}ο λογος – *En archè èn ho logos* - *in The Beginning there was the LOGOS*» – or actually: Universal Spirit – or the plenitude of creative Thought (NOUS) – or still else: *Divine Omnipresence ... —*

Arrived at this point of our transcript of the dusty manuscript, we permit ourselves to make readers attentive to the deep metaphysical understanding concealed behind such a derivation of Creative Thought. Our author could have, from the beginning, used the term of «parable» instead of «hyperbolic»: This would both graphically and philosophically have fulfilled the same purpose, but at the same time would have included the parable as a symbolic way of philosophical tuition.

Exactly the same way, thus, the multiple thought-nuclei coincide when we look at the beginning of biblical Genesis the author points at here: LOGOS – the fundamental Thought – the Prime Idea, translated by Gœthe as «the Deed» {resp. the DATH in the tree of the Sephiroth}, and in official Bible translations given as the WORD - or finally the Mason's ‹VERBUM DIMISSUM›. – Here, at the limit of what a human mind is capable to approach – at the LIMES, as our author names it, and which to Initiates of Antiquity was a stream to be fran-chised; - here all concepts and terms coincide, that means: fall together and apart. Here is also the turn where we can find a direct connection between biblical Genesis and the first verses of the Gospel of John :

«In the Beginning there was the WORD, and the WORD was with GOD, and GOD WAS THE WORD ... »

Are not this «WORD» and author's «divine PRIME IDEA» one and the same?
And are not both issuing out of «CHAOS»? – And are not both these origins
together the same as what we name GNOSIS – or PRONOIA – the *eternally*
pregnant, *all-embracing Forethought* – the one we encounter in the Chinese DE, and in the lecture for the *«Missa in immaculatam conceptionem Vir-*
ginis Mariae» – and in almost exactly the same words again in the old texts of
Babylon and India (or in biblical *Prov. 8:22-35; resp. Jes. Sir., 14:5 ss.*):

«The Lord possessed me in the Beginning of His ways. – I was there ere He
accomplished the first act of creation. I was there since all eternity, even ere
Earth was created. Yet no Abyss was there, but already I was engendered. Yet
no source sprung out of Earth, nor was towered up the mass of the mountains.
– I was born even before the hills. – Neither Earth nor streams had He created,
nor fastened Earth at her poles. When He unfolded the Heavens, I was already
there; – when to the abysses He gave their limitations; when He wrote an
inviolable Law for all the Worlds; when beyond the Earth the Air He fastened;
when the sea He closed within her shores; and when to the Waters a Law He
prescribed, lest they transgress their limits; – when her foundations He set
to Earth, I was there already, ordering everything … » —

To say more would not fit our modest cognizance; but instead we should
like to direct the reader's attention to a respective passage in Mystery of the
Cathedrals by FULCANELLI, where he speaks about the Arch-Mother and Arch-
Matter: «Mater Ea» – Materia Prima, Prima Mater, viz. prime Matter. [2] - And
while our author happens here to quote the Gospel of John, let us also
mention that albeit John is said to have baptized «only» with WATER, convent-
ional representations of John baptizing Jesus show the dove of VENUS
COLUMBA, i.e. VENUS OURANIA – emanation of Spirit, i.e. FIRE – hovering above
the (earthly) person of Jesus: ♀[3]. *On the other hand, the myth lets Venus be*
born from the Sea! Could this mean that according to its nature the VERBUM
DIMISSUM is comparable to Prime Waters ▽ *rather than to Primary Fire* △ *? –*
Or does it correspond to perfect union of both as shown by the RHOMBUS ◊ *and*
by the Seal of Wisdom – Sigillum Sapientiæ Salomonis – SAL/SOL-AMMON ✡ *?*
– Let us go back to what says our author! – He thus continues:

True: The IDEA indicated here must not be understood as an ‹idea›
in common current speech, but much more as an ‹idea of the idea›,
in a divine sense.

Evenly true: viewed in a strict sense, we are unable to define the ori-

---

[2] *Fulcanelli: Mystery of the Cathedrals and esoteric interpretation of hermetic symbols of*
the Great Work [of Alchemy]. – Editions Pauvert, Paris, 1st orig. edition 1926, p. 91:
Maria, virgin and mother, there represents VISIBLE *shape. Elias – the Sun, God-*
Father – is the emblem of the INVISIBLE *Breath of Life (esprit vital). From the union of*
these two principles emerges SENSIBLE *Living Matter, subdued to rise and fall follow-*
ing the laws of transformation and progress. This, then, is JESUS: SPIRIT INCARNATE; –
the FIRE INCARNATE, *enclosed in earthly things as we ‹know› them– JÈS.*

[3] Compare also in *Aquarius Genesis*: Legend to pic.10 and frontispiece, as well as comments
to Theses 2, 4, 7, 8, 11, 12, and the table of symbols, p.155.

gin and precise properties of *any «idea»*, and even less are we able to explain the term of an *«idea of an idea»*. On the other hand, even the sole imaginability of these terms should give the lie to our own elucidations of the matter – and so would any *prime particle of Matter*, were we able to *imagine* it and therefore express it in terms of a mass; for, as soon as it were possible to *imagine* it, it should evenly – at least in this imagination – become susceptible of subdivision («dissection»), as explained earlier. – See *Dao-De-Ging*, loc. cit., N° 01.

Rather, our ‹verbal mongrel of an *«idea of the idea»* actually acquires its true significance as it – the ‹*idea of an idea*› – in its definite unimaginability as *divine idea* is completely withdrawn from human scope and seizure. – Whatever we are yet able to see, or hear, or sense, or perceive in any other way, can, as such a perception, become real only by some *«idea of ours»* – preconceived WHERE and HOW?

A table, to take our first example, becomes capable of existence as a bodily ‹thing› only on the basis of our *idea of a table*. This idea ‹moves› on the *i-axis* of the *hyperbola I* towards the value of *F* ; There it is reflected, and on the *hyperbola M* ‹returns› into dimensions of what we call a ‹mass›. Only now it becomes accessible to our physical awareness ... which is WHAT *precisely?* – Like our antique predecessors who named *«desire the father of thought»*, we now might in turn name the *idea* – namely the *concrete idea* – the *mother of perception*:

It is only by *intensification, condensation and conglomeration* out of itself and by itself, that a PRIME IDEA makes possible the formation of an IDEA; and the latter again generates, by its intensification, condensation and conglomeration, a sensitive or psychical perception – and thereby – as a third step – a physical manifestation and subjective sensual experience. It therefore is «no wonder» that all human inventions and developments lag far behind whatever we might call «Nature», considering that from the first idea to the physical realization (e.g. of a table) an *at least twice infinite* path needs to be covered!

Seen that way, no invention, no development, and hence no progress of any kind could be possible, if not from time to time a ‹divine spark› should dart from one Infinite to the other, so that through the spiritual en-lightening, or «flash of genius» thus generated, Eons burn down to nothingness, so that on this plane as well all dimensions (and limits!) of human imagination break down: time and space dissolve, and for a tiny little instant, divine universality becomes seizable.[4]

Should now anybody like to accuse such conceptions to be ridi-

---

[4] *Fulcanelli loc. cit. p. 92 describes this by the rapture of «the old Master who in anxious attention questions and scrutinizes the evolution of mineral life, and finally, overwhelmed by evidence, contemplates the wonder which his faith has allowed him to penetrate for a short instant!».*

culing all human science, and therefore to be ‹heretic›, nihilistic and pernicious? This should mean to completely misunderstand our statements, and to downright attempt turning them into their complete contrary. In fact, we here not only have discovered evidence of the Divine – namely of direct emanation of God Himself – but also have moved up our human dispositions so much closer to God's Breath and His Plan! That is why of all creatures in the Universe Man alone is capable – and even destined – to receive and transform Spirit which in Truth always is of divine origin, and therefore entirely divine and indivisible itself:

«For whatever has come to be, has come to be by the One, and without It nothing has come to be what has come to be ... » - no human work either! – *«And the Light [today still] shines in Darkness, but Darkness [until today] did not grasp it.»*

Here, some might also want to advance Nietzsche who in his epistemology concluded that everything is but *idea* («imagination»), and who despaired in this ‹knowledge›, arguing: *«Why live on, knowing that everything is nothing but illusion?»* —

Instead, we have seen that the trail from an idea (inspiration) to a vision (imagination) is very, very long: Many errors are possible, and so are *false imaginations* on the basis of *genuine ideas*. – But even false imagination is still far from being an *illusion* – i.e. a mockery from the mirror-world of Spirits: It is rather the effect of Lucifer who, always on the lookout, offers to us vain humans a clear thought with one hand, while with the other seeking to ensnarl and blindfold us by some shadow, the stench of which should certainly suffocate us, were we not protected by the eternal Grace of God.

Under such preconditions it is really astonishing that we who are nothing but a tiny dot amidst universal Creation – are in any position at all to create for ourselves such a wondrous and polyvalent world picture which, even if fundamentally consisting in «just so ideas» and their energo-magnetic emanations (‹images›), nevertheless offers us everything we need to get closer to Truth – i.e. to the Spirit of God. Name it self-delusion or whatever you like: Given that it helps us advance on our path towards full consciousness, we value these illusive *images* – these *imaginations* – to be evenly earthly and divine!

Should we then throw away our lives as we unmask this awesome «idea-image» of a Universe – this «collective illusion» or «collective auto-suggestion» built up during so many eons? –

Of course not! To these illusions we owe both experience and consciousness. Their ‹physical› outlet› makes possible every evolution, physical or spiritual – independent of whatever interpretation we might apply onto this «physical world»! – We, little humans, are even called to play our role together with the absolutely necessary *Unique Prime Actor,* or *Agens* needed (*«unum necessarium»*) to allow for both the idea and its materialization to be brought into being. – This is why we, humans, are part of divine Creation ourselves – not just as very special creatures, but as responsible, *divinely human co-creators!*

Here the manuscript stops. – How was it going to end? What final conclusion – what inspiration – what philosophical ideal perhaps was it the unnamed author intended to bestow on his readers as a viaticum? – And what might have been the fundamental motive behind the whole tract? Was it to prove the existence of God? Or was it to explore the origin and inner meaning of all that exists – of the existing Creation as well as of what still needs to be created? – We are unable to decide the question but believe to hold a possible conclusion in our hands; and this we add here, hoping that it differs not too much of the original intention of the anonymous author. We thus dare to conclude this tract –adopting his style and argumentation – like this:

«Thus we find ourselves at the point of intersection of the world of ideas and that of material realities: at the *Limes* – i.e. the common origin of all axes of all our hyperbolic spindles (the third of which is formed by the *Hierarchy of the Heavens*) – namely, where all dimensions – as many as there might be – «fall together», both collapsing and uniting: ‹There› where there exists the Prime Source of whatever we might call ‹divine›, ‹there› in Truth also lives *New Divine Man!*» —

Other lectors of this tract may chose a different ending as they please; – to us, the above given addendum passes for an essence of all thoughts developed until here. – And so we step back over the ‹Limes›; - back into the world of vulgar humanity, which we are better acquainted with ... —

Appendix 5-A

The Pictures

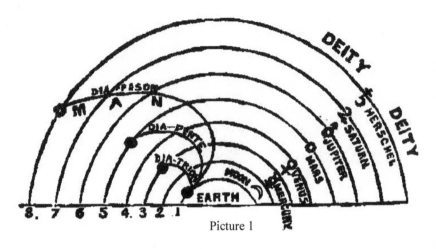

Picture 1

Picture 2

Picture 3:

Picture 4.

Picture 5

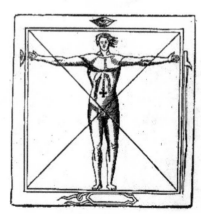

Picture 6

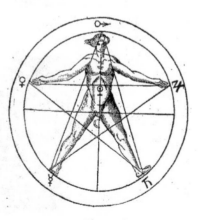

Picture 7

Picture 8A

Picture 8B

Picture 9

Picture 10

Picture 11

Picture 12

Picture 13

Picture 14

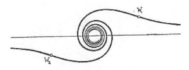

Picture 15-A: Lituus

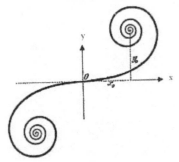

Picture 15-B: Klothilde

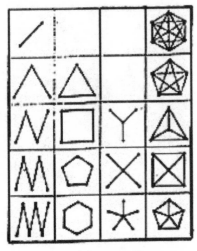

Picture 16: Ramsey-Signs:
(Metatron-Cube = SON!)

Picture 17

Picture 18-A

Picture 18-B

Picture 18-C

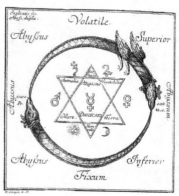

Picture 19

Picture 20

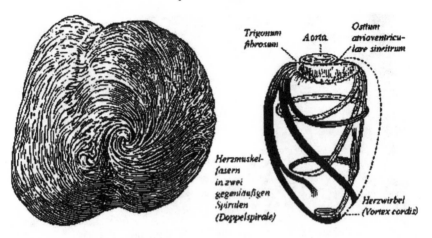

Picture 21
(Double Spire at the apex of the left ventricle,
Triskell at the apex of the right one)

Picture 22

Picture 23

Picture 24

Picture 25

Picture 26

Picture 27

Picture 28

Picture 29

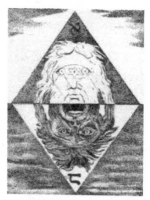

Picture 30

Picture 31

Picture 32

Picture 33

Picture 34

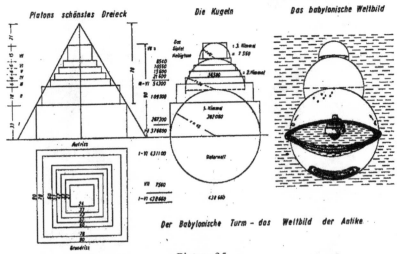

Picture 35

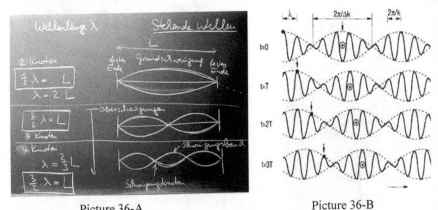

Picture 36-A

Picture 36-B

Picture 37

Picture 38

Picture 39

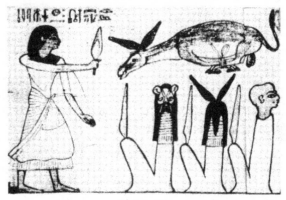

Picture 40

Picture 41

Appendix 5-B
Comments to Pictures

FRONTISPIECE I: Deir el-Bahari, inside the monumental temple of Pharaoness Hatshepsut: The side-temple consecrated to Goddess Hat-Hor:
   The Pharaoness (or her belligerent son Tut-Mose, because of the blue ‹war helmet›?), being nursed by Hat-Hor with the *Milk of Wisdom.*

FRONTISPIECE II: Archaic facial painting of an Australian Aboriginal, with the typical ‹*Hyperborean Double-Helix*› (see symbols, pictures and text).

PIC. 1: The *Dictionary of Phrase and Fable* (London, Paris, New York, 1899) under the term DIAPASON, says. *«Following the Pythagorean system, the world is a piece of harmony, and Man the full chord consisting of a fundamental or tonic, its major third, its just fifth, and its octave».* – The diagram shows not only a whole octave but also how Man is contained in it as a microcosmos: *«Man touches Deity, passes through all the planets, and touches Earth. Because he touches Deity he has an immortal soul, and because he runs through the Planets, the Planets influence his nature.»* – The symbols in the picture are displaced by one, however.

PIC. 2: *«Eadem Mutata Resurgo – Transformed I resurge as the same»*: The rotating helix is a symbol for death, transmutation and resurrection.

PIC. 3: A thin rod held into softly flowing water produces a small turbulence that seems to disappear at once. In reality, it is a chain of swirls and counter-swirls achieving minimal disturbance of the flow: The swirls neutralize each other reciprocally. Similarly, KARMA – the Law of absolute equilibrium throughout the Universe – always compensates causes and effects in such a way that harmonious balance of Macrocosmos, Cosmoi and microcosms is granted for.

PIC. 4: Two stamps made of ceramic (Çatal Hüyük, Turkey), officially dated to the time of 6'000 b.C. – One seal shows the ‹*Hyperborean double helix*›; the other the latter's evolution to give the *Arian Sun-Wheel* ⊕ – the SWASTIKA. The inverted arm and the central eye show that manifestation of the CHRISTOS cannot be spoken of yet: Anon only the divine ‹eye of the Father› ‹◉› is – semi-consciously – experienced.

PIC. 5: Celtic bronze-clasp. *Crucifixus* and *Pantokratès* simultaneously. – Especially remarkable: the four spirals (the four world-periods) as a *pectorale* of the Christ. They appear to form sort of a Swastika. The curious *recumbent crescent of the Moon* (→ Isis!) on Christ's belly can be observed also on sculptures of Christ in Romanic churches.

PIC. 6: ‹Vitruvian Man› standing in the Square below the all-seeing eye ‹◉›: The flying ribbon (‹*phylacterium*›) emphasizes the deliberate Symbolism: In traditional Symbolism, phylacteria *always* indicate the presence of some *secret* or *hidden meaning* (occultism).

PIC. 7: ‹Vitruvian Man› standing in the *Pentacle or Pentagon*. His head and extremities form a *Pentagram.*

PIC. 8A: The fact that from the classical helix, or *Fibonacci-Curve*, both the *Pythagorean Triangle* and the regular *Pentagram* can directly be deducted; – also, that at every intersection of the *Spiral* with a point of intersection of the *Pentagram* a *six-pointed star* ✳ is formed – symbol of the *solar Christ-Light* (Venus) – all this will hardly surprise vulgar Scientists. Contemplated in-depth however, all this is a great *wonder of Nature*!

PIC. 8B: The phenomenon as defined mathematically in pic. 8A occurs again in the shape of mussels. – The ‹mussel of St James› is, even today, mystically linked with the *«Path towards Compostela»* – the pilgrimage towards an old sanctuary of primitive Christianity dedicated to Jacobus, a son of Jesus; – or to Jacobus, brother of Jesus, (‹known› as ‹*Joseph of Arimathia*›, i.e. *Rama Theios – divine fool*). – In Alchemy, this *«Pilgrimage towards Compostela»* is an allegoric alias for the labors yielding the famous ‹*Compost*› – well-proportioned mix of substances for the *Sublimations*.

PIC. 9: Even most spiritual humans show engraved in their finger prints the sign of deep unconsciousness: the *Hyperborean Double-Helix*: ◉ !

PIC. 10: The WISDOM-STAR OF SALOMON with its solar central point ☿ is the classic symbol for the *physical Philosopher's Stone* – i.e. Christ-Spirit «incarnate» in absolutely purified ‹philosophal› matter, crystallizing as an *Icosaeder*. The Rose over the southern transverse nave of the cathedral of Basel/Switzerland shows the resurrected Christ – microcosmically: New Divine Man – donned with the purple cape of Priest-Kings, and in a gesture signaling the Rune *Ýlhaz* – ᛉ. The naked chest forms a Pentacle with the sternum as its center. Thus, CHRIST is here linked to both the cipher FIVE (MERCURY) and the cipher SIX (VENUS: ♀), viz. VENUS COLUMBA, with the magical symbol ⚥, and the ‹Sun-wheel› ⊕).

PIC. 11: The classic *Labyrinth* is a typical symbol for the path of humanity: Involution and evolution; – centripetal and centrifugal consciousness; – the path inwards for self-knowledge, and the path outwards to achieve knowledge of Cosmos, Macrocosmos and God Himself. – Without the path through captivity in matter and ‹Death›, no liberation by the Light can be. – Here: The Labyrinth of Knossos (Kreta) – with its myth of the Minotauros is the most significant allegory for the path to redemption during the AGE OF TAURUS (ca. 4500-2200 b.C.).

PIC. 12: The SON – the CHRISTOS – sitting in the (feminine) Mandorla, escorted by the four cosmic Elements – not as a judge over the World, but as Ruler through LOVE! – Toulouse, church St. Sernin.

PIC. 13: Mosaique at Sassoferrato/Italy, today in the Glyptothek, Munich: The Sun-Hero, here MITHRAS, as the 13TH ÆON in the heart of the Zodiac. *The sign of Aries is missing*! The Lady beneath the tree, and the *three* nude ‹Parvuli› (Mt.18:3) are ordinarily explained as *«Earth and the Four Seasons»*! The snake curled around the neck of Lady Nature like an Ouroboros and which one of the two infants seems to seize, indicates a higher meaning. The Parthian *Sagittarian* (*Ares!*) in his monks cloak (Lord over life and death) can hardly mean ‹Winter›, but appears to *guard the closed book of Esotericism.* – He could also be a Persian Wise – *Sophi, Sufi* or *Schaffis* – or an *Alchemist*, for: The *putto* in the left corner reminds EROS and BACCHUS (*‹Liber›*). His right hand holds a *stone* or *phiole*; his left *a pair of crucible tongues.* Below this, we see a pistil in a white *vessel*, half-hidden by the foot of SOPHIA and concealed under the hem of her robe (remember double meanings of symbols!) The Twins (Gemini) might also indicate the ‹Two Natures›, or the two paths of initiation as mentioned in the commentary: the solar (‹Cain›) and the lunar one (‹Abel›).

One more explanation could be: The solar SON in the middle of mani-fested Creation, born from the MOTHER resting below, while the FATHER «dwells in the Dark» as say sacred texts. The whole would then be a very carnal – i.e. *visibly incarnate* representation of the Macrocosmos.

PIC. 14 : The Celtic *Triskell* does not occur in sacral Mathematics but in popular handicraft, preferably in silver, corresponding to *feminine nature.*

PIC. 15-A : The Double-helix, ‹enhanced› to become a well-defined geo-metrical figure has its precise mathematical equation as the *Lituus.*

PIC. 15-B : Equally, if the Double-helix is ‹unfolded› to become the *Solar S,* this can be mathematically defined as the so-called *Clothilde.*

PIC. 16: So-called Ramsey-Signs (no public explanations accessible any more). Top line: The ‹Metatron Cube› is a symbol for the SON or Medi-ator; – curiously in line with *I* – i.e. X, i.e. the SON.

PIC. 17: A Celto-Germanic Sun-wagon: The Celestial Sphere and the Sun-Horse are undissolvably tied to the *laws of the physical Quaternary* and its *wheels*, i.e. the physical Cosmos.

PIC. 18-A: The word CHRISMA comes from terms connected to *unction* and *Initiation* (a CHRISTOS is a *Transfigured One*, and as such an *Anointed One!*) – The Chrisma had a great signification already in *Mithraism.* – In the *«dwel-ling of a Mithraic Bishop»* by the Mithræum in *Augusta Raurica* (Basel, Switzerland), was found this little object. Archeologists say: *«This find shows that centuries before Christianization in Switzerland an officer in Roman service (!?) was wearing the Chrisma ... to close his tunica».* – Augusta Raurica is known to have had its own Mithraic Bishop! – *Mindful of the great fancy of the Roman army for the cult of Mithras* we humbly ask: How could a Roman officer charged with annihilation of Celtic lore live in a Celtic High-Priest's home, «close his tunic» with this tiny pin, and then even *drop it*?! – Pic.18-B and pic.25 indicate a much more plausible application.

PIC. 18-B: Lucky amateurs of Symbolism might encounter a large half-relief like in pic. 25, where besides famous *martial Taurobolide Mithras* appear two small images of a *Mithras-Priest* in typical ritual poses: 18-B reminds a medical doctor holding a patient's hand in the position required for some operation. We believe: The (once gilded?) silver needle of Augusta Raurica was used for a ritual act: The extremely small «fibula» was used to effect a small wound and ‹inject› some *scorpion's poison* at the crossing of *Vena Cephalica* and *V. Basilica*, thus effecting a death-like fever-trance *during three days*; see Sanctus Ardoynus: *De Venenis.* Basel, Peter Perna, 1562; – item: SCORPIO). – The little instrument with its chrisma- or scorpio-shape was held as pic. 18-A shows it; the tip was a ‹sun-ray› («of Mithras»?) to apply this ritual little wound as an *Initiation: Bleeding*, as the term still is in today's French with its *enseigner* and *Seigneur*.[67] – For complements to this interesting subject, see commentaries to pictures 18A, 18C and 25. –

PIC. 18C: The other small half-relief (see pic.18A and B) shows the Candidate as a «Parvulus», kneeling. The Mithras-Priest appears to perform the ritual of *imposition of the hands*, plus the one of *signature ⊗ on the forehead* (see text, and the relic of it in today's baptism with water).

PIC. 19: An oft reproduced picture, printed for the first time in famous *Aurea Catena Homeri* (Frankfurt & Leipzig, 1723). – Its title is flanked by the motto : *«If you don't understand what is earthly : how would you understand what is heavenly? ...»* – There clearly is question of a *Compendium of Creation* in view of the Great Work in the *Minutus Mundus* of Alchemy: *«... All and everything is nothing but exactly this all-embracing World Spirit in a more or less condensed state of existence»*. This book connects *The Work* to the school of Pythagoras, with Mose, R. Fludd and H.C. Agrippa. – Expressions like ‹chain› and ‹rings› refer to the interconnection of all creatures and processes in the Universe as well as to the ‹Golden Chain of Universal Tradition› (compare with god OG ‹spewing up› a chain).

PIC. 20: The ‹Power with the Lion Head› – AUTHADES of the *Mysteries of Pistis Sophia*, ascribed to Valentinus. – In Persian Tradition: the ‹Great Charioteer of the *perfect vessel*› (Cosmos); the ‹Æon of Eternity› named *Zervan-Akarana*, i.e. infinity of Space and Time. As the *Lord of this World – Yaldabaoth –* he stands on the Earth Globe (that old Persian Initiates knew the spherical shape of the World is long documented also in the tales of *1001 Nights*). – In his right hand, he sways the whip, in his left a torch; for he is also Lord over cosmic luminaries (‹Saba-auth›). His wings show him to be a celestial creature – angel or demon, hence also *vibrations* – or *waves*. His wavy hair signifies a *Being of Fire*.

Gnostics connected SABAOTH to the *Quaternary,* interpreting him as the *fourth beacon of the Sevenfold Light, which* crushes the human Ego-personality. – The *four characters on his body* then remind the *four seasons,* the four ‹Corners of the World› and the four World Eras (‹Yuga's›). His heightened sex in the precise center of his features highlights both the Duals of contraries and the central cosmogonic ‹dilemma› of the Earth Period: *conscious sexuality and genderism,* the higher octave of which is intensely linked to both divine *Fire Ether* ♁ and *spiritual creativity* ♀.

Other representations show him with a *thunder-bolt on his chest,* the *Crescent of the Moon* between shoulders and wings, and holding the Staff of Power plus another object (a torch) – or else: *«transitioning into eternally young Mithras in the center of the Zodiac»* (see pic. 13 and its comment), and other similar things.

The snake *curled around him five times and crowning his head,* shows that *a fifth force is driving him.* It also indicates Infinity of Time and Space, and moreover the Great Law (ASHA), to which even the macrocosmic Father-God, AHURA MAZDAO, obeys. – Another interpretation to the curled snake might be the supracosmic origin of the «inner-most Mystery» –

AIYN-SOPH-AUR, Prime Source and Navel of Creation, ‹empty› center of the ⑨. – The original statue shown here is preserved in the Vatican!

PIC. 21: The muscles of the heart ventricles run as two spirals in counter-course, «allowing for maximum contraction» (equilibrium of alternating forces rather). The apex of the left ventricle shows the turning-point of the ‹Hyperborean› (centripetal) double-helix ⑨. The turning-point in the apex of the right ventricle – seat of the core vibration of the microcosmos – shows the (centrifugal) ‹Atlantean› Triskell ℛ ; and because of the counter-course of the fibers there results as a *transition between the two*: the Solar *S.* – Regarding *Aquarius Genesis*, these relations are of high significance! (Picture taken from: Th. Schwenk, *Das sensible Chaos* – adapted according to Spalteholz, *Atlas of Anatomy for Surgeons*).

PIC. 22: The fact cannot possibly be ‹pure chance›: that of all beasts an elephant in Europe (!) with his *trunk completely unrolled* was combined with this double-helix, cast open to give the *Solar S.* – The association of the two odd exotic elements is too close one, and so is their common symbolic import, namely *unfolding* of spiritual consciousness in matter.

PIC. 23: When the Seeker becomes a Finder (‹Trobador›), i.e. when he has found his PATH and begins to follow it, he at first does so «in the fear of God» and under the sign of the CROSS – the central light that also is in the center of this image. However: Fear of God does not mean *dreading* a jealous, angry God, but *positive awe* – i.e. *marveling* at the discovery of wonders on one's way. Irradiated by the Seven Lords of Destiny, and in continuous zeal to achieve equilibrium and harmony in all activities (the balance on the table), the Candidate strives for self-knowledge, following the Hermetic sentence: «He who knows himself, knows the Universe!». –

Amidst the world of physical Elements he grows in his love for God, for humanity and for himself. Thus, around him and inside him the union of contraries unfolds in LOVE: This is the Path to Perfection.

Hidden under the mystical concept the present picture offers also the alchemistic one. The latter demands that its Disciple precede the *materia – mater ea* – on each operative step of purification and transformation so that the ‹philosophal earth› becomes the *Philosopher's Stone*, and the operand a ‹Spiritual Master› and then an *Adept of the Stone* – thus a Transfigured one – a CHRIST. Equally Tradition over many centuries postulates that a human who as an ‹Emissary of the realm of Spirit› decides to found and build up a school of initiation (e.g. Pythagoras) must have reached, in autonomous self-initiation, every step or ‹Degree› he wants to animate in his Community, by initiating other humans. – Anything else would be (and often was, too) charlatanry – or illusion!

PIC. 24: The ‹birth of the MITHRAS *out of a rock*› reminds Alchemy and its myth of JESUS born in a *cave*. Mystics compare this ‹cave› to the *heart* as the dark *microcosmic cave* wherein the Redemptor must be born (*Béth-Lèhèm* – semit. *house of flesh*). – Incidentally, the present picture alludes to the *«lozengé»* thus reminding the latter's heraldic interpretation of the *waked Heart* (see commentary to *Thesis 4*, especially on p. 73).

Pɪᴄ. 25: Mithras as a *Taurobolide*. An esoteric exegesis is inevitable here while the exoteric meaning is only alluded to. First of all it is important to underline that there is no question of a «heathen sacrifice of a bull» as some say, but the image of overcoming the *earthly nature* of the Initiand himself, with the bull as ‹scape goat›. It is a rite about self-sacrifice:

«Earth is virginal, and bloody, fiery and fleshy», says a manuscript by *Markus Gnosticus*[68]. *Thus the Neophyte* becomes a *Candidatus* – a *purified* or *pure one* (candidus = pure, white). This is confirmed by a report of the *baptism with blood* (A. Schütze, *Mithras*; loc. cit) – a cross-over between *baptism with water* (*purification* through ‹ablution from sins›) and *baptism with fire* (true dowsing with blood). – This kind of ‹forcible rebirth› is probably what the gospel of John points at (Jo.1:13). –

That the tail of the bull ends in *three ears of wheat*, thus reminding *Ceres* and also *Cain*, does not hamper this understanding. – The *Snake* always accompanying Mithras may mean the macrocosmic vital energy in accordance with *Ophites* – or else EL-SHADDAI thirsting for the blood streaming from the sacri-ficed (sancti-fied) bull (see legend to pic's 18).

The recurring *scorpion* undoubtedly plays a most important role in the cult for Mithras (see pic's. 18.): The description of Ardoynus in his *De Venenis* (loc. cit.) is easily applicable to above interpretation. The scorpion's poison could be kept handy in some phiole into which the little ‹fibula› was dipped for its use: On the Rhine no live scorpions are found.

All this may seem abstruse, but it corresponds absolutely to the character of the Mithras-cult, where devotion, bravery and self-conquest had to be demonstrated (thereof the passion of warriors for this cult). – The relative idiom *«take the bull by his horns»* is beautifully explained on a famous vase of Kreta showing a group of youths as ‹*Tauromachoi*›.–

In the big in-folio of 574 pages: *Santis Ardoyni Pisavrensis medici et philosophi præstantissimi opus DE VENENIS* ... (Basel, H. Petri & P. Perna, 1562), pages 436 through 473 are dedicated to the scorpio: this is more than half of *«Liber Octavus»* – *«Book VIII: About Bites and Pricks of Small Poisonous Animals With or Without a Sting»* – and the largest chapter of the whole tome! All classical Persian Arabic (!) and Greek authors are quoted here, naming medicaments and theriacs (*theriaca*) for the treatment of a prick of a scorpion. The latter is characterized as *«similar to the prick of a big insect»* – hence *not lethal* – namely in the following way:

Symptoms are partly reminding a *trance*, partly a *ritual death*. Surprisingly, there are mentioned *«scorpions with a tail of gold* (the little instrument in pic. 18-A?). – The other «colours of scorpions» correspond to the *progress of the Great Work of Alchemy* (‹Peacock's Tail›), where the scorpion is a symbol for the *Sublimationes*. This corresponds (alchemically) to the *Second Work* – or (mystically) to the second of three *initiation steps* (Degrees). – It may not entirely be excluded that there was a custom to keep in some box scorpions the size of a hand, to partly *tame* them (like tarantulæ today) – and then ‹put them to use› at the occasion. Tamed snakes for the purpose of initiations and other rituals were known in some temples of Egypt (and so are still cobras in the USA). Also there is known the use of scorpions by Romans as an oracle (putting two of them to fight in a pan with sand, and a charcoal fire underneath) …

The vault beyond the *Taurobolide* in pic. 25 is not a cave as is often stated, but a cloudy sky as visible in sculptures of gothic cathedrals, too. Below this heaven, seven stars – the seven ‹planetary-Lords›; – maybe likewise the seven chakras. – SOL and LUNA support the firmament. – *Beyond Heaven*: six trees; in front of each one a flaming altar. – Each of these pairs corresponds to a sacred hill for Canaanite cults as reviled on and on in the Ancient Testament (e.g. 1.Ki.2). – *On Earth*, below the snake, the number of the *seven altars of full self-sacrifice* in honor of the Godhead is complete. This corresponds to an initiation school of today, or any similar Order with seven Degrees. The altar lacking in the apex of the representation is replaced by the main part of the image: Here the Initiand seems to be acquiring the Degree of THE RAVEN, the latter peering down encouragingly from heaven, while the Candidate looks up to him as if asking for help (see pic. 26; *corvus* ↔ *corbus* ↔ *cista Bacchi*).

PIC. 26: The *Scala Philosophorum* of Alchemy has its counter-part in the series of initiations (7 Degrees) in Mithraism as represented in this mosaique (Mithræum of Ostia/Italy). Details to explain these steps would be quite enlightening, but too extensive in the present context. However we need to mention that the top field of the mosaique is no votive tablet but means *attained beatitude* (inscription: FELICISSIMUS). – The latter may be attained by who, finally freed of all seven veils of ignorance, *enters the state of Perfection*: The Adept, the Transfigured in his apotheosis, has sacrificed even on the seventh altar, and thus has become … a *‹god›*!

PIC. 27: The cloister of the cathedral of Tarragona/Spain: Crucifixion scene with the typical deflected wrists; Longhinus and a mercenary with his sponge with vinegar. – Some special features here are: The wake, confident expression on the face of the Christ, and his very visible navel, plus the aureole bearing the *Templar-Cross*: ⊕. – Behind the crucifixion: acanthus leaves. – On both sides of the head of the Christ (on *heraldically inverted sides*, but with the same diameter as the aureole, hence connected to it) a Crescent ☽ and a *Sun* ☉. The latter once more alludes to the Christ as a Sun-God: *Twelve* flower petals stand around the heart of the blossom (the 13th Æon), itself being a Sun symbol ☉. This Sun-flower is thus also a *sun-wheel* ⊛. Adding to this the *neighboring Moon* ☽, there results the *Chrisma* ⊛, so that this representation as well is in harmony with the arch-old star-wisdom around the cosmic Christ. The same capital thus shows the Trinity of Father ☉, Mother ☽ and Son ⊕ – so to speak as an Aiyn-Soph △ ‹standing on its head›. The heads of the three figures and the three *celestial bodies* ☉, ☽ and ⊕ = ♁, *penetrate each other* as two Triangles: △ and ▽ – thus forming the Salomonic seal of wisdom: ✡. This is of great significance! The whole capital is crowned by seven hardly visible, ornamental *Aries-signs*: ♈.

PIC. 28: A picture from the *Chrysopoeia Cleopatræ* – one of the rare (ophitic gnostic) female Alchemists. Specific authors (especially *Zosimos*) mention her as a proven Adept of the Philosopher's Stone. The high significance of this representation is elucidated in *La Clef des Douze Clefs de Frère Basile Valentin / Schlüssel zu den Zwölf Schlüsseln von Bruder Basilius Valentinus* (loc. cit.; only printed edition – Basel, Edition Oriflamme, 2006 – note. 52).

PIC. 29: One of the beautifully painted cassettes at the ceiling of Romanic church St. Martin in Zillis (Grisons / Switzerland) dated from 1130 a.C. The *Light-Force* in the announcement by the angel is shown by THREE *white light-flashes* bolting from his fingertips; – a physically realistic representation as still used in today's *comic strips* (French: *bandes dessinées*, i.e. *ribbons of images* like in Zillis).

PIC. 30: The ambiguity of the Lord of this World, between white and black – Light and Darkness – is clearly represented in this famous graph by ‹Eliphas Levy›, showing the Head of Zohar. – See also The ‹*Mysteries*› *of Pistis Sophia*›, loc. cit.; p. 36.

PIC. 31: Medallion with a representation inspired from Sumer. The inscriptions say, on the left: IALDABAOTH, on the right: HAGIEL(?). – The right hand holds the Staff of Power (see Book of Jasher); the left a little ‹chest› (¿‹cysta›?) reminding the little casket carried by Sumerian ‹gods› on most of their images (¿a ‹radio set›, or a ‹storage battery› for extraterrestrials?).

PIC. 32: Church of Bégude de Mazenc (Drôme Provençale/France): An *Adept of the Philosopher's Stone*, viz. a *Transfigured* of the mystical path, wears the crown of a ‹*Celestial King*›. But at the same time he presents on a silk cushion the *Crown of Thorns* of the ‹*Imitatio Christi*›. He seems to declare: «*Who aspires to the former, must first accept the latter!*»

PIC. 33: This serpent in a pharaonic tomb has the sun-symbol of cosmic Trinity for an eye: ℛ – but as the eye it is, it might also be interpreted as the supra-cosmic eye of the Aiyn-Soph-Aur 𓂀. The former interpretation is supported by the text distinguishable on the margin containing the expressions *Ra-*☉*-neb*: «Re [is] the Lord».

PIC. 34: Cultic and prophane utensils of the Celts are preferably adorned with solar and/or star symbols. Here the typical Celtic *Sun-wheel* on a gilded bronze shield-buckle.

PIC. 35: From R. Schubart: *Der Babylonische Turm* in: ANTAIOS, vol. II., p. 240 ss. (see source index):
Here sacred geometry of the *Tower of Babel* is analyzed with the result that numerology, onomatology, sacred geography and antique Traditions were used as the basis for the conception of this tower. The Babylonian image of the Divine as well as Babylonian Magick also was the frame for Jewish rituals of sacrifice, resp. proportions and outfit of the altar as reported for the ‹first Salomonic Temple› in the Bible. The latter, Archeology proves, was in fact a Syrian (actually Omridic) building, really.

Most interesting here: the obvious *Platonic relations* as given in *Pentateuch* (!), and the *numeric value* 26 (= 2 x 13) throughout the relative verses in AT reporting the Tower, especially *Genesis* 10:1-26 (!), viz. chapters 21-26 (!). – They are accompanied by the copy of Accadian cuneiform

‹*Esagila Tablets*› dealing with the *Temple of Esagila* = *Marduk*. The tablets give the precise measures of the Tower (always connected to the number 26) and mention the spherical shape of the world with the value Pi = 3.1444. – Said article gives all these details together with cosmological exegesis of a three-layer-world, following the concept: *Head– Heart – Body*, as it later appears in the *Tree of Sephiroth* and in Hermetic tradition. Relations between measures, angles and built volumes found by above author are most impressing: Fiery {equilateral} Triangle, Divine Eye, Hexagon, Heptagon, and the number 26 both as flanks of the Heptagon *and* the numeric sum of יהוה – IHVH – the ‹NAME› = ‹SEM› – whence the appellation of *Semites* as THE *People of the Name* (of EL-SHADDAI).

PIC. 36A: Standing waves simultaneously show both a dynamic and a static nature. Understood as *zero-amplitude* (statica, tonica) with three amplitudes of overtones and three undertones, there would result a septenary (quasi a ‹*Lambdoma*›). – All seven together then would represent the tones of a musical octave: In other words, there result *49 planes of vibration*, as declare the *Scholia to the Aquarius Genesis*. Precise values of these ‹over-› and ‹undertones› are as irrelevant as is the non-applicability of the expression «*tones*» on this highest dimensional plane.

PIC. 36-B shows no «zero-wave» (straight line), but the typical cyclic transformation of all creatures (*transgress through the zero-point* = ‹death› viz. birth): The zero-wave is in fact no wave in the usual meaning: Amplitude zero, longitude infinite, frequency zero = ‹eternal life›. – This would then be *New divine Man*: a god immortal, and subject to no more changes.

PIC.37: This Mithraic artifact found in Denmark is full of universal Symbolism (graphically completed by editor of present book):

The *equilateral triangle* (Trinity!) is the basic element of the sun-wheel (divided into six equal parts like the *Chrisma*; – see pic. 18-A). – *On the (heraldic) left*, the typical Mithraic shewbread with its incised equilateral Cross, whence may be concluded that *the right side* was showing the *chalice* (Holy Grail): – Both are part of the Mithras cult. Of it, among others, the ‹Christian› rite of the ‹Last Supper is derived. The center of the triangle is filled by a *Phœnix* (with its feather-crown and specific tail). Beyond the back of the bird slithers the oft mentioned snake – its head probably pointing downwards like in pic. 25. – The whole triangular composition is dominated by a recumbent Crescent (the MOTHER, the soul), a Latin Cross † (4 Elements, Matter, the Son?), and, third, a sun symbol ○ (the FATHER, Spirit). To these correspond the three steps of initiation (triple rebirth according to soul, spirit and body – or: Baptism with ‹Water›, Spirit and ‹Fire›), after which the Transfigured «ascends to the Father» as a ‹Sun› /‹Son› – here as a MITHRAS, or CHRIST).

Here, too, an interpretation taken from operative Alchemy is indicated: The *bread* may correspond to the MATERIA PRIMA ♁, the calix to the VITRIOL; and the three symbols on top to the STONE TO THE RED, the STONE TO THE WHITE, and the ELIXIR. – Or again: MOON, CROSS and CIRCLE as MERCURIUS ☿ in his/her/its three main forms in the Great Work: the chalice indicates SULPHUR; – the shewbread with its CROSS

(Fire, Light!) points at the SALT – *Sal Christi*, or *Christ-al* – as indeed they often are represented and commented in alchemistic literature.

PIC. 38: The alchemist as a bishop reuniting cleft Nature (Dichotomy!) by the Sacred Marriage: Plate XXI of the *Viridarium Chymicum* by Stolcius de Stolcenberg (Frankfurt, Jenni, first printed edition 1623).

PIC. 39: The Platonic bodies as symbols for proportions and rhythms of the Universe and its planetary orbits etc. ...

PIC. 40: The guardian of the Holy Grail has turned his back to both natural magick and IAI, the Dionysian Ass: IAO (see p. 99 and 235 s.): Holding in his hand the fragrant Lotus Flower of the New Born Soul, he goes on and on (see: Lao Dse, *Dao-De-Jing*, ♙ 56, following the German translation by M.P. Steiner in: *Dao-De-Ging – die Gnosis im Alten China.*– Text and commentaries (German). – *Basel, Edition Oriflamme*, 2013. – It says:

« ... *If one have a family and be loved – or if one be lonesome and neglected – If one harvest sympathies and profits – or if one experience hate and losses – If one live in a noble condition and in magnificence – or if one be of a low condition and poor ... – When a human has really achieved IT, he goes on: A Sage is one who has really achieved IT, and goes on ...*

PIC. 41: The Disciple has turned his back to the Black Crocodile – symbol of being born to die on the Wheel of Life and its Dichotomy. He is an Anointed One by his bond with Spirit. Having become a GOLD-HORUS, he holds in his hand the Anch – insignium for attained eternal divine Life!

ALMOST ALL PICTURES TO THE PRESENT BOOK are taken from classic, i.e. baroque or antique, iconography. This is rather inconsequent a fact, given that the text of *Aquarius Genesis* and the commentaries to it use a *very different language* than usual initiation literature. – It therefore is appropriate to emphasize that today's new Era gives way to completely new values and categories – and therefore to a new iconography as well: A world of symbols where – against all odds – mundanely human and humanly divine spiritual aspirations are intricately entwined – dynamically and sometimes harmoniously, but sometimes in a chaotic and even destructive muddle. – But new Creation MUST come out of Chaos!

THE PRESENT IMAGE shows this fact very clearly: A flag featuring a local football-club, hanging at the front side of a christian church and wearing a biblical motto. – This football now clearly shows a *tripartite Yin-Yang-Sign.* – This innovated old symbol signals that the world continues to consist of pairs of Duals – but that there is also *a third way* coming up: The classical EITHER … – OR … is being replaced by a «not-only … but-also … and-moreover … ». – The Universe is on the brink of revealing spiritual forces and vibrations that will completely change our physical world! – Above image also hints at *new DNA chains developing in humanity*!

Appendix 6

Notes to the Scholia

MAGNA MATER THRONANS – Ishtar, Ninti, Ereshkigal or Sophia – on her High Throne: In our days, the deeply veiled Goddess is lifting her seven veils. At her side stands the Sage Initiate, Priest or Priest-King, favored by her and as such *adopted as her child*. He only reaches unto her knee (as did humans compared to giants resp. gods in the beginning of times). Inclining his head, the Initiate seems to clasp his *atramentum*, and some writing tablets already filled.

Half-relief in the kingdom of Osroënia (capitals in the 3rd century: Haran and Odessa. Haran is the cradle of new western spirituality whence Abram started westward. Odessa in turn was one of the top initiation centers from Antiquity into the 9th century a.C., world-wide.

224

Notes To The Scholia

[1] Following *Rabbi Samson Raphael Hirsch* who appeals to the TALMUD as a witness, the word *Thorah* should be read kabbalistically – not only as TAROT, but also as TAU-RHO. – Translated into Greek letters, this means: τρ resp. TP. – Hebrew language formation (hebraization of originally Semitic, Greek or Latin expressions) currently inverts or mirrors original vowels or syllables. The same goes for Yiddish, and – not surprisingly – also for the formation of the American and English languages.

Applying this ‹rule› to the trio of expressions TORAH/TAROT/TAU-RHO – and for TP, there results (through mirroring) the sign used as a paragraph mark *in all computers, worldwide*: ¶ or ¶. – This means: With *each paragraph mark in every text on every Computer throughout the whole world* – unconsciously –*Thorah and Talmud are magically invoked*!

Reading› now the mark ¶ as a *hieroglyph* (i.e. a sacred pictogram), – in minuscules thus τρ — we get ♓, resp., even closer, as ♑ – the zodiacal sign of *Capricorn*. – This is an *Atlantean Era* – and thus the Era where the magic of Kabbalah appears to have its origin!!

[2] See *Corpus Hermeticum, the translation into Latin by Marsilio Ficino* (print of 1503) ; – loc. cit. orig. fol. 14-R ss. (see advertisement at the end of the present book, p. 243).

[2-A] See Max Heindel, *The Rosicrucian Cosmo-Conception*, with relative definitions and descriptions; – and Rudolf Steiner, *How to Attain Knowledge of Higher Worlds* – and other articles and books of R. Steiner.

[2-B] These last two paragraphs clearly aim at the renewal after a cosmic cataclysm: establishment of *«a new Heaven and a new Earth»* (Apoc.)

[3] Quoted in: Fulcanelli, *Mystery of the Cathedrals*. – German edition Basel, Edition Oriflamme 2004. – English translation not recommendable. – Same for: Fulcanelli, *Dwellings of the Adepts*. – Basel, 2008; see ad on p. 242.

[3-A] The word *scienti-fic* expresses by itself the *skillfully artificial* character of academic ‹knowledge›: ...*-fic* from lat. *facio = make-up → fake.*

[3-B] See: P. Martin, *Esoterische Symbolik heute* ... – French: *Symbolisme Esotérique Actuel* .... Basel, Edition Oriflamme, 2010, viz. 2011. (trad.: *Esoteric Symbolism today – in daily life, language and initiation.*)

[4] Bab-El = House of the Sun/God. – Fulcanelli in *Mystery of the Cathedrals* (loc. cit) interprets *Ba-bel* as *Door towards the Lord [of the Sun]*. – In ANTAIOS, Vol. II (in German; ed. Mircéa Eliade and Ernst Jünger; Stuttgart, Klett, 1961), R. Schubart in his article (trad.): *The Babylonian Tower – World-model of Antiquity–* names the Tower of Babel a *«Compendium of universal Symbolism»*, allowing – together with Mithraic Symbolism as below – to draw most rewarding conclusions (see our pic.33). –

[5] See *Popol Vuh, Edición íntegra*. – Clasicos Universales, ISBN 84-95994-26-7 (Madrid, 2005); part III, chapter 5, where we read: *«Alas! – We forsook our language! – What have we done? We are lost. Through what have we been seduced? Just one was our language when we came to Tulán; we were created and shaped after one single form. It is not good what we have done!» – Thus spoke the Peoples under the trees and in the thicket [of the prime forest]* – «¡Ay! ¡Hemos abandonado nuestra lengua! ¿Que hemos echo? Estamos perdidos. ¿Por qué fuimos engañados? Una sola era nuestra lengua, cuando llegamos a Tulán;

habiamos sido creados y formados de una sola forma. No está bien lo que hemos hecho — dijeron los pueblos bajo los árboles y los bejucos ...

[5-A] see: Edmond Bordeaux-Székély, *The Essene Book of Creation*. International Biogenic Society, 1989. – And: The Beatles: *The Yellow Submarine*.

[6] In fact, in ARISTOTELES we read: *«The so-called Pythagoreans were the first to study Mathematics ... and came ... to the conviction that its principles are the principles of whatever exists ...*

«Given thus that everything else in its whole nature appeared to be adapted to Numbers, but Numbers to be the first foundation of whole Nature, they concluded the elements of Numbers to be the elements of whatever exists, and the entire Heaven to be Harmony and Number». (Aristot., *Metaphysica*).

[6-A] Elaine Pagels & Karen L. King, *Reading Judas – the Gospel and the Shaping of Christianity*. – Penguin, 2007.

[6-B] *«Apparently these, too, believed the Number to be the Origin, i.e. [ground-]matter for whatever exists, and for its conditions and its states of being; but the elements of Number to be evenness and unevenness, the former being unlimited, but the latter limited; the (Number) One however to be derived from them both (as it is both even and uneven) – every number instead [to be derived] from the One; – and Number to be, as said before, the entire Heaven».* (Aristoteles, *Metaph*.)

[6-C] *Deus est sphaera infinita cuius centrum est ubique, circumferentia nusquam* – God is an infinite sphere, the center of which is everywhere, and its circumference nowhere. – The origin of this currently quoted phrase is subject to discussions: There are named Jean de Meung, Dante, Master Eckhart, Nicholas de Cues, Giordano Bruno, Alanus ab Insulis, Robert Fludd, Pascal, and Leibniz.

[6-D] See Jesús Zatón, *Geometria Sagrada – Bases naturales, cientificas y pytagoricas*. – French: *Géométrie Sacrée – Bases naturelles, scientifiques et pythagoriciennes*. – Librairie Pentagramme, 2016.

[6-E] Loc. cit. p. 326; quoted in: Jean Markale, *Le Druidisme – Traditions et Dieux des Celtes*. – Paris, Payot. – German: *Die Druiden – Gesellschaft und Götter der Kelten*. – Bertelsmann, München, 1987, p. 229.

[6-F]The last full-length novel of German author Hermann Hesse, the *Glass Bead Game,* was published in 1943 (Penguin, Hammondsworth, 1975). – Also published under the title *Magister Ludi*.

[7] Comp. Papus, *The Kabbalah*; original edition around 1857. – And: A. Frank, *The Kabbalah*; 1st ed. Leipzig, H. Hunger, 1844; English editions available for both.

[7-A] This group reminds the Zoroastrian motto: *«To know, to be able, to want, to dare, to do, to be silent».*

[8] *Nag-Hamadi Scripture of Pistis Sophia by Valentinus Gnosticus.* New English translation: Prof Dr. Hurtak. – See also: *The Gnostic Mysteries of the Pistis Sophia* – comments by Jan van. Rijckenborgh; Haarlem 1992.

In *Dictionnaire Encyclopédique du Christianisme Ancien* (DECA), the Church of Rome names *Valentinus Gnosticus* a heresiarch – i.e. an arch-heretic. On the same page (!) DECA affirms however, Valentinus to have been a Bible Theologist influenced by Platonism, who «*only slightly digressed from still not clearly defined limits of orthodoxy*». Nevertheless he was burned alive in Rome in 160 a.c., for being a Heresiarch. DECA (on p. 2568) gives ample information also on the contents of the ‹*Gospel of Pistis Sophia*›; but uttering doubts about the authorship of Valentinus for whatever text ... – the old: «*what may not be, cannot be!*» ...

[8-A] Peter Selg: *Rudolf Steiner und Christian Rosenkreuz.* – Arlesheim, Verl. Ita Wegmann-Institut, 2011 – ISBN 9783 905919-25-7.

[8-B] C.W. Leadbeater: *Het Astraalgebied – zijn tooneel, bewoners en verschijnselen.* – Amsterdam, Theosophische Uitgevers Matschapij, 1905.

[9] *Dao-De-Ging – Die Gnosis im Alten China. Vollständig neu aus dem Chinesischen ins Deutsche übersetzt und aktuell erklärt.* – Basel, Edition Oriflamme, 2013; – loc. cit., ⚯ 25 and ⚯ 34.

[9-A] See. R. Steiner, *The Secrets of Biblical Genesis.*

[10] See. J. v. Rijckenborgh, *Dei Gloria Intacta – the Christian mystery of initiation to the holy Rosicross for the new age.* – Haarlem, Rozekruis Pers, several languages and reprints.

[10-A] See Werner Greub: *Wolfram von Eschenbach und die Wirklichkeit des Graals* (transl: ... *the reality of the Grail*). – Dornach 1974. – pp. 170 – 300.

[11] Loc. cit., pp. 147 ff.

[12] Academic historians make of ancient Ethiopia an Egypto-Roman province that «became christian during the 4th century», and derive its name from αιθιοπς – aithiops, «meaning blackness of faces (αιθος – aithos, charred black)»!!. – But ops not meaning *face*, but *eye*, a more likely origin appears to be αιθοψ – aithops, fiery, flashing, sparkling. –Ethiopian texts found in Egypt have produced pre-christian and gnostically Christian writings – e.g. the Ethiopian version of the ‹Thora› and the Book ENOCH, authored mainly in the 2nd century b. C. (as writes François Martin in the best (French) edition – Archè, Milano, 2000).

[12-A] We recommend thorough pondering over these somewhat complex parallel relations of terms, concepts and manifestations alike: This is crucial to understand the whole enhancement of, and in, *Aquarius Genesis*!

[12-B] Emanuel Swedenborgh: *De Telluribus in Mundo Nostro Solari, quæ vocantur planetæ: et de telluribus in coelo astrifero: deque illarum incolis; tum de spiritibus & angelis ibi; ex auditis & visis.* – In English known under the short-title: *Earths in the Universe.* – 1st lat. ed. 1758.

[12-C] See: *Dao-De-Ging*, Ed. Oriflamme 2013; loc. cit., ⚯ 73 & commentary.

[12-D] See *Mutus Liber – The Silent Book of Alchemy.* – German ed. Amsterdam, 1991, Edition Weber: Beautiful fac-simile of the full-page copper plates of 1677, with the introduction and comments by E. Canseliet, F.C.H., Disciple of Fulcanelli, and a foreword by Jean Laplace, disciple of E. Canseliet; – French edition with plates in reduced size, black & white only: Paris, Suger, 1986. – Loc. cit., plate I and its commentary.

[13] The book *Chilam Balam of Chumayel* of the Itza-Maya's of Yucalpetén (Yucatán) comments like this: «*Before, there was no Heaven. The* WORD *was born from itself in Darkness* ... – Another translation has: *God the Father was created solely by His own power, in Darkness* ....

[13-A] M. Hirmer: *Aegypten.* – Verlag Hirmer, Munich, 1967.

[14] R. Schubart in: *The Babylonian Tower*; see in-depth comment to pic. 35.

[14-A] *Nag Hamadi Scriptures*; loc. cit.; pp. 115 ss.; – quoted from the *repentance of Sophia* according to the *Secret Book of John*, Nag-Hamadi Codex (NHC) II,1; III, 1; IV,1:

> Then the Mother began to move around. She realized that she was lacking something, as the brightness of her light diminished. She grew dim because her partner had not collaborated with her. –
> I said: «Lord, what does it mean: she moved around?» – The Lord laughed and said: «Do not suppose that it is as Mose said, "above the waters". No, when she realized the wickedness that had taken place, and the theft her son (Yaldabaoth) had committed, she repented. When she became forgetful in the Darkness of Ignorance, she began to feel ashamed. She did not dare to return, but she was agitated. This agitation is her moving around».

[14-B] See *La Clef des Douze Clefs de Frère Basile Valentin – Der Schlüssel zu den Zwölf Schlüsseln von Basilius Valentinus*; – loc. cit., note 108 to that text (comp. note 28 to present pictures).

[15] See: *The Zend Avesta of Zarathustra. Translated from the Zend Hieroglyphs by E. Bordeaux-Szekély*. – International Biogenic Society 1990.

[15-A] See: *The Zend Avesta of Zarathustra*, loc. cit.

[15-B] Thus given in *Sohar*, according to Daniel Matt, famous Sohar-translator into English (see: http://tinyurl.com/h3ufc7v: A YouTube film about *Jewish Gnosis* with, among others, four excellent *Jewish gnostic cabbalists*.

[15-C] But following the modern way of thinking, vibrations (waves) are time cycles: Whence then comes this contradiction? – Answer: Through our low way of thinking which impedes our conceiving *anything*, *what so ever*, without connecting it to some *physically ‹object-ive›* imagination!

[16] *Cologne Mani Codex* (*Codex Manichaicus Coloniensis*, with parts of Mani's life and teachings). – The earliest original Manichean work in Greek. – See: W. Sundermann, *Mani's Revelations in the Cologne Mani Codex and in Other Sources*, in L. Cirillo et al., eds., *Codex Manichaicus Coloniensis*, Cosenza, 1985

[17] Loc. cit.; in its first chapters.

[17-A] We emphasize the difference between *physical* and *material* Creation, the former including also etheric manifestations of every kind.

[18] Robert C. Meurant, *The Myth of Perfection of the Platonic Solids, chapter VII*. – An excellent paper! (on site: http://tiny.cc/mwggry).

[18-A] *Phi* – Φ – the mysterious mediator to reach the *Golden Section*.

[18-B] One should not dismiss these explanations as pure speculations. No, for deep meditative understanding they really show the true course of ‹Spirit coming into Flesh› – now not expressed in mystical stereotypes but in a language where mystic view and precise Science combine, and thereby finally can be mentally *apprehended*, and thus spiritually *comprehended*.

[19] *Popol Vuj* – loc. cit., p. 153-155. – See also Fulcanelli's book: *Mystery of the Cathedrals*, chapter *Mystery of the Cathedrals*, section VII. French Rev. 22:16, for «*root*» uses «*drageon*» = «*a root runner*» (assonance to «*dragon*»). – This reptile today has re-acquired a meaning beyond its myth (comp. the *Tablets of Emerald of Toth, the Atlantean*, Tablet VIII; –

and also: R. Steiner: *The Gospel of John.* – Hamburg, 1908).

[19-A] A term absent in English Heraldry: German Heraldry calls a multiply *lozangé* escucheon ‹*geweckt*›, thus offering an alchemistico-phonetic cabalism with «*Wecken*» *(cake with a rhomboïd pattern)*, and *geweckt (wake)*. Now, as every *escucheon* is a symbol for the carrier's *heart*, a *lozengé* is also a *waked heart*, ready to receive the baptisms of Water and Fire ...

[20] See. *Corpus Hermeticum*, in German after the Latin translation by M. Ficinus, loc. cit supra. – Everard's English translation of 1650 is spurious.

[21] R. Steiner: *The Orient in the Light of the Occident.* Dornach, 1942. – And also: R. Steiner: *The Gospel of John.* – Hamburg, 1908.

[22] Therefore the fact that natural shielding of the Earth against sunrays is diminishing, has a much higher than just earthly impact, namely a cosmic and even macrocosmic one: The new Era is indeed the Age of *Incarnation of the Christ Spirit* (a vibration!) not just in *one human*, but *in all humans of good will.* – Whoever will meet given preconditions regarding *conscious growth in Knowledge and Love*, will be admitted also to the Sun-Mystery of the CHRISTOS. – Who will prove *unable or unwilling* to follow this invitation, will inevitably be «*burnt to ashes*».

[23] Physical appearance of the cosmic CHRISTOS originally was the basis of today's Christendom. But at the same time it meant to be the end of an Era during which Love (i.e. the Christ-Power) had to be prepared *from the outside by an Elohim* (JHVH), until humanity would have reached the maturity to receive directly, and grasp freely, this Mystery: With the *rise of the ‹Star of Bethlehem›* ✭ commenced the Era where the solar Love-Fire of the CHRISTOS *can be experienced by every single human, and be realized by every single individual*, too. As a matter of fact, here lies the tragic of Judaism as well as of Christianism: that the *Disciples of both* didn't fully cope with the impact of this event: the beginning of a new cosmic Era (PISCES!) for a first spiritual ascent of Humanity.

A. Schütze adds (following a book by E. Bock, *Das Alte Testament und die Geistesgeschichte der Menschheit* – (trad. *The Old Testament and spiritual history of Mankind)*– translated ad-hoc:

«*Strictly orthodox Judaism increasingly saw Sun-veneration as an abomination, because it (Judaism) more and more limited itself to a one-sided, image-less, inwardly moral and psychic piety ... The fight between ‹Heathendom› and ‹Judaism› ... has repeated itself in the Church of Christianism. This fight ended with a provisional victory of ‹Jewish› spirituality, i.e. a spirituality alienated from Cosmos. True Christendom instead unites picturesque tenderness for Nature with the rigidity of a purely spiritual inward piety of prayers.*»

[24] This explains relations between the *macrocosmic Seven Spirits before the Throne of God*, and the seven *cosmic* ELOHIM. The *Seven Planets* are their visible *macrocosmic* parallel – *as mediators for intra-cosmic forces and vibrations animating the Macrocosmos.* Their relative *supra-cosmic* antagonists are the seven invisible vibrations (each of them again fanned out sevenfold) with *their* seven fundamental sounds, forces and colours – all combining to give the ‹white gold› of the all-embracing, divine vibration also named *Septuple Spirit* (see commentary to *Thesis 2*).

[25] Quoted in: G.R.S. Mead, *The Mysteries of Mithras.* – Edmonds, USA, 1993.

[26] See also: Greub, *Wolfram von Eschenbach und die Wirklichkeit des Graals.* – Dornach, Freies Geistesleben, 1981.

[27] Throughout this book, conventional language often lacks adequate expressions for new concepts and relations un-described ever before. It therefore was necessary to create corresponding new terms. – Lectors are bidden to accept and follow these ‹invented› idioms.

[28] Kabbalistic Temurah regarding letters and numbers very similarly says: «*Aleph* – א, *the 1 – is death and life: Unthinkable abstract principle of whatever is, and of whatever is not ... – Teith,* ט *(9), archetype of primitive femininity, attracts Life, hence shapes will evolve, step by step. – Jod:* י *(the 10, or ‹hand›) is the counter-part of the One in this game: without it nothing could exist. – Beith* ב *is the archetype of all ... containers: the 2, without which nothing could exist*».

[28-A] → J.F. Blumrich, *Kásskara and the seven worlds. History of humanity according to the tradition of the Hopi Indians* (1979).

[29] In the *Book of the Chilam Balam of Chumayel* conveying Traditions of the Itza-Maya, Venus is named «*the jewel on the chest of the Sun*».

[30] Following M. Heindel, R. Steiner and others, at the beginning of each Era the preceding ones are recapitulated in ‹quick-motion› – akin to a human embryon mutating from a monocyte to a fishy and an amphibian state and to human – *with in between the reptilian phase as a divider in evolution* – and with related particularities such as the reptilian brain.

[31] Nikolai Rainow, *Legends of the Bogumiles*; quoted in the periodical *Pentagram*, Nr. 3/2006, p.13.

[31-A] The book *Nag-Hamadi Scriptures*, loc. cit. p. 119, gives some details: «*Yaldabaoth said to the rulers around him: "Come, let us make a human being after the likeness of God {as reflected by the waters}, and that it be similar to us, so that this human image may give us [the(ir)] Light" ... »* – enumerating a multitude of demons contributing to this: « *... and the mother of them all is Matter ... she stands in their midst, for she is illimited and mates with all ... and by her all are nourished. The four top demons are ... {sorrow, pleasure, desire, fear}* ». *From these four demons come the passions ... »* {follows the latter's enumeration}.

Now a *spiritual human body* is created, but is unable to move. The ‹Mother› thus bids the ‹merciful FATHER-MOTHER› for help: He sends 5 lights to YALDABAOTH, in place of the latter's 5 angels. These enjoin Yaldabaoth to breathe some of his spirit (which comes from his mother, but he ignores that) into the face of Adam. – Now the body begins to move and is powerful and illuminated: «*Adam was* more *intelligent than the Creator and First Ruler* (YALDABAOTH). *The Archons tried to annihilate Adam, and throw him into the deepest depths of Matter ... the* FATHER-MOTHER *sent him a help – Life ... and ... taught Creation about the Path leading upwards ... »* – {Ensues creation of Eve-Zoè} ...

[31-B] See P. Martin, *Esoterische Symbolik Heute / Symbolisme Ésotérique Actuel*, loc. cit.; – in both German and French editions on pp. 52 s.

[32] Henricus Cornelius Agrippa ab Nettesheim, *Occulta Philosophia* ... – Colonia, Sotèr, 1531. – English: *Three books of occult philosophy*, annotated by Donald Tyson (2005; – ISBN 0-87542-832-0) In one of the corresponding pictures (II, p. 164), Man stands *upright inside a* SQUARE-below the Eye ◉ and with the CROSS **+** on his Solar-plexus. – On p. 166, he stands with spread legs in a PENTAGRAM – with ☉ on the Solar-plexus, ☽ on Sexus, the five Planets surrounding him. – On p. 167 he stands spread wide in a *lozangé Square*, surrounded by the twelve signs of the Zodiac; on the next, he stands half-spread as a slim Pentagram inside the CIRCLE (Zodiac) with the CROSS, ⊕. – In the *sixth picture* (II, 170), he stands as a Cipher ONE I inside a magic Square of sixteen congruent TRIANGLES in which there are inscribed also the RHOMBUS ◊, and the LIGHT-CROSS ✕, and the CROSS OF MATTER **+**.

[32-A] This is VENUS COLUMBA (see text). – The Name JESOUS moreover also means *The Fiery One* (*Jès – Fire*).

[32-B] See J. v. Rijckenborgh, *Dei Gloria Intacta*. Haarlem, Rozekruis Pers, several languages and reprints since 1977; – pp. 88-93, re. *Venus-Initiation.*

[32-C] These elucidations must still leave untold many things, just because many things remain unspeakable, and accessible to inner vision only ...

[33] H.P. Blavatsky, *Universal Doctrine*, 1893; Vol.I: The Stanzas of Dzyan.

[34] See the beautiful cassettes at the ceiling of the gothic church of St. Martin in Zillis (Switzerland), dating from 1130; – pic.29 in the present book.

[35] See Appendix 3-B: *Cain and Abel Today.*

[36] The term *«intelligent» here means a combined activity of head and heart.* The term *slyness* means the sort of intellect issuing from animally human blood and spinal fluid (→ ‹Kundalini›). – See also: R. Steiner: *the Temple Legende and the Golden Legend* – concerning so-called «Atlantean Slyness» of some of the first Post-Atlantean tribes.

[37] The lunar Goddess (ISHTAR-ISIS-ASHERA) reflects, among other, names in the Old Testament like ASHER, a ‹tribe from JACOB›. – ISHTAR, i.e. Iset-Er or SUBLIME ISIS is the ever pregnant, ever maidenly, Goddess-Mother of Sumerians, the SHAKTI of Hindu's. – PHIL-ISHTAR, i.e. PHIL-ISET-ER, Eng. *Phil-Iset-ine*, became *Palest-ine*. – ‹Christian› MARIA is derived from MAMA / MARI, the Babylonian Mother-Goddess *par excellence*: She is ERESHKIGAL-NINTI of Sumer. ISET is her Egyptian name, changed into ISIS by Greeks and Romans (IS = Moon; -t = feminine ending; – also SITA of the Hindu's). All these stand on the recumbent Crescent, with an Aureole of 12 stars around their head Therefore, ISIS became MOTHER MOON, spouse of FATHER SUN (RE,), recalling the *Tabula Smaragdina* of *Hermes Trismegistos*. Thus the «small celestial light» ☽ like a loyal spouse follows the Great Sun, Great Helios or SHEM-ER (Sublime Sun) that became ‹SUM-ER›. ISET-ER was revered as the greatest ‹female› manifestation of God, and SHEM-ER as His greatest ‹male› manifestation, *but for the Initiated never really as God Himself.* – This has nothing to do with human genders!

Interestingly, *Mercurius* (*Hermes*) is both a member of the *Trinity*, and as Planet in our solar system, *«the Son closest to the Father».* – He therefore has the significance of THE SON – and that of a Mediator as mentioned by all pantheons (precisely Hebrew METATRON). As such we find him in Alchemy, and again as another analogism to the CHRIST in our solar system.

[38] See: I. Finkelstein, N.A. Silbermann: *The Bible unearthed. – Archeology's New Vision of Ancient Israel and the Origin of the Sacred Texts.* – The Free Press Inc., 2002. – And in *Genesis of the Grail Kings*, loc. cit..

[39] I. Finkelstein and N.A. Silbermann loc. cit., give archeological proofs that SALOMO – if at all – lived *centuries later* than insinuated by biblical ‹History›; – and also that the little nomad tribe of Hebrews at that time had neither the skills of an ‹Intelligentsia› (writing, architecture etc.), nor the means (money, transport facilities, horses, labour force etc.) to build such a big temple. – Nor could they realize the great military exploits mentioned in the Bible. Moreover, the *notoriously forbidden iron tools* did not yet exist! We thus may rightly sustain the «40'000 horses of Salomo» to be an antihistoric fiction as are the «1000 spouses» with whom, following a Roman catholic Encyclopedia, he *«never did anything indecent»* – *«nihil contra pudorem fecit».* A statement (to comment it mildly) hardly compatible with usages and traditions of the Orient at any time …

[40] A. Schütze: *Mithras.* – loc. cit.; pp. 156 s.

[41] Jonathan Tubb: *Peoples of the Past: Canaanites.* – ISBN: 9780714127668.

[42] See: *Reading Accadian Prayers and Hymns,* edited by Allan Lenzi; necnon (Collective): *Sumerian Hymns and cult songs,* at: http://libroesoterico.com/biblioteca/ Textos%20sagrados%20y%20antiguos/Sumerian%20Hymns.pdf

[43] Thus quoted in Laurence Gardner: *Genesis of the Grail Kings, loc. cit.*

[44] See: Rudolf Steiner, *The Temple Legend and the Golden Legend.* – Loc. cit., pp. 219 and 235.

[45] See: 4.Mo.21:8-9 – and also: *Der Schlüssel zu den Zwölf Schlüsseln von Bruder Basilius Valentinus/ La Clef des Douze Clefs de Frère Basile Valentin* (French and German), loc. cit, supra – note 52, p.299.

[45-A] See: Fulcanelli, *Dwellings of the Adepts,* vol.I, part II, sect. VI:
«This image for which only a few vague indications and simple hypotheses exist, never was an idol as thought by many, but only a full emblem of the secret tradition of the Order [of Knights Templar], used mainly outwardly, and as an esoteric paradigm, as a seal of the Order and as a sign of affiliation. Reproduced on jewelry, on front gablets of Commanderies, and on tympanons of chapels, it consisted in an equilateral triangle pointing downwards: the hieroglyph for WATER, *the first created element according to Thales of Milet who affirmed:* «God is this Spirit who created all from Water». – *A second, smaller equilateral triangle pointing upward was put in its center, in place of the nose in a human face. It stood for* FIRE, *or more accurately, Fire enclosed in Water, or the divine spark, i.e. animation of the flesh:* LIFE *inflated into* MATTER. *«On the basis of the inverted triangle stood a very large* ᚻ – *the Greek ‹Èta›, the horizontal beam of which was cut in its middle by a small circle. This symbol in hermetic steganography designs Universal Spirit, ‹Creator Spiritus› – God. –*
«Inside the big water-triangle, just above the fire-triangle, one could see,

like eyes, [heraldically] on the left, a circle with a crescent Moon in it: ☽, *on the right, the sun-symbol* ☉. *– Directly below the small triangle there was added the cross standing on a circle,* ♁, *thus producing the double hieroglyph of the active principle of Sulphur* ♀ *combined with the passive principle and solvent of all metals – ‹quicksilver›. Oft there were added some lines pointing downwards from the tip of the water-triangle, which a profane spectator would not recognize as the expression of a light-beam, but as sort of a little beard ...*

«As a purely hermetic expression regarding the Great Œuvre [of Alchemy] the expression of Baphomet *derives from the Greek root* Βαφευς, *dyer, and* μης *for* μην, Moon; *except one prefere* μητηρ, *genitive* μητρος *– mother or womb, which gives the same moon-like meaning ...*

«Βαφειν means dip and dye ... , leading us thus to symbolic baptism (Mètè), equally expressed by the term of Baphomet ... *– This, then, is the Holy Grail containing the evcharistic wine: liquid of spiritual fire; – vegetative live and vivifying fluid, instilled into physical things».* – (End of quotation from Fulcanelli).

[46] See Edmond Bordeaux-Székély: *The Essene Book of Creation*. – International Biogenic Society, 1989.

[47] *The Mysteries of Pistis Sophia*. – loc. cit., p.36

[48] *The Mysteries of Pistis Sophia*. – loc. cit., p.30

[49] Fulcanelli, *Mystery of Cathedrals*., chapter *Paris*, section III-B.

[50] Grimm-Brothers: *The tale of Snow-white and the seven dwarfs*. – The name *Snow-white* aims at the purity of the Original Soul in Paradise. The ample version of the story like the famous animated film by Walt Disney, does not begin in Paradise though, but with the ragged human soul in our physical world of ‹Good› and ‹Evil›, under the dominion of jealous JHVH-Yaldabaoth (*«Who is the fairest of them all!?»*). – The *Prince* on his white (*solar*) horse plays the role of the *Sun-Hero* – the CHRISTOS.

[51] See *Nag Hamadi-Codex* II, 5, translated by Roger A. Bullard – contained in creation myths: *Hypóstasis tōn Archontōn* – meaning: *The essence/ characteristic of the Archons.* (*Hypóstasis* = substance, foundation, realty, ranking. – *Archontes* = Governors, Powers). – An extensive text about the Archons and creation of Man is contained in: *Nag Hamadi Scriptures, ed. Marvin Meyer*, New York, Harper Collins, 2008; – loc. cit., pp. 115 ss., chapter: *The Secret Book of John*, subchapter: *The Human appears.*

[52] Many explanations for the term *Ouroboros* – ουροβορος – are possible, and this also in parallels, not just as alternatives: *«Ouro-» alone* can mean: *space, distance, limitation, Good Wind (Spirit!), luck, the good moment, a mountain, guardian, protector or supervisor, a drawn furrow or ditch* – and also: *(a)ur = Fire/Light.* – The Etymology: ϝορσϝορς (pronounced *vorsvors*): *Boros* alone has an arch-Celtic root: *bèra*; – i.e. *bear* and *birth*; – and also the one of *«vor»* (ϝορ) *– de-vour (!), gulp down.* – *Ouroboros therefore contains parallels to the Hindu god Vishnu ... —*

[53] Sun Dse: *The Art of the Right Strategy.* Translated also as: *Truly overcomes who never fights.*

[54] See *Appendix 3-A* in present book: *The End of Wrath, or why Eve was created.*

[54-A] Normal people never create a thought, but just *undergo instigations*!

[55] *The ‹Mysteries› of the Pistis Sophia* – loc. cit, p. 79.

[56] The most common name – ‹Devil› can be explained etymologically in many ways: Latin *Diabolus* (from Greek διαβολος – *dia-bolos*, French *diable*, ital. *diavolo*) – may be understood as *The One hurled down* (from Heaven). – The Old-German *Deubel* (in vernacular: *Tüüfel, Düübel* a.s.f.) might rather derive from a solar term: *Ziu-Bel – Deus Beël – God Baal*. – Christendom – along with Judaism – would have perverted the *solar God of Light* into the *Lord of Darkness*. In catholic Christianity the latter even has a higher ranking than Jesus Christ Himself (see. P. Martin, *Symbolisme Esotérique Actuel;* – loc. cit. chapter 8.8, and picture). – *Beel, or Baal,* although strongly condemned especially in late Jahwistic teaching – is the ‹Sun-God›, to which also relates the famous Tower of Babel: «*Ba-B-El – door towards the Lord God*», viz. *House of God* – see note n° 4 above.

Concerning YALDABAOTH (another ‹cherished› Devils figure), see comment to Thesis 7 of *Aquarius Genesis*, along with pic. 20 *and its legend.* – French *diable* moreover indicates APOLLO (another *Sun-God!*), meaning the cult of ABELIO *in the Pyrenees during the first centuries of our Era*: DZJU-ABELIO. Here we prefer the term *Ziu* (for lat. *Deus/Zeus*) – ‹pagan› Father-God, thus cosmologically the Sun again. – ZEUS JUPITER of Antiquity could also be heard as DZJU-PATER, or, leaning towards Pelasgian or Sanskrit: ZJU-PITR, *God-Father* ...

Another, relatively young but somewhat doubtful, source for the term *Diabolus*, corresponding to what is said above, could be Islamic *Dzju-Iblis*. This would prove the circumspection with which «orthodox» religious language inside the judeo-islamo-christian ‹concordat› has been, and still is, thoroughly ‹harmonized›.

The denomination AHRIMAN, from Persian AHURA MAINYIU, already commented on above – besides YALDABAOTH – occurs particularly often in esoteric texts of the 20[eth] century. Both do not mean antagonism of physical Light and Darkness, but rather the opposition of fullhearted YES and extreme emotional negation. – In short, the Dual of Knowledge and Love (‹Light ›) – and Ignorance and Hate (‹Darkness ›).

Among AZTECS viz. INCAS, this ‹Counter-God› was TEZCATLIPOCA. – Many further expressions can be derived from the *fight of established institutions* against teachings with some ‹sun-cult› as their core doctrine. – Hence veneration of the ‹Solar Light› that is *all Love* – and understood *by every inner priesthood* as source of *Gnosis* – the one positive Religion aiming at true *Love, Freedom, Brotherhood and Redemption of all humans of good will.* – Actual veneration of the Sun as a natural body by true Initiates was meant allegorically; – but behind this allegory stands a clear inner realty: The one true innermost source of whatever can be expressed by the term of LIGHT in its highest sense, namely as the ● which *on the cosmic plane* is indeed emanated by the cosmic Sun (see text!).

[57] First Theosophist Valentin Weigel (1533-1588): *Das Buch vom Gebet («Gebetbüchlein»).* (transl.: *The Book About Praying*). 1st printed edition since its *editio princeps* in 1612, Basel. Edition Oriflamme, 2006; p. 139.

[58] ‹*Gospel*› *of Pistis Sophia.* – loc. cit. p. 62

[58-A] *Dao-De-Ging* – *Die Gnosis im Alten China.* Here translated ad-hoc into English from the German edition by Edition Oriflamme, loc. cit.

[59] The book *Nag-Hamadi Scriptures* {loc. cit.; p. 115 ss.}: gives a passage from the *Secret Book of John*, demonstrating shape and impact of the Kingdom of Wrath under the regiment of the Prince of this world – YALDABAOTH. The enumeration of the names of the ‹Powers and Rulers› under YALDABAOTH is interesting, as many of them re-appear in biblical and other myths which are *younger* than the final version of biblical Genesis, while the present enumeration is older. It says:

«[Yaldabaoth] is the first ruler, the Archon who took great power from his mother. Then he left her and moved away from the place where he was born. He took control and created for himself other Æons with luminous fire which still exists. He mated with the mindlessness in himself and produced authorities for himself.

«The name of the first is ATHOT, whom generations call the [reaper]. The second is HARMAS, who is the jealous eye. The third is KHALILA OUMBRI. The fourth is YABEL. The fifth is ADONAIOS who is called SABAOTH. The sixth is CAIN, whom generations of peoples call the sun. The seventh is ABEL ... The ninth is JOBEL {*Yubal!?*} ... The twelfth is BELIAL, who is [Lord] over the depth of the underworld.

«YALDABAOTH installed seven kings, one for each sphere of Heaven in order to govern the Seven Heavens – and five to reign over the depths of the Abyss. He shared his fire with them, but he did not give away any of the light-power he had misappropriated from his mother. For he is ignorant darkness.

«When Light mixed with Darkness it made Darkness shine. – When Darkness mixed with Light it dimmed the Light and became neither light nor darkness, but rather gloom. – This gloom Archon has three names: The first name is YALDABAOTH, the second is SAKLA, and the third is SAMAEL. He is wicked, with the mindlessness within him {compare to what *Pymander* tells *Hermes* about *entities lacking Mind!*}

He said: „*I am God, and there is no other God besides me*", for he quite ignored where his own power had come from.

«The rulers each created seven powers for themselves, and the powers created six angels each, until there were 365 angels. {The seven high powers became the seven days of the week!}. Their names: The first is ATHOT, and he has the face of a mutton. The second is Eloaios... the face of a donkey. The third is ASTAPHAIOS ... the face of a hyena; – the fourth is IAO {another allonym for JHVH, as are the next} ... the face of a snake with seven heads; – the fifth is SABAOTH ... the face of a snake; the sixth, ADONIN ... the face of a monkey. – *The seventh*: SABBATAIOS ... the face of flaming fire. – Yaldabaoth has many faces more ... he could show whatever face he wanted ... {In another list of 7 more powers, 5 more allonyms for JHVH appear}. –

«Yaldabaoth organized everything after the pattern of the first Æons that had come into being, so that he might create everything in an incorruptible form. Not that he had seen the Incorruptible Ones. Rather the power that is in him, that he had taken from his mother, produced in him the pattern for the World Order.

«When he saw the Creation surrounding him, and the throng of angels around him that had come forth from him, he said to them: *„I am a jealous god, and there is no other god besides me".* – But in announcing this, he suggested to the angels with him that *there is* another god. For, if there were no other gods: of whom should he be jealous?»

(End of quotation from Nag-Hamadi Scriptures).

[60] This indicates the cycle of a ‹Day of Revelation› or ‹Day of Brahma›, described by the seven planetary phases which again are divided into seven periods, according to Universal Doctrine. Compare Max Heindel: *The Rosicrucian Cosmo-conception*, and the works of R. Steiner, along with the theosophical teachings of H.P. Blavatsky, and others.

[61] The fact that biblical History in the AT evolves according to Celtic norms and usages is described comprehensively by *Jean-Paul Bourre* in his book: *Les Celtes dans la Bible* (Paris, Laffont, 1990). The ‹GEIS› is sort of a curse with its menace bound to *unavoidable conditions*. This can be observed for both the situation in ‹Paradise› (either eternal unconsciousness in ‹sleeping death› or the wheel of births and deaths with their painful physical experiences) – and for the curse of the 13th Fairy in the tale of *Sleeping Beauty* (‹self-caused› death by the *thorn of the spindle* at the age of sexual maturity). A death that cannot be eschewed – but tempered by the *protective spell* of the 12th Fairy (salvation through LOVE'S first kiss). – The notion of ‹GEIS› rather frequently appears in Celtic lore – also in the *Edda* – and explains itself as an onomatopoiesis from the cry of the *jay* (from French: *geais* – both the same phonetics: GEIS).

By the way: *Initiation to the 8th and 9th Spheres* in Hermetism is conveyed by a kiss as well! – See Note 65 hereafter.

Bourre in his book *dismantles* a two-hundred years old doctrine about ‹Indogermanics›, contrived by school-historians who affirm the Celts to have migrated *from the far East* to Gallia and Britannia (the regions where prime Celtic culture and lore were the most firmly rooted and influential!):

«It is a historical fact: The so-called Indo-Europeans reached Asia Minor around 3000 b.C. – They are part of the first wave of migrations originating from [Atlantis and] North-West Europe – C'est un fait historique: Les ‹Indo-Européens› ont atteint l'Asie Mineure 3000 ans avant J.-C. Ils appartiennent au premier courant migrateur, venu du Nord-Ouest de l'Europe». – They really were the few ‹western› survivors of the Atlantean Catastrophe, and as the *carriers of the flare of ancient wisdom* carried the Eternal Knowledge across the devastated and spiritually impoverished world: From the coasts of the Ocean eastwards to the Indian Ocean – and back again some 2000 years later: from India to Spain. – One of the remnants of that tradition is the cult of the *Inextinguishable Light* in Christian and Islamic churches/mosques, viz. the *Pure Eternal Fire* on the altars for AHURA MAZDÃO in Ancient Persia. This cult hardly differs from Chaldean Tradition and its *Star-Wisdom*.

To every clearly thinking human it is obvious that the different regions in the Near East, bearing names like *Galatia, Galicia, Galilea, Golan, Gilead* etc. did not *give* their name to, but *received* it from, those Westerners, – just as settlements in America since the 16th century were named after the origins of the settlers (see *La Clef des Douze Clefs* ... – *Der Schlüssel zu den Zwölf Schlüsseln* ... – loc. cit., note 75, Ger. & Fr.).

[62] Jacob Bœhme: *Forty Questions Regarding The Soul.* – By this phrase, Bœhme proves that he was initiated into the Great Work of Alchemy!

[62-A] See J.W. v. Gœthe: *Doctor Faustus, Part I.* – The scene in the ‹witch's kitchen› completes, and explains itself by, the present text.

[63] See *Jubiläums-Gesamtausgabe 400 Jahre Rosenkreuzer-Manifeste (1614, 1615, 1617)* ... *in softly modernized German.* – Basel, Edition Oriflamme, 2016; – loc. cit. p. 230: *Antwort der ... Bruderschaft deß RosenCreutzes auf Etzlicher an sie ergangene Schreiben* (ed. Molter).

[64] In the NT, Jesus says: *«I have not come to invalidate the Law, but to fulfill it».* – What Law is He referring to? In biblical book *Exodus*, Mose brought *only one law*. – When he had «broken the first tablet», he «wrote down» the version known as the *Ten Commandments*. This new Law however, the Eldest of the tribe(s) and the priests subdivided into *a hundred laws* preserving their particular ambitions and interests. Since the era of Pharisees, a numberless amount of subdivisions and interpretations (Mishnah, Mitzvoth, Talmud) came up. – Most probably Jesus meant the Unique Universal Law He transmitted to His Disciples – and in the meaning as reported by the *Essene Gospel of Peace* (loc. cit.). – The *Secret Book of Cathars* denounces the Laws brought by Mose as given by Yaldabaoth, i.e. «Sathanas» – possibly because of the words of Paul in Rom 7:7-8: *«I'd have not known misdeed but for the Law; – and desire not either, had not the Law said: "You shall not desire". For without a Law, misdeed is dead».* – Real autonomy erases complexes of indignity and guilt, giving way to realization of the One Commandment given by Jesus.: *«... and your neighbor as yourself»*: Thus, «misdeed» is dead, not due to fear of punishment or damnation, but out of Love for God and ‹neighbors'›!

[64-A] See: *Confessio Fraternitatis RC (1615)*, as per note 63 here-before.

[65] See *Interrogatio Johannis, The Secret Book of Cathars.*

[66] Rœlof van den Brœk: *Hermes Trismegistus. – Inleiding, Teksten, Commentaaren.* – Amsterdam, In de Pelikaan, 2006. – loc. cit.. p.234: *De Inwijding in de achtste en de negende sfeer.*

[67] *Mysteries of Pistis Sophia* – loc. cit., part II: *Questions of Maria Magdalena regarding the soul*; p. 133 – 143.

[68] The *Dictionnaire Roman, Wallon, Celtique et Tudesque* ... (Bouillon, 1777) has : SEIGNÉ, ou SAIGNÉ, (i.e.) *marqué: signatum*!

In medicine, the ancient French term *seigner* (today: *saigner*) meant *to bleed a person.* – In both politics and butchery instead it meant: *to drain the blood off.* – The *result of ritual bleeding* is there named *Seing* or *Signe*: English *sign.* – The Nouveau Dictionnaire Français-Latin ... (Paris, 1833), under the term of SEIGNEUR (*i.e.* Lord, but etymologically: the one who *marks* a person, e.g. a slave, by a *bloody sign*) has also the translation of: *Summus rerum moderator* – the tenant of the highest Degree of initiation in the *cult for Mitras* – i.e. the one who *orders, directs, and starts up the highest acts* as does a Priest and *Hiero-phant* on a cultic (ritual) plane,.

[69] Quoted in: M. Berthelot: *Les Origines de l'Alchimie.* – Paris, 1885; – Reprint: Osnabrück, Zeller, 1966 (in French). – Loc. cit., chapter: *Sources Gnostiques*, p. 63.

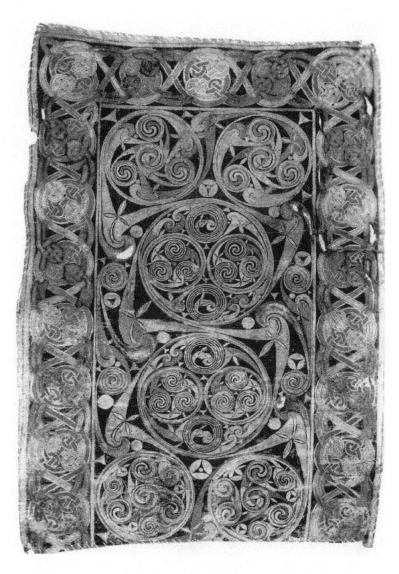

An illuminated page from the *Book of Durrow*, composed around 675 a.C.
in Ireland: The first richly illustrated British MS with the four Gospels
and some additional texts. – Older than the famous ‹*Book of Kells*› (8th century) these colours and the composition of interwoven *Celtic Triskells*
and *Gothic plant-ornaments* remind of some patterns of the culture of
the peoples of Mayapan flourishing at the same time.

Masonico-alchemistico-Rosicrucian Epitaph of a knightly, most probably Templarian Lady (the wrath): Cemetery at the former Sun-Sanctuary near Montluel, Dépt. Ain/France; (El = *Helios, Sun*; *luel* – maybe *lev-El, = lever du soleil = sunrise* ?). Above the ‹*Square of the Building*›, and carried by the *Four Pillars* (devotion, joy, steadfastness and serviceability), are arranged the four steps of purification, birth of the New Soul, ‹Spirit-Birth› and Transformation, with a Phœnix soaring up from a heap of blazing coals (Transfiguration). – The whole composition is crowned by the *Occitan Rosicross of The Temple*, protected by a tower with *twelve pinnacles.*

Epilogue: Up to the focus of Life!

When human occupants of a *microcosmos*, have accumulated during an uncountable number of lives an unconceivable amount of experience, and feel the archetypical longing for a definitive goal – a definite focal point for all their thoughts, feelings and aspirations – then it may occur that ‹inside him or her› a new, higher intelligence awakes. They then *understand and experience* the call of the central Love-Fire emanating from the Heart of the Universe. In it, they *vaguely perceive* the primary source of whatever may be called Light and Life – the Aiyn,: ξ – and suddenly they are able to *recognize* THE PATH leading there: At once they perceive the effects of both this light and this focus calling them – attracting them – inspiring them!

What is it that reacts to this call?

It is a tiny little relic of a divine essence that has survived in the human heart – in spite of degeneration and education, and against all egocentric ambitions and suspicions – like a little seed waiting for an opportunity to revive ... and to re-establish its original glory, *as it was in the Beginning*!

Thus awaken new senses, a new consciousness, and a new will. – Thus develops a new way of thought, with new words, and new deeds. Even with unchanged daily activities and prophane occupations, the ordinary worldly human has become *a neophyte* who, if he dares to step on the *Path towards the Focus of Life*, following it as *a Candidate* in every moment – steadfast and in joy – *must and will*, by virtue of universal spiritual Laws in time become a *Master*: a Master above and beyond whatever is mortal in him; – a Master of the *Spiritual Philosopher's Stone*!

Who strives after this sublime aim anchored in new consciousness is no seeker any more, but a finder – a *Trobador*: The ideal of the ‹Prodigal Son returning home› will become and remain a lamp before his feet – at the service of *all Humankinds* in the Universe!

Expressed in the language of *Aquarius Genesis*, this means: Through an inner urge the ordinary earthling strives to *return* to the focus of all Life – the Zero-point of Energy ● – the spiritual Love-Sun of the prime Beginning! – Who ever starts and remains consequent in doing so, will be transformed from a vulgar earthling ♂ to a spiritually dominated ♀ *Soul Man*. – Thanks to *new thought, new awareness and a new will*, Man will achieve bondage with the Spirit ⊕ – and even re-union with the Spirit: ⊗. This is the new *Spirit-Soul Man* ☉, he who will definitely transfigure to become *New divine Man* – reunited with the FATHER, as a brilliant ✳!

Other Books Published by Edition Oriflamme

P. Martin (ed. M.P. Steiner): Lodges, Orders And The Rosicross: Rosicrucianism in Lodges, Orders, and Initiatic Societies, since the turn of the 16ᵀᴴ century. – The ‹red thread› and innermost goal of all spiritual teachings and Traditions is: knowledge of the Cosmos, of Man, and of the God: Thus resulted so-called Universal Doctrine, named, in one word, Rosicrucianism. – This scrupulously documented and richly illustrated book shows how inner knowledge came from the East, preserved, passed on and expanded throughout time and space. – It wishes to lessen distrust, increase knowledge, and thereby encourage humans to consciously add to *truly human life in Freedom, Brotherhood and Love*. – PB, 192 pp., 131 pictures, some of them full page. – ISBN 9783952426258 .– E-Book-Edition: ISBN 9783952426289.

Fulcanelli: Mysterium der Kathedralen *und die esoterische Deutung der hermetischen Symbole des Großen Werks*. Vollständige deutsche Erstausgabe nach der dritten franz. Ausgabe (Paris 1964) mit drei Vorworten von E. Canseliet, F.C.H. Übersetzt und herausgegeben von M.P. Steiner. Mit 49 ganzseitigen Tafeln und 1 Frontispiz. – 348 SS.ISBN 3-9520787-2-7.

Fulcanelli: Wohnstätten der Adepten – *Die hermetische Symbolik in der konkreten Wirklichkeit der Heiligen Kunst des Großen Werks*. (Original-Titel: *Les Demeures Philosophales*). Vollständige deutsche Erstausgabe nach der dritten, erweiterten franz. Ausgabe (Paris 1964 / 1979) mit den drei Vorworten von Eugène Canseliet, F.C.H. Ins Deutsche gebracht und eingeleitet durch M.P. Steiner. Mit Zeichnungen von Julien Champagne und späteren Photos sowie mit vier zusätzlichen ganzseitigen Tafeln, davon zwei in Farben. – 2 Bde. In 1 Bd.. – PB, 624 Ss. – ISBN 3-9520787-7-8

Der Schlüssel zu den Zwölf Schlüsseln von Bruder Basilius Valentinus / La Clef des Douze Clefs de Frère Basile Valentin – German & French. Weltweit erste Veröffentlichung des Manuskripts eines unbekannten elsässischen Adepten des Steins der Weisen, verfaßt um ca. 1700: Ein alchemistisch-rosenkreuzerischer Kommentar zu den *Zwölf Schlüsseln der Philosophie* von Basilius Valentinus. – Reich illustriert; mit ausführlichen Anmerkungen und bibliographischen Hinweisen. – Teil I: Französische Transkription des MS, Text und deutsche Übertragung jeweils parallel auf der Gegenseite. – Teil II: *Vom Stein der Uralten* und *Zwölf Schlüssel der Philosophie* (ill. 2. Ausg. von 1602). Übers. u. Hrsg.: M.P. Steiner; – Einführung und Anmerkungen: P. Martin. – PB, 348 Ss. – ISBN 3-9520787-4-3. – Bilingue: en Français et en Allemand.

Valentin Weigel: Das Buch vom Gebet
Das ‹Gebetbüchlein› von V. Weigel, dem ersten deutschen Theosophen, Vorläufer von Jacob Bœhme und J.G. Gichtel – in heutigem Deutsch herausgegeben nach dem Erstdruck von 1612. Ein Meilenstein der Geistesgeschichte, auf dem Weg zu freiem Denken und Glauben. – Mit einer Einführung und Anmerkungen von P. Martin. – Geb. m. S-Usl.; 152 Seiten, illustriert. – ISBN 3-9520787-5-1. – € 23.00 /.

J.G. Gichtel: Theosophia Practica – *Eröffnung und Anweisung der dreyen Principien und Welten im Menschen ...* — Nach der 3. Ausg., o.O. (Amst.?) 1736. – Mit 1 doppelseitigen und 4 einseitigen Farbtafeln des Originals sowie 5 weiteren ganzseitigen, meist farbigen Abbildungen, Titelblatt-Reproduktionen und Vignetten. – Aus dem barocken Deutsch sanft in heutiges Deutsch gebracht und durch P. Martin mit einigen Anmerkungen und mit einer Einleitung versehen, die dieses Buch *zum ersten Mal bibliographisch vollständig und korrekt kommentiert*. – Ppb.; 172 Seiten; – ISBN: 978-3-9523616-0-3; – € 21.00.

P. MARTIN: ESOTERISCHE SYMBOLIK HEUUTE, *im Licht des Alltags, der Sprache und des gnostischen Wegs der Selbsteinweihung.* **(2010)** – Die Elemente der universellen Symbolik und ihre geistige Wirksamkeit, mit Beispielen aus Alchemie, Mythologie, Hermetik und Heraldik neben konkreten Fällen aus der unmittelbaren täglichen Gegenwart. Eine anschauliche Übersicht über die wichtigsten Symbole; eine Einführung ins selbständige Analysieren fast aller Symbole; Erklärung ihrer ständigen Gegenwart und unvermeidlichen magischen Wirkung. – PB., 120 Ss., 28 Farbseiten, 54 Abb. im Text, mit über 100 Literaturhinweisen, einer Symboltabelle und einem Wortverzeichnis. – ISBN 978-3-9523616-1-0. –

PIERRE MARTIN: LE SYMBOLISME ÉSOTÉRIQUE ACTUEL *sous l'aspect du langage et de la vie quotidiens, du Chemin gnostique et de l'Auto-initiation.* **(2011).** Les éléments du Symbolisme Universel dans les traditions de l'Alchimie, de la mythologie, du Hermétisme, de l'héraldique, et du présent actuel. – Avec des exemples concrets de nos jours. Une introduction à l'analyse autonome de presque tous les symboles, leur omniprésence, leur effet magique *dans la vie moderne.* – Traduction Française, édition corrigée et augmentée. – Broch., 124 pp. – Avec un index bibliographique, un index des expressions spécifiques, et une Table de référence des symboles les plus courants. — ISBN 978-3-9520787-6-1; € 16.00.

LAO-DSE: DAO-DE-GING (TAO-TE-KING) – DIE GNOSIS IM ALTEN CHINA.. **(2013)** Vollständig neu aus dem Chinesischen ins Deutsche gebracht und kommentiert, mit Anmerkungen von P. Martin. – Die Übersetzung aufgrund dreier ‹Urtexte› berücksichtigt über 30 frühere westliche Übersetzungen in 6 Sprachen, zahlreiche heutige chinesische Übersetzungen und Kommentare sowie Sitten und Gebräuche des 6.- 4. Jh. v.Chr. Sie wurde von chinesischer Seite für gut befunden. Einige Textvarianten werden diskutiert; der Kommentar beleuchtet *drei Ebenen:* Das tägliche Leben von Jedermann – die Lehren an ‹den Weisen›, ob Herrscher, General oder spiritueller Lehrer – und die Ebene des inneren spirituellen Wegs. – Einige seltene, fürs Verständnis hilfreiche Abbildungen zeigen sichere Fakten zu bisher nie gewagten Übertragungen des Texts. – **AUCH ALS ‹e-Book› ERSCHIENEN!** PB., 352 Ss., mehrere Farbtafeln, Reproduktion des chinesischen Texts in bis zu drei Fassungen. — ISBN 9783-952361689.

P. MARTIN (ED. M.P. STEINER): LODGES, ORDERS AND THE ROSICROSS: *Rosicrucianism in lodges, orders, and initiatic societies, since early 16th century.* This scrupulously documented and richly illustrated book shows how inner knowledge came from the East and evolved during the last 500 years –preserved, passed on, surviving and expanding through time and space. – It wishes to lessen distrust, increase knowledge, and encourage lectors to consciously enhance *truly human life in Freedom, Brotherhood and Love.* PB, 192 pp., 131 pictures, some of which full page. – ISBN 9783952426258, – E-Book-Edition: ISBN 9783952426289.

CORPUS HERMETICUM, LATEINISCH UND DEUTSCH (2014): Die lateinische Übersetzung aus dem Griechischen durch Marsilio Ficino (1468) nach dem Zweitdruck (Mainz, 1503), jetzt präzis ins Deutsche übersetzt. – Das Corpus Hermeticum – ein Text von poetischer Schönheit und höchster philosophischer Genauigkeit – spannt den Bogen von aristotelischer Elementenlehre bis zur Quantenphysik! – Lat. Facsimile des Drucks und deutscher Text auf gegenüberliegenden Seiten. –Einführung, vertiefende Anmerkungen d. Hrsg., illustriert. – ISBN 078395242624l.

M.P. STEINER (HRSG.): DAS WEISHEITSBUCH JESUS SIRACH UND DIE PASSION JESU CHRISTI IN DEN HOLZSCHNITT-TAFELN VON BURKHARD MANGOLD. (2014). – Bibliophiler Druck dieses *vorchristlichen Weisheitsbuchs,* mit den Holzschnitten des großen Basler Künstlers, ergänzt um die Serie von ihm selbst handgedruckter, hand colorierter Tafeln mit seinen Handnotizen. – Die Serie *Passion* ist die Krönung von Mangolds Holzschnitt-Kunst. – Einige Farb-Repros seiner Werke. – Einf.. d. Hrsg.. – Kart. m. S-Usl., Format 19.5 x 27.5, 186 Ss. – ISBN 9783952426227.

M.P. STEINER (HRSG.): JUBILÄUMS-GESAMTAUSGABE 400 JAHRE ROSENKREUZER-MANIFESTE (1614 1615, 1616); ERSCHIENEN 2016 –. Zum ersten Mal alle drei Manifeste in einem Band, mit drei Zusatz-Kapiteln sowie 10 Sendschreiben an die und Antworten aus der RC-Bruderschaft (1612-1618). – Alles sanft in ein heutiges Deutsch gebracht, mit sprachlichen, historischen und philosophischen Anmerkungen. PB 288 Ss.. – Illustriert. – ISBN 9873524262-72.

AL-GHAZALI: BRIEF AN DEN JÜNGER («AYUHA-'L-WALAD»)
Arabisch und Deutsch jeweils parallel auf der Gegenseite. – Nach der französischen Übersetzung von *Tufiq as-Sabagh*, und mit dem Vorwort von *George H. Scherer* zur 1. Auflage (mit dem Lebenslauf von *al-Ghazali*; – Beyruth,1951 Deutsch von M.P. Steiner, mit einer kleinen Einführung in Geschichte und Esoterik der Sufi-Philosophie versehen durch P. Martin. – Ppb., 124 Ss., 3 Tafeln (1 Porträt von *al-Ghazali*) und 4 Vignetten. – ISBN 3-9520787-9-4 – € 15 / CHF 21.00.

AL-GHAZALI: LETTRE AU DISCIPLE («AYUHA-'L-WALAD»)
Textes Arabe et français, face à face. – D'après l'édition de Beyrouth (1959). – Traduction française par Toufiq as-Sabagh. – Préface de G.H. Scherer à l'édition princeps de 1951 (avec la Vita de Al-Ghazali), et une introduction à l'histoire de l'Arabie Ancienne et du Soufisme, par P. Martin. – Broch., 140 pp., 5 planches (portrait de *Al-Ghazālī*), 1 carte géographique, et 4 vignettes. – ISBN 978-3-9520787-6-1.

M.P. STEINER (HRSG.); AUS DEM GEISTIGEN ERBE DER ESSENER – EVANGELIUM DES FRIEDENS UND BUCH DER SCHÖPFUNG. (2017). – Mit der spannenden Geschichte der Entdeckung der Originalmanuskripte in den Geheimarchiven des Vatikans, 1927, also 20 Jahre vor Qumran. Diese Texte lassen Jesus fern von aller Kirchendogmatik als Eingeweihten, Heiler und Lehrer von unmittelbarer Liebenswürdigkeit erscheinen. – PB, 120 Ss., illustriert u.a. mit ganzseitigen Abbildungen nach dem Sonnengesang von Franz v. Assisi (1250). – ISBN 9783-907103-005.